Prophetic Oracles of Salvation
in the Old Testament

Prophetic Oracles of Salvation in the Old Testament

Claus Westermann

Translated by Keith Crim

T&T CLARK
Edinburgh

Translated from the German
Prophetische Heilsworte im Alten Testament.
© 1987 Vandenhoeck & Ruprecht, Göttingen.

Translation © 1991 Westminster/John Knox Press

Originally published in the United States of America by
Westminster/John Knox Press

This edition published under licence
from Westminster/John Knox Press by

T&T Clark
59 George Street
Edinburgh EH2 2LQ
Scotland

First published 1991

ISBN 0 567 29197 9

British Library Cataloguing in Publication Data
Westermann, Claus
Prophetic oracles of salvation in the Old Testament.
1. Bible. O.T.   2. Salvation
I. Title
234

Printed in the United States of America by
R. R. Donnelley & Sons Co.,
Crawfordsville, Indiana

Contents

Foreword

My book *Grundformen prophetischer Rede* was published
in 1964 (5th ed. 1978; English translation, *Basic Forms of
Prophetic Speech*, 1967). The title appeared to many as
rather presumptuous since the book dealt only with the
forms in which judgment was announced. This remained on
my conscience until my retirement and moved me to investigate the prophetic salvation oracles, a task which is now
complete. But to say complete is again to say too much. It is
clear to me that in many respects this work is merely a
sketch and is in need of further work and correction. Above
all I must apologize for not having more fully discussed the
previous work in this area. Because of the large number of
texts involved, fuller discussion was hardly possible. I am
also aware that I have probably said many things that others
before me have said similarly. Here too I ask for pardon.

There is really only one thing that I hope this study will
achieve, that it will make clear the necessity of an investigation of the prophetic salvation oracles in the context of all
these oracles in all the prophetic books. The nature of prophetic proclamations of salvation in the exilic and postexilic
period can only be determined in terms of the total textual
evidence.

Only on that basis can the conclusions of this study be
evaluated: that in Israel during the exilic and postexilic period we can identify two groups of salvation oracles which

7

stand in sharp contrast to each other, a contrast which corresponds to that between prophets of salvation and
prophets of judgment in the preexilic period.

I wish to express my sincerest thanks to Dr. Eberhard
Ruprecht for his helpful review of the manuscript and to
Mr. Harry März for his kind help in securing books for my
research.

For whatever else should be said in a foreword, consult
my article "Zur Erforschung und zum Verständnis der
prophetischen Heilsworte" (*ZAW* 98, 1986, 1–13), where I
gave a preview of the results of this research.

April 1987   Claus Westermann

Abbreviations

BWANT	Beiträge zur Wissenschaft vom Alten und Neuen Testament
BHS	*Biblia Hebraica Stuttgartensia*
BKAT	Biblischer Kommentar: Altes Testament
BZAW	Beihefte zur *ZAW*
E.T.	English translation
HSAT	Die Heilige Schrift des Alten Testaments
JB	Jerusalem Bible
JPSV	Jewish Publication Society Version
NJB	New Jerusalem Bible
OTL	The Old Testament Library
REB	Revised English Bible
RSV	Revised Standard Version
THAT	*Theologisches Handwörterbuch zum Alten Testament*, ed. E. Jenni and C. Westermann, 1971–76
ThB	Theologische Bücherei
WMANT	Wissenschaftliche Monographien zum Alten und Neuen Testament
ZAW	*Zeitschrift für die alttestamentliche Wissenschaft*

Introduction

Anyone who sets out to investigate the prophetic oracles of salvation in the Old Testament immediately encounters difficulty in defining them precisely and thus in arranging and grouping the many texts involved. A first reaction would be to investigate the oracles of each of the prophetic books separately and to group them according to the time periods we find in the history of prophecy in Israel. This was the method used by S. Herrmann in his *Die prophetischen Heilserwartungen im Alten Testament* (BWANT, n.s. 5, 1965). But in so doing one encounters the problem that even today there is no agreement as to which of the oracles that are contained in the book of the prophet Isaiah, or the prophet Hosea, were really spoken by that prophet. There is still uncertainty over what the presuppositions of such a study should be.

It has become clear to me (and the following study will corroborate it) that the oracles in the various prophetic books, both in their form and in their content, agree with one another to an astonishing degree or are at least quite similar. To be sure, they display characteristic differences, but the points at which they agree or are similar are clearly predominant. From this we may conclude that the oracles of salvation in the prophetic books belong to the same distinctive tradition, just as do the oracles to the nations. This tradition must then be studied as a whole, and the grouping

of the oracles of salvation must be based on the totality of
the texts of salvation oracles in all the prophetic books.

In reality anyone who has even once read through all the
salvation oracles in the various prophetic books must be
struck by the extensive agreement and the many similarities
among them. That thus far no conclusions have been drawn
from these similarities that would help with the exegesis
and closer definition of these oracles is the fault of the exegesis conducted thus far. This exegesis is for the most
part—though not always consciously—determined by the
literary-critical method and is dominated by the first question it poses, that of authorship. It immediately becomes
involved in the question of whether or not a passage is
"genuine." The words that are deemed "genuine" are ac-
corded precedence over those that are not. Thus the dominant concern is always to identify the major personalities
involved (Herrmann, p. 5). And this evaluation is then im-
posed on the texts. The unavoidable consequence is that
the scholar who has made this determination is more inter-
ested in the "genuine" passages in the specific prophetic
book. The history of research in the prophets reflects this
evaluation in that attention devoted to the "nongenuine"
texts is much less than that given to the "genuine." As a
consequence of this discounting of texts, commentaries on
the individual prophetic books give little or no attention to
passages in other prophetic books that are regarded as not
coming from the prophet in question.

The literary-critical method has given rise to the conception that a prophetic saying contains the thoughts of that
prophet (R. Kittel, *Gestalten und Gedanken in Israel*), which
then found their literary expression in the written oracles.
But the sayings of the prophets are not simply statements;
they are addressed to specific hearers. It is this that finds
expression in their spoken form. They are words of a messenger (L. Koehler), words that Yahweh gives to the
prophet (*wayyehi debar yhwh 'el*), so that he may speak
them to the people of Israel. The word of the prophet is a
component in a procedure that moves from God by way of
the prophet to the people. Our task is to investigate this
procedure and its components: to discover the Hebrew
dabar as an event in time, to which belong the starting
point, the goal, and that which is said in the progress from

the former to the latter. But if the content of what is said is separated from this process, the prophetic word as such can no longer be understood.

What has been said thus far applies to the prophetic oracles of judgment as well as to those of salvation. We must now investigate the distinction between them.

Oracles of judgment are limited to one part of the history of Israel, but the oracles of salvation are found throughout that history. The prehistory of the prophetic oracles of salvation begins with the promises to the patriarchs and continues in various forms of salvation oracles in the early history of Israel. Its posthistory extends into apocalyptic literature. The prophecies of judgment are confined to a particular time in Israel's history, the individual phases of which are defined by the activity of individual prophets, from Amos to Ezekiel.

The situation is quite different for the oracles of salvation. Only a few of them can be ascribed with certainty to one of the prophets of judgment. The greatest number arose anonymously in the period between Deutero-Isaiah (a few are probably earlier) and the conclusion of the prophetic canon. The context of the vast majority is not to be regarded as the work of an individual prophet unknown to us, but in the total tradition of this period. These anonymous oracles were, individually or in small collections, added to or inserted into the various prophetic books by those who transmitted them. This followed a process similar to that which shaped the folk proverbs. This is seen with particular clarity in those oracles of salvation which arose as supplements to specific prophecies of judgment from Isaiah, Hosea, or other prophets. But in terms of the history of tradition it is false to ascribe them to disciples of these prophets, for they arose only when the specific proclamations of judgment had been fulfilled.

The primary result of literary-critical exegesis is that to the present day the prophetic oracles of salvation have been classified together as "expectation of salvation," or "hope of salvation," as if that were obvious. In the collection of articles in *Eschatologie im Alten Testament* (ed. H. D. Preuss, 1978), for example, there is, so far as I can see, no exception to this procedure. On the other hand no one speaks of "expectation of judgment." A proclamation

(*Ankündigung*) is not the same thing as an expectation. In the Old Testament the semantic domain of hope and expectation belongs exclusively to the language of the Psalms, especially the confession of trust, and not to the language of prophecy. It can occur that a prophet is given a message to proclaim that contradicts his hope. The questionable nature of the designation "expectation of salvation" for the prophetic proclamation of salvation is clear in that it does not correspond to the terms for messages of judgment; the latter are appropriately termed "proclamations of judgment." This can be explained by the concept that lurks in the background that the messages of salvation are expressions of the thought or concepts of the specific prophet. In my opinion it is not responsible scholarship to take it for granted that the prophetic messages of salvation should be termed "expectation of salvation," when this is in direct contradiction to the language of these messages.

There is a further reason why it is important to recognize that the prophecies of salvation in the prophetic books are intended as proclamations. This identity as proclamation is clear and unambiguous at an earlier stage of prophecy, especially in Deutero-Isaiah, where in one group of messages there is a distinction between the announcement and the fulfillment of the proclamation. But we can see at a later stage the transition from proclamation of salvation to expectation of salvation. This can be observed in a variety of changes in the language of salvation oracles. This change from proclamation to expectation in late stages of the oracles cannot, however, be identified and taken into account if the exegete *a priori* equates proclamation of salvation with expectation of salvation. Although it is not always possible to draw a sharp distinction between the two, these stages in the history of the prophetic oracles of salvation are unmistakable.

An Analysis of the Oracles of Salvation

If the prophetic oracles of salvation constitute in themselves a fixed, independent tradition, then objective criteria for the exegesis of an individual oracle can be derived only from a survey of the total corpus of such oracles. A preliminary task is the investigation of the oracles of salvation scattered in the individual prophetic books. But because the oracles in all the prophetic books are in extensive agreement, this in itself is not sufficient. In addition, it is necessary to develop from a survey of all the prophetic oracles of salvation a grouping of these oracles on the basis of their structure and content.

First, a distinction must be made between the preponderant majority of oracles of salvation found in collections of such oracles in Deutero-Isaiah, Jeremiah, Ezekiel, Trito-Isaiah, Micah, and Zephaniah, or as additions to or insertions into collections of oracles of judgment, on the one hand, and on the other hand those found in reports of a situation in which an oracle of salvation was given, as we find them in the historical books. We encounter the latter only in the books of Isaiah and Jeremiah, and possibly also in Ezekiel.

Second, as for the large number of salvation oracles in collections, we must distinguish between a major group (Group 1), and three secondary groups found in all the prophetic books.

Third, there is a further distinction between those oracles that are addressed to an individual and those addressed to a community. In the patriarchal narratives at the beginning of the history of these oracles as it stretches throughout the whole Old Testament, we find oracles of salvation addressed to an individual, even when by the individual the whole family is meant. In the prophetic books, the oracles are for the most part, and in Deutero-Isaiah exclusively, addressed to Israel, the people of God. But there are also oracles addressed to individuals. A further distinction is that after the catastrophe of 587 B.C. the prophetic oracles of salvation are addressed to the "remnant," those who have survived the catastrophe; in many cases the "remnant" is explicitly addressed. This presents a new aspect of the oracles.

Fourth, there is also a difference in the length of time between the giving of the announcement and the arrival of that which has been announced. If the oracle is addressed to an individual the lapse of time between proclamation and fulfillment is usually brief (for example in the promise of a son: "At this season, when the time comes round . . . "; 2 Kings 4:16). In such cases a sign is often added to the promise, as in Isaiah 7:14–16. For this brief time span the perfect tense is appropriate in such an oracle, which originally was given only to individuals. In oracles to the people, the lapse of time is greater; thus the future tense is used.

Fifth, it is also necessary to explore the content of what is proclaimed. Various things can be meant by the word "salvation"; it can be an act or a state (*Zustand*). The proclamation can be of an act of deliverance or a state of well-being, or of the two together. This difference is expressed in the form of the oracle, and thus form and content cannot be separated. This distinction enables us to group the main oracles according to objective criteria. A proclamation of deliverance follows a fixed, unvarying sequence: Distress; cry for help (lament); the cry is heard; deliverance. A large number of oracles of salvation consist solely of the proclamation of deliverance.

An oracle of salvation may be given not only in a threatening situation but also in a situation of misery and adversity. Here a proclamation of a future situation of well-being is appropriate. This can take two forms. First, a proclamation of blessing can follow one of deliverance, a promise that announces a time of blessing and prosperity. It is found early in Israel's history coupled with a proclamation of deliverance and has its own roots and its own history. Second, after the collapse of 587 B.C. we find the proclamation of the restoration of a state of well-being. Both these forms have in common, in contrast to a proclamation of deliverance, that the promise of blessing and the proclamation of the restoration of a state of well-being do not follow a fixed order of events, but the motifs are presented alongside each other. The proclamation can move into a description, in which the proclamation of the new course of events is either reduced to an introductory formula such as "In that day . . ." or is omitted completely. This distinction between the act of deliverance and the state of well-being is of basic importance for our understanding and analysis of the oracles of salvation. It goes back to the distinction between God's activity in deliverance and his activity in blessing. The two together constitute God's saving activity. Typical of *Group 1* are the oracles of Deutero-Isaiah, who proclaimed Cyrus, the ruler of a foreign nation, as Israel's liberator, commissioned by Yahweh (Isaiah 45). Since thereby Israel also acknowledged the political rule of the Persian

Empire as the will of Yahweh, this had consequences for Israel's relationship to the other nations. Those who survived the fall of the Babylonian Empire can be included in the invitation to accept deliverance and well-being. The additional oracles of salvation belonging to Group 1 also follow the pattern of Deutero-Isaiah's proclamation.

Next we consider the other groups of prophetic oracles of salvation. The extensive similarities among the oracles of salvation in all the prophetic books are also found in the three smaller secondary groups 2, 3, and 4. It is especially striking that in all the prophetic books there are only these four groups, and none of the groups is found only in one or two of the books. This confirms that all the oracles of salvation belong to one strand of tradition.

The texts of *Group 2* are for the most part short and are generally supplements to other texts, with which they agree in form and content. They always consist of two parts and are seldom expanded. They proclaim destruction of Israel's foes and at the same time salvation for Israel. The simple form underwent two developments. In one set of texts the motif is added that the destruction of the foes will be achieved explicitly by Judah-Israel, and in the other that Judah-Israel will take possession of the land of their foes. At a later stage the form of the twofold proclamation underwent two expansions in two steps, which mark the transition to apocalyptic. In the first expansion the approach of the foes precedes their destruction, and in the second the twofold proclamation is expanded into larger compositions that present an apocalyptic drama.

Strictly speaking, groups 3 and 4 cannot be included among the prophetic oracles of salvation. As for *Group 3*, in the majority of the prophetic books, but especially in Jeremiah, we encounter conditional proclamations of salvation, which are derived from deuteronomistic paraenesis, and have there their original and appropriate place. They show the transition from prophetic proclamation of salvation to deuteronomistic paraenesis.

Group 4 consists of texts in which the prophetic proclamation of salvation is combined with a motif of the piety of late Wisdom literature—the fate of the pious and the fate of the wicked, or in which this motif replaces the prophetic proclamation.

This analysis enables us to delineate at least a few essential features of a history of the oracles of salvation in postexilic times. This, however, is possible only through the investigation of all the oracles in categories derived from the total corpus.

The oracles of salvation in the proper sense (group one) can be tabulated as follows:

Deutero-Isaiah	35 texts
Isaiah 1–39	29 texts
Minor Prophets	34 texts
Jeremiah	38 texts
Ezekiel	15 texts
Trito-Isaiah	6 texts
Total	157 texts

In addition there are 39 texts of Group 2 (the twofold proclamation), and texts that are related to the prophetic words of salvation but cannot be included among them. Group 3 (conditional proclamations of salvation) includes 34 texts; and Group 4, the pious and the wicked, 16 texts.

The prophetic books include collections of oracles of salvation: Isaiah 40–55; parts of Isaiah 56–66 (60–62), and perhaps also parts of Isaiah 32–35; Jeremiah 30–33, and perhaps also 3:6–4:4; Ezekiel 33–37 (38–39; 40–48); Amos 9:11–15; Micah 4–5; Zephaniah 3:11–20; parts of Zechariah. All the other oracles of salvation are scattered outside these collections, added to oracles of judgment or to folk proverbs, or inserted between them. They were first collected in the process of compilation of the prophetic books. This is illustrated by the oracles that are found in the same or similar form in different prophetic books (e.g., Isa. 2:2–4 and Micah 4:1–3), or in the same book at different places (e.g., Jer. 23:5–6 = 33:15–16).

It should be noted that prophetic oracles are also found in the Psalter, there transformed into praise of God. An example is Psalm 147:2–3: "The Lord builds up Jerusalem; he gathers the outcasts of Israel. He heals the brokenhearted, and binds up their wounds."

PART ONE

Oracles of Salvation

1

Oracles of Salvation
Before the Time
of the Writing Prophets

The Period of the Patriarchs

These oracles belong to the form of society defined by the family or the tribe. For the material dealt with here, see my book *The Promises to the Fathers* (1980) and the exegesis in the second volume of my Genesis commentary, *Genesis 12–36* (1985). The individual promises have their own tradition history within the history of the patriarchal tradition, and their history continues alongside other traditions. For example, the promise to multiply the people evolves from the simple form "I will multiply your descendants" (Gen. 16:10) to the proclamation "I will make you a great nation" (Gen. 12:2), which was intensified to "a multitude of nations" (Gen. 17:4).

The promises to the fathers have a remarkably rich history down to the oracles of salvation of the postexilic period. The promise of new pasture as deliverance from trouble became the promise of the land of an advanced civilization and then the promise of possession of the land, which is connected with the promise of deliverance from Egypt. We encounter it in a changed form in the promise of return from exile back to "the land which I promised to your fathers." The promise of the birth of a son developed into the promise of the savior king. The promise to multiply the nation is found again together with the proclamation of deliverance from exile. The promise to be present to help is transferred from Moses to Joshua (Josh. 1:2–6) and is found again in the assurance given to the prophet Jeremiah (cf. Ex. 3:2 and Jer. 1:8). The promise of blessing is united with the promise of the land, continues in a variety of forms, and then is united with the proclamation of deliverance in Deutero-Isaiah and elsewhere. The promise in the Priestly document, "I will be your God," occurs again in Ezekiel and in the covenant formula. In later additions to the promises to the fathers, the unconditional promises are changed into conditional promises, as in the deuteronomistic redaction of the book of Jeremiah and elsewhere.

From the Exodus to the Occupation of the Land
(The Period of Wandering)

The Promise of Deliverance and Possession of the Land

From the book of Exodus on, God's activities are directed toward the group, and this is expressed in the difference between the promises in Genesis 12–50 and those given later. The promises to individuals become prominent again only beginning with the settlement of the land. At the beginning of God's activity with the group we find a promise (Ex. 3:6–8) which has significance for the whole history that begins here, the promise of deliverance from Egypt. This is seen especially in the so-called historical credo, Deuteronomy 26:5–9, the significance of which Gerhard von Rad emphasized. This significance is not based solely on the one experience of deliverance. It includes a sequence of events: Distress, the cry to God, God hears and gives his promise, deliverance. This sequence preserved the strength of its distinctive tradition down to the exile and beyond. It is on this basis that Israel's God remained through all Israel's history the God who saves, whose activity was experienced in the sequence of events of distress, promise, and deliverance. If we look ahead to the proclamation of Deutero-Isaiah, which announced the new exodus, the new deliverance from slavery, we can see the way in which this promise had determinative significance for the history of Israel. Even though it took on written form only in much later times, this does not lessen any of its significance. The sequence of events depicted here can be traced back to early times, and this shows the way it agrees with the promise of a new land in which to live, a promise that in Genesis 12–50 could only be cast in terms of deliverance. In contrast to Genesis 12:1–3, Exodus 3 shows the situation in which the promise of deliverance is given, a promise that includes the entry into a new homeland.

Thus the promise of the land in Exodus 3 cannot be separated from the promise of deliverance. The new land makes a new existence possible for the people who cry out to God in their time of need. The promised land is the place where deliverance is realized. In this respect too the repetition of the Exodus promise in Deutero-Isaiah corresponds to the original promise.

The books from Exodus to Numbers, and especially Deuteronomy, are characterized by attention to the occupation of the promised land as the second part of the already fulfilled promise of deliverance from Egypt (Ex. 6:1–8; 13:5, 11; 32:13; 33:1; Num. 11:12; 14:16, 23; 32:11; Deut. 1:8, 35; 4:31; 6:10, 18, 23; 26:1–3; and thirteen additional passages). We will consider below the way in which the promise of the land was transformed in Deuteronomy.

The programmatic significance of the promise in Exodus 3:6–8 becomes clear in that its author drew on all three forms of this promise that was basic to Israel's history: the assurance of salvation (perfect tense, "I have heard your cry . . . "); the proclamation of salvation (future tense, "I will lead you forth . . . "); the depiction of salvation (present tense, " . . . to a good and broad land, a land flowing with milk and honey"). All three formulas recur in the history of the oracles of salvation, though expressed in differing ways. Throughout the Old Testament, the Exodus promises are recalled again and again.

The Promise to Be Present with the Leader

In Exodus 3:12 God promises Moses, "I will be with you," and at the change of leadership from Moses to Joshua (Josh. 1:5) God promises, "As I was with Moses, so I will be with you." Spoken in a later setting, this is the same promise that the patriarchs had received, in both cases a promise for the journey. Here too it is a promise directed to an individual, but to the leader of a group under way, so that it

involves the welfare of the group as well. As was the case
with the patriarchs, this promise is given directly by God to
the leader, without any intermediary. It forms part of the
prehistory of prophecy because it reappears in the call of
the prophet Jeremiah (Jer. 1:8), "Be not afraid of them, for
I am with you to deliver you." It is also found in the promise to the people in Deutero-Isaiah.

From the Entry Into the Promised Land to the Monarchy

The Conveyance Formula: Oracle of Salvation as Answer to a Question Asked of God

The predominant form of the promise at the time of the
occupation of the land (the period from Joshua to the
Judges) is the so-called conveyance formula: "Behold, I
have given into your hand . . . " In the patriarchal narratives instruction is combined with the promise (Gen. 12:1–
3; chs. 46, 48), and similarly this formula is combined with
instruction. The question is always posed by the leader, and
it is he who receives the answer. This indicates a similarity
to the promise to be present with the leader. In the early
period, questions were put to Yahweh by casting lots, as
described in 1 Samuel 14:41–42. The answer was a yes or a
no (1 Sam. 14:36–42; Judg. 1:1–3). In correspondence to
the question, the answer is in two parts, instruction and
encouragement ("I have given . . . into your hand"). The
situation is always the same. Before making an important
decision the leader asks God what he is to do. It is clearly
distinguished from the situation in which an oracle of salvation is given, where the preceding lament sets the stage for
the oracle. There is no immediate danger to be faced, but
the leader needs God's instructions. God's answer to the
question can resemble an oracle of salvation, where the instruction is supported by the assurance, "I have given . . .
into your hand" (Josh. 2:24; 6:2, 16; 8:1, 18; 10:8, 19;
Judg. 3:28; 4:7, 14; 7:9, 15; 18:9; 20:28; 1 Sam. 14:12;
17:46; 23:4, 7; 24:5; 26:8; 1 Kings 20:13f., 28; 22:6, 12,
15; 2 Kings 3:18), or where the statement inserted into the
story stands by itself. The promise of victory is limited, with
few exceptions, to the time of the occupation of the land
and the wars fought in that time in the name of Yahweh.

It is difficult to say whether the question addressed to God and the prophet's answer in the form of the conveyance formula was continued in the later period of the monarchy or whether it was a scribal formulation of the late period. In 1 Kings 20:38 deuteronomistic language can be recognized in that a reason precedes the formula of conveyance: "Because the Syrians have said . . . , therefore I will give all this great multitude into your hand, and you shall know . . . " Second Kings 3:13–20 recounts a miracle performed by Elisha; verse 18 says, "He will also give the Moabites into your hand." In the story of David and Goliath the conveyance formula is quite changed. David himself is certain that the Lord "will give you into our hand" (1 Sam. 17:46–47).

After the occupation of the land the rite of consulting Yahweh by casting lots came to an end (with the exception of specific cultic rites). If a king now wanted to consult Yahweh he turned to a prophet (1 Sam. 22:5; 1 Kings 12:21–24; 22:5–12; 2 Kings 3:17–20; 8:7–11; 22:12–20). The answer, however, can vary greatly from one instance to another, as, for example in 1 Kings 12:21–24 and 1 Samuel 22:5.

There are also other assurances of victory. In 2 Kings 13:14–19 Elisha, by a symbolic action, gives the king assurance of victory over the Syrians. In 1 Samuel 15:1–3, Samuel, in deuteronomistic language, gives Saul assurance of victory over the Amalekites. Especially significant is the story in 1 Kings 22. Here is it the prophets of salvation who promise both kings victory, and the conveyance formula with the assurance of success is reinforced by a symbolic action (v. 11). At first Micaiah ben Imlah also gives assurance of victory (v. 15), but then in a vision he predicts defeat (v. 17). Here the prophet speaks critically of the conveyance formula and denies that in this case it is the word of Yahweh. Similarly, that formula is never used by the writing prophets. In its proper significance it is restricted to the period of the settlement in the land, though it does occur later.

The Message of the Seers, Portrayal of Blessing

A portrayal of blessing that is also a promise is found as early as Genesis 49:10–12. It is a promise of blessing for

Judah, combined with the promise of a king to come from
the tribe of Judah (v. 10). Under his rule, rich blessing will
come to the land, a state of blessing and abundance (vs. 11–
12). The king is the mediator of blessing. The blessing
brings fertility to the land and also expresses the beauty of
the king (cf. Psalm 45). The closest parallel is Numbers
24:5–7, a saying of the seer Balaam, foretelling here too the
fertility of the land and praise of the king. The sayings of
Balaam find their place in the Balaam episode at the final
phase of the journey through the wilderness, directly before the entry into the promised land. Indeed, the promise
in Exodus 3:6–8 had already contained a portrayal of blessing in the words " . . . to a good and broad land, a land
flowing with milk and honey." This is echoed in the account
of the spying out of the land (Num. 13:27) and then under-
goes rich development in Deuteronomy (6:3b, 10–11; 8:7–9;
see also 7:12–13; 28:3–6).

Just as in the promise in Exodus 3:6–8 an allusive description of the land is added as a supplement to the promise of
possession of the land, so in Deuteronomy 8:7–9 there is an
expanded description of this beautiful land, a portrayal of
blessing. Thus to the promise of deliverance there is added
the promise of blessing (cf. Gen. 12:1–3). The reason that
the same portrayal of blessing is found in the words of a seer
in Numbers 24:5–7 is that the seer, as someone who sees
into the distances of time and space, has control over effica-
cious words (according to Num. 22–24 he can both bless and
curse). By pronouncing what he sees in the distance he
makes it effective and brings it to pass. Thus it is understandable that in 1 Samuel 9:9 the work of the prophet is seen as
the continuation of the earlier work of the seer: "Formerly
in Israel, when a man went to inquire of God, he said,
'Come, let us go to the seer.'" See 1 Samuel 3:1b for the
parallelism of "word of the Lord" and "vision." Thus it is
understandable that in later times the word of the seer and
the portrayal of blessing were again combined with the word
of the prophet. The late portrayals of salvation in the words
of the prophets (e.g., Isaiah 11) correspond to the portrayals
of blessing in the tribal period and in the words of the seers.
This connection is unmistakable in the proclamation of a future savior king: the king is here the bringer and the mediator of blessing, as in Genesis 49:10–12.

The distinction between God's activity in deliverance and his activity in blessing as seen in the history of the oracles of salvation in the Old Testament is evident in the differences between two traditions, each with its own forms of speech, and also in that the promise of deliverance comes first and the promise of blessing is added to it. (Cf. C. Westermann, *Blessing in the Bible and the Life of the Church*, 1978.)

Oracles of Salvation in 1 Samuel–2 Kings

With the beginning of the monarchy and the resultant changes in the state, differentiations arose in the form of the oracles of salvation. Oracles addressed to the people as a whole and those addressed to individuals developed in different streams of tradition. There was also a second change. The oracles to the patriarchs had been given directly, without any human intermediary. In the period of the tribal wanderings the oracles addressed to the group were given through the leader, and those to the leader were given directly. From the time of the monarchy, however, the oracles were given only through an intermediary, whether they were directed to an individual, to the people as a whole, or to the king.

Among those who mediated God's word there developed with the establishment of the monarchy a division between priest and prophet. The priesthood had its beginning with the settlement of the land, while the office of prophet, which began with the monarchy, had its forerunners in the man of God, the seer, and the ecstatic.

Oracles That Announce the Deliverance of Individuals

The text of 1 Samuel 1:17–20, 21–28 corresponds to the promise of a son in the patriarchal narratives and has the same structure: the plight of childlessness; the lament; the lament is heard and a child is promised; the birth of the child. This story differs from the earlier promises of a son in that the story of Hannah is the introduction to the story of Samuel and is told only because the child that is born here has significance for Israel, as is the case in Judges 13. Further differences are that the one who announces the promise is a priest and that the lament and its answer are elements in worship at the temple. The constant elements and the variable are easy to recognize.

In 2 Kings 4:8–17 Elisha promises the Shunammite woman a son. In the story we can identify the same structure: childlessness, lament, the lament is heard, proclamation, the birth of the child. There are clear echoes here of Genesis 18.

In 2 Kings 8:7–15 and 20:1–7 illness is the problem. The diseased Ben-hadad sends Hazael to inquire of Elisha, and Isaiah goes to see King Hezekiah, who is ill. The oracle is an answer—spoken through the prophet—to the plea of one in trouble. In 2 Kings 22:18–20 the problem is a threat to the people, and Josiah sends to ask the prophetess Huldah for help. Her answer is a pronouncement of judgment on Judah, vs. 15–17, but this is followed in vs. 18–20 by an oracle of salvation concerning Josiah's personal fate.

In the miracle stories of the Elijah-Elisha tradition the miracle is generally reported without a word or proclamation, but such a word is found in a few places. An example is 1 Kings 17:14: "For thus says the Lord the God of Israel, 'The jar of meal shall not be spent . . . ' " See also 2 Kings 2:21; 3:17; 4:43; 7:1. In these five passages the proclamation has no essential function and could have been omitted. These statements introduced by the messenger formula represent a later stylization of a miracle story about a man of God in order to make these stories agree with those of the deeds of a prophet. In the proper sense of the term they are not oracles of salvation.

The oracles of salvation given to those suffering from childlessness or those who are ill were included in the books of Kings, because those to whom they were given played a direct or indirect role in the history of the kingdom. Thus we may conclude that both were common in the period of the early monarchy and were widely known. They were spoken by a man of God, a prophet or a priest.

Oracles for the People in Time of Need

First Samuel 7:3–15, a story with strongly deuteronomistic flavor, tells of rescue from the Philistines. The oracle of salvation has been made conditional, but the structure can be recognized: the threat of war, the cry for help, the cry is heard, help is given. The oracle itself is to be found in the context: "If you . . . direct your heart to the Lord . . . he will deliver you out of the hand of the Philistines" (v. 3). It is also to be seen in the stone that is set up as a memorial of the Lord's deliverance (v. 12).

First Samuel 12:14, 19–22 is similar. Once again the oracle is blended into a deuteronomistic speech, but the elements can be recognized. In v. 14 the oracle is made conditional and in v. 22 it is cultically paraphrased; compare 2 Kings 13:23.

In the account of the Assyrian siege of Jerusalem in 2 Kings 19:2–6, King Hezekiah's servant brings the king's lament before Isaiah, who answers, "Say to your Master, 'Thus says the Lord: Do not be afraid because of the words that you have heard. . . . Behold, I will put a spirit in him, so that he shall hear a rumor and return to his own land'" (vs. 6–7).

This is a typical oracle of salvation, given by a prophet in the name of Yahweh to a king in a situation of danger for the people, and it is limited to that situation. The oracle is in two parts, but abbreviated. In place of the verb in the perfect tense stands the assurance, "Do not be afraid," which presupposes God's coming to the help of the people.

Another oracle in an Assyrian siege is 2 Kings 19:14–34. The text is composite. In vs. 14–19 Hezekiah goes before God in the temple with the Assyrian letter threatening Jerusalem and pleads for deliverance. The prophet Isaiah imparts the assurance of being heard: "Thus says the Lord, the God of Israel: Your prayer . . . I have heard" (v. 20).

Following this assurance in the perfect tense is a proclamation of salvation in the future tense: "Therefore thus says the Lord concerning the king of Assyria, He shall not come into this city. . . . By the way that he came . . . he shall return" (vs. 32–33).

This self-contained account was later expanded. In vs. 21–28 a message of judgment on Assyria is inserted, and vs. 30–31 contain a later oracle for the "remnant." The oracle in vs. 32–33 was later expanded in vs. 34: "For I will defend this city to save it, for my own sake and for the sake of my servant David." (Compare 2 Kings 20:6, which is also a · typical prophetic proclamation of salvation, given by a

prophet to a king in the name of God after the king brought
the plight of the people before God in the temple.)

The oracle is limited to this situation, and the lament of
the king for the people in the temple is an act of worship.
The oracle is spoken not by a priest but by a prophet because the situation is a historical crisis, in which the prophet
is the mediator of the divine word. The oracle is in two parts:
the statement that the plea has been heard (v. 20), and the
proclamation of liberation (vs. 32–33). The proclamation is
formulated in terms of the retreat of the foe in accordance
with the situation. In such a direct threat the oracle for Israel
has its original and proper expression in the form of a message of woe for Israel's foes. The oracle about the "remnant"
in vs. 30–31 is from the exilic or postexilic period.

Oracles Directed to Kings

These oracles differ from those previously discussed in
that they do not involve deliverance but blessing, mediated
through the institution of kingship. They involve God's
choice of a king, anointing, and the promise of a dynasty.

Samuel's anointing of Saul is introduced by the words,
"Stop here yourself for a while, that I may make known to
you the word of God" (1 Sam. 9:27), and at the anointing
Samuel says, "Has not the Lord anointed you to be prince
over his people Israel? And you shall reign over the people
of the Lord and you will save them from the hand of their
enemies round about" (10:1). First Samuel 1:13 and Second
Samuel 3:18 are similar. In 2 Samuel 7:8–11a the divine
choice and the anointing of the king are secondarily combined by the Deuteronomist with the promise of Israel's deliverance from their enemies, in agreement with the
historical account, according to which the first kings were
installed because of the Philistine threat. In later accounts of
the choice of a king by a prophet no oracle of salvation is
hinted at (1 Kings 11:29–39; 2 Kings 8:7–15; 9:1–10).

The Nathan Oracle (2 Samuel 7) is the sanction for the
establishment of David's dynasty. In the strict sense chapter
7 is not an oracle of salvation but an affirmation given in the
name of God. Its special significance is seen in the expansions in vs. 8–16 (L. Rost) and the many later echoes of the

oracle. The original sanction in vs. 9b and 11a contains two elements: the promise of greatness and honor (a name) for David, and the permanence of his house. This sanction is expanded in several ways. Verses 8b and 9a look back on the choice of David and the experience he has had thus far of God's support. In verses 10 and 11a the promise to the king is combined with that given to the people of Israel, which is framed by the twofold promise to the king (vs. 9b and 11b). There are reminders here of God's promise to be with the people and to give them the land. The significance of the dynasty is explained in vs. 12–15 (v. 13a, the building of the temple, is a late addition).

In 1 Kings 3:4–15 greatness and honor are promised to King Solomon, and the permanence of his kingdom is confirmed. The case is the same in 1 Kings 9:1–9, but the promise is made conditional in deuteronomistic language. This marks the preparation for the conclusion of the deuteronomistic portrayal of Solomon's kingdom, in that Solomon is accused of falling away from Yahweh.

We should also note the confirmation of a dynasty by a priest in 2 Kings 9:1–9, which reminds us of 1 Samuel 2:30.

The sanctioning or confirming of the kingdom to David and Solomon and to their dynasty in the name of God does not belong to the oracles of salvation in the sense of being a proclamation. It is not a question of deliverance but of permanence. The "promise" to the king of greatness, honor, wealth, and wisdom is the language of celebration and homage at the royal festivals.

The transformation of this confirmation of the dynasty to a merely conditional confirmation in 1 Kings 9:1–9 and in Psalm 89 indicates the limits of such confirmation. These passages have their importance for the further history of the oracles of salvation in the Old Testament in that the promise of a coming savior king is based on such passages.

From Unconditional to Conditional Promises of Salvation

The transformation of a previously unconditional promise (2 Samuel 7) into a conditional promise is seen most clearly in 1 Kings 9:4–9:

If you will walk before me, as David your father walked . . . ,
keeping my statutes . . . , then I will establish your royal
throne over Israel for ever, as I promised David your father.
. . . But if you turn aside from following me . . . , then I will
cut Israel off from the land which I have given them. (Cf. 1
Sam. 7:3–4, in a speech by Samuel; 1 Sam. 12:4, 19–25)

The message that the prophetess Huldah gave to Josiah
presupposes a conditional oracle: "Because your heart was
penitent, and you humbled yourself before the Lord . . . ,
I also have heard you, says the Lord" (2 Kings 22:19).

In these passages the language is deuteronomistic. Since
here the proclamation of salvation is limited by being conditional, or (in case the condition is not complied with) by
the announcement of judgment, the proclamation of salvation loses that which makes it a promise—its being unconditionally reliable. This breach in the proclamation of
salvation is caused by its being tied to obedience (1 Kings
9:4). The priority given to the following of God's will over
the authority of the promise must have come about
through a gradual process. In this process that which was
distinctive, the prophetic proclamation of salvation given
with full authority, was lost. Here it is the deuteronomistic
school that is speaking, for whom the prophetic oracle of
salvation is a matter of the past. Another hallmark is the
greater lapse of time between the issuing of the proclamation and its fulfillment. This greater time span is necessary
to allow for the decision between obedience or disobedience to be made in the course of history. The early oracles, which were not conditional, assume a more limited
period of time between the giving of the oracle and its
fulfillment.

Appeal to the Earlier Proclamations of Salvation

Characteristic of the deuteronomistic school is their appeal to earlier proclamations of salvation and to their fulfillment. Interconnections in the history of Israel may be
seen in that oracles which had been given to Moses and to
David are regarded as fulfilled at a later time. Such an
appeal finds clear expression in Solomon's prayer at the
dedication of the temple.

[Thou] hast kept with thy servant David my father what thou didst declare to him; yea, thou didst speak with thy mouth, and with thy hand hast fulfilled it this day. (1 Kings 8:24)

For thou didst separate them from among all the peoples of the earth, to be thy heritage, as thou didst declare through Moses, thy servant. (v. 53)

Blessed be the Lord who has given rest to his people Israel, according to all that he promised; not one word has failed of all his good promise, which he uttered by Moses his servant. (v. 56)

Joshua 23:14 (deuteronomistic) is similar. See also 2 Kings 13:23; 1 Kings 9:4–5, 12, 15. The great emphasis placed in these passages on the fulfillment of the promises ("his good promise") shows the interest the historians had in the continuity of that history which rested on the "functioning" of the proclamation of salvation. Though cast in other words, Isaiah 52, written about the same time, toward the end of the exile, is similar.

This is related to the use in many passages of the promises to the fathers as a motif for God's contemporary acts.

But the Lord was gracious to them and had compassion on them . . . , because of his covenant with Abraham, Isaac, and Jacob, and would not destroy them; nor has he cast them from his presence until now. (2 Kings 13:23)

For thou didst separate them . . . to be thy heritage, as thou didst declare through Moses, thy servant. (1 Kings 8:53; cf. 56) (See also 2 Kings 20:6)

This latter group of passages indicates that for the Deuteronomist the old promises still had power beyond their first fulfillment. Even in later generations they could still move God to be mindful of his people. It should be noted, however, that for the Deuteronomist only the promises to Moses and to the patriarchs had this "classic" significance. In spite of its great significance, the proclamation of salvation to David had been invalidated by the disobedience of the royal house, but in this connection no mention is ever made of an oracle given by a prophet. This is probably due to the awareness that the significance of the prophets from

Amos to the exile is found in their proclamation of judgment, and that the oracles of salvation contained in their
writings have only partial and limited significance.

Conclusion: Oracles of Salvation
Prior to the Writing Prophets

The oracles prior to the time of the writing prophets
show that in the history of Israel there was never a period
without oracles of salvation. They also show that each oracle is determined by the situation in which it is given. One
part of the situation is the form of society: family, wandering group, tribes occupying the land, people under the
monarchy. The differences are found in the nature of what
is announced or promised. In this, however, there is an unequivocal constant: the proclamation of an act of deliverance. We find it in the promises to the patriarchs, in the
proclamation of salvation to the wandering tribes and to the
people under the monarchy, whether to the people as a
whole, or to individuals, or to the king. It is missing only in
the time of the occupation of the land, but we may say that
it is implicit in the formula by which the land is given to
them. Occurrences of that formula are limited to this period
of the history. Only in these sections do we find the assurance of victory, and it is never given by a prophet.

Alongside the proclamation of deliverance we find the
promises of blessing, beginning in the time of the occupation of the land (Balaam). They are glimpses of the future,
and as such they can be combined with the proclamation of
salvation. However, they remain separate down to later
times, and as a depiction of a situation, the promise of blessing remains distinguishable from the proclamation of deliverance. The proclamation of deliverance is the distinctive
feature of the historical books. It was combined with the
promise of blessing only in the prophetic oracles of salvation in the exilic and postexilic periods.

It is blessing that is at issue in God's words to kings to
confirm and guarantee the permanence of the institution of
the monarchy. Greatness and fame promised to the king are
coordinated with victory in war. In the late Old Testament
period the confirmation and guarantee of permanence is
found in modified form and applied to Israel.

A note on the usage of terminology: Since "promise" is the traditional designation in the Pentateuch (promises to the fathers), but in the prophetic books it is "proclamation of salvation," the two terms can be regarded as synonymous.

PART TWO

Prophetic Oracles
of Salvation, Group 1

2

Deutero-Isaiah

Deutero-Isaiah's message as contained in chapters 40–55 is, as a whole, a proclamation of salvation, a situation not duplicated in any other prophetic book. The reason for this is that the proclamation is concentrated on a single event, the liberation of Israel from Babylonian captivity. A further difference is that here we do not have individual oracles one after another, as for example in the collection in Jeremiah 30–33. Rather we have a coherent whole consisting of various literary forms and combinations of such forms, and the main lines of the composition can be recognized. This can be seen in the framework provided by the prologue in 40:1–11 and the corresponding epilogue in 55:8–11, 12–13.

The fact that this is the only complex of oracles of salvation in the Old Testament that can be dated with certainty and whose historical context is known makes it necessary to begin here with our investigation of the oracles of salvation.

The various literary forms in Isaiah 40–55 are all used in connection with the message of salvation; they do not, however, merely announce deliverance but seek to make the proclamation both understandable and convincing, especially in the passages attacking mistaken beliefs. They also set the messages in the great historical context of God's dealings with his people, past and present. The proclamation made in the present is expanded to include the past and the future.

The past is included by the intensive and variously repeated references to God's saving actions in the history of
his people, almost exclusively in proclamations and assurances of salvation. It is done in reminders of the guilt that
Israel has brought on itself in falling away from God (in
controversies such as Isaiah 43:22–28), and of the necessity
of God's judgment on his people as the response to their
apostasy (also in controversies), but also in remembrance of
the suffering that God in his acts of judgment had to bring
upon his own people (this only in the proclamations of salvation, such as 48:5–11).

The future brings the liberation that Deutero-Isaiah proclaims, but it is not like God's earlier saving deeds in every
respect. The prophet distinguishes between the "new" and
the "former things." It is something new, because the liberation from Babylonian captivity is accomplished in a different manner—through the Persian king Cyrus, whom God
has commissioned, and not through the armed forces of Israel. We read of this in the texts that speak of Cyrus and
open a new perspective into the future. In addition there
are the messages of judgment that deal with the divine nature of God, that is, with the distinction between God and
the gods.

The purpose of this expansion is to explain these proclamations of salvation as part of a historical sequence which is
based on the whole of Israel's history, which can even be
said to encompass that history. Yahweh "created" this people for himself, he "chose" them, he showed them faithful-
ness along the road they traveled, he has "graven" them on
the palms of his hands (49:16). But these people have
turned from him, have been unfaithful to him, have fallen
away from him. Thus God must bring judgment on them; he
has had to give up "Jacob to the spoiler, and Israel to the
robbers" (42:24). This could have meant the end of Israel's
history. That is has continued is solely because of God's
mercy on his people. That God has turned once again to his
people is shown in that he suffers under the judgment that
he has had to bring upon them: "For a long time I have held
my peace, I have kept still and restrained myself" (42:14).
Thus the suffering that Yahweh has had to bring upon his
people, and that he himself finds heavy, breaks forth in the
lament of the people, "How long?" When God turns again

to his people they are liberated, gathered together, and brought home. The deliverance is followed by blessing on the future of the people whom God has freed, a future that will now be open also to the nations.

While the list of motifs from the earlier saving deeds of God down to the return of the exiles has its points of correspondence with the traditional oracles of salvation, in Deutero-Isaiah when the prophet speaks Yahweh's words of judgment on the peoples and the oracles about Cyrus we find a new and distinctive extension of his activity for his people. This is revealed in his work as creator (40:12–31) and as Lord of the whole world, in much the same way as we find it in the praise of God in the Psalms. Out of this extension emerges that which is new, reaching beyond liberation toward the future of the people of God. It is this that makes liberation possible through Cyrus the Persian king without any necessity for Israel itself to contribute to this liberation, or to defeat or destroy the oppressor, and thus the future is open to all. It is the inclusion of the praise of God in the Psalms that makes possible this broadening of the future. The words by which God brings the gods to judgment show that there can be only one creator and lord of history (41:1–5).

41:4 "Who has performed and done this?"
44:6b "I am the first and I am the last;
besides me there is no god."
(See also 41:21–29; 43:8–15)

But this One is able to transform that which is future into that which is present (41:21–29).

The inner coherence of the individual literary forms that Deutero-Isaiah uses is derived from the situation in which he proclaimed his message of salvation. He made use of the form of the oracle that responds to the lament of the individual, which continued to be given throughout the time of the catastrophe, as Lamentations 3 shows. The prophet could make use of this tradition and build on the relationship of personal trust which we know from the Psalms, e.g., Psalm 23, and which endured in so many forms in personal crises. (See R. Albertz, *Persönliche Frömmigkeit und offizielle Religion,* 1978, 188.)

Deutero-Isaiah's proclamation will now be explored from

two aspects: first, in a very brief discussion of the literary forms which the prophet used, and second, in a survey of the motifs in the sequence just discussed in which God's history with his people is set forth. This sequence recurs in a number of oracles following the time of Deutero-Isaiah. The significance of Deutero-Isaiah's proclamation can be fully grasped only through its working out in the oracles of the exilic and postexilic periods.

The Development of the Message in Its Various Forms

The Promise of Salvation (Oracle of Salvation)

This form is found only in Isaiah 41:8–13, 14–16; 43:1–7; and 44:1–5, but there are echoes in 54:4–6 and 51:12–13. It occurs only in Deutero-Isaiah and in passages that borrow his style. Deutero-Isaiah himself developed this form by analogy to the oracle of salvation to the individual, and especially the oracle to the king as found in a large number of Assyrian texts. (See M. Weippert, "Assyrische Prophetien der Zeit Asarhaddons und Assurbanipals," in F. M. Fales, ed., *Assyrian Royal Inscriptions*, Orientis Antiqui Collectio XVII, 1981, 71–113; E. W. Conrad, "Second Isaiah and the Priestly Oracle of Salvation," ZAW 93, 1981, 234–246; and idem, "The 'Fear Not' Oracles in Second Isaiah 34," ZAW 96, 1984, 129–152.) When Deutero-Isaiah directs to the people as a whole the reassuring words "Fear not," originally meant for an individual, he is personifying the people and intensifying the oracle as a message of comfort. His personal message derives its direct appeal to the human heart from these assurances of deliverance, as voiced in the initial words of the book, "Comfort, comfort my people!" The giving of comfort is a personal, matter, as when a mother comforts a child.

The divisions of the promise of salvation (with various expansions) are the call of reassurance (fear not); the basis of reassurance in the perfect tense or a nominal form; and the future-oriented basis, identical with the proclamation of salvation.

The Proclamation of Salvation

This constitutes the future-oriented basis of the assurance and can be an independent element or combined with other forms. The message of God's openness to the people is addressed to their plight, answers their lament, and announces the coming change for the better. Apart from these elements, which are basic to them, the proclamations of salvation are structured in various ways. The basic outline is provided by the lament of the people, in the petition for God's intervention, and in God's action. In all the texts the intervention that is proclaimed is limited to the act of deliverance. Nothing is said about what follows. The conclusion often consists of the praise that the one rescued offers to God, or the acknowledgment of God's deeds on behalf of the people, God's defeat of peoples and kings.

Proclamations of salvation as independent units are found in Isaiah 41:17–20 (following the assurance of salvation in 41:8–16); 42:14–17; 43:16–21; 45:14–17 (fragmentary); and 49:7–12.

The Proclamation of Salvation in Larger Units

Isaiah 49:14–26

This unit is in three parts: 14–20, 21–23, and 24–26. The tripartite form of the lament is the basis of this composition: The lament against God, "Yahweh has forsaken me" (v. 14); the personal lament, "I was bereaved and barren" (v. 21); the complaint against the foes, "Can the prey be taken from the mighty?" (v. 24). In each of the parts introduced in this way, a word of salvation is given that corresponds to the lament. The composition brings the connections between the proclamation of salvation and the lament of the people to clear expression.

Isaiah 51:9–52:3

Here is a different type of composition, determined by the three imperatives from the same verb root at the beginning of the three sections: 51:9–16; 51:17–23; 52:1–3. The meaning of this sequence of imperatives is explained by the third, the call to move out from captivity, "Loose the bonds from your neck," which is also a proclamation of liberation. This is preceded in the first part by the cry for help in the lament of the people in 51:9a, "Put on strength, O arm of

the Lord" (cf. Ps. 44:24, 27). Isaiah 51:9b–10 points back
to God's earlier mighty deeds. The pledge of rescue in 12–
16 answers this cry for help by pointing to God's power as
Creator, as in 40:12–31.

In part two the cry at the beginning is repeated with variations and is now directed to Jerusalem (51:17a). This reminds us of God's judgment on Jerusalem and then
describes it in detail in vs. 21–23, with the proclamation
that the "cup of his wrath" will now be turned away from
Jerusalem.

Part three, 52:1–3, is again introduced with an imperative and calls the people to rise up in freedom. (On the text,
see my *Isaiah 40–66, A Commentary*, OTL, 1969; probably
51:11 belongs here at the end of the passage.)

The sequence of the three parts of 51:9–52:3 is then as
follows:

> God's earlier saving deeds (51:9–16)
> Israel's apostasy and God's judgment (51:17–23)
> God's return in grace (all three parts)
> Deliverance from captivity (52:1–3)
> [Perhaps here, the return (51:11)]

The Commission to Cyrus and the Fall of Babylon

These oracles too have as their purpose the proclamation
of salvation, but they all deal with what is new, the deliverance of Israel from captivity in Babylon.

Isaiah 44:24–45:7

This passage is a unified, self-contained oracle, bounded
by the corresponding verses 44:24, "I am the Lord, who
made all things," and 45:7, "I form light and create darkness. . . . I am the Lord, who do all these things." The center of the whole oracle is the royal oracle to Cyrus in 45:1–
3, which assures him of success in his campaign against Babylon. The framework consists of the introductory messenger formula, expanded through first-person statements in a
chain of participial phrases (44:24–28), and the conclusion
(45:4–7), which declares that the oracle to Cyrus is given
"for the sake of my servant Jacob."

The distinctive feature of this oracle is that the proclamation of salvation which it contains (v. 26b) is not ascribed to the God who chose Israel to be his people (45:4a), but to the creator of heaven and earth (44:24b, 27 and 45:7; compare 48:12–15 with 51:12–16), who as such is the Lord of history (45:1–3).

Isaiah 45:9–13

Three verses of this unit (11–13) belong to the oracles of judgment. Yahweh answers charges that bring into question his actions for his people. The answer corresponds item by item with the charges (44:24–45:7). As creator of the world and of humankind (v. 12), Yahweh can command Cyrus and prepare his way, so that God's people can be liberated and his city rebuilt. The two woes in vs. 9–10 are probably later additions (K. Elliger).

Isaiah 45:18–46:13

This unit is a composition in three parts: introduction, 45:18–19; the nations, 45:20–25; and Israel, 46:1–13. It presupposes the oracle to Cyrus in 44:24–45:7 and addresses those who are offended by it (note the three negative statements in 18–19 in the style of dispute oracles). As creator of heaven and earth God alone is God (cf. 44:24). He did not create the earth void, but made it suitable for human habitation (only here). God created the earth as a dwelling for all the peoples. The allusion to Genesis 1 is continued in vs. 20–25. Verse 19 is the introduction to 46:1–13 and is to be understood in that context.

The oracle in 45:20–25 is quite similar to the oracles to the nations, but the second exhortation, v. 22, "Turn to me and be saved, all the ends of the earth!" goes beyond them. This is found only here in Deutero-Isaiah; only here are the "survivors of the nations" addressed. The fall of Babylon (46:1–4) will no longer mean the destruction of all its inhabitants. There will be "survivors," as there were after the catastrophe that befell Israel, and to them the exhortation in vs. 22–24 is addressed. The triumph of the victors is delayed, and in its stead we have this invitation. Isaiah 45:20–25 is in sharp distinction to the spirit of the oracles that follow Deutero-Isaiah. Group 2 of the oracles of salvation are a marked contrast to what is proclaimed here.

The first two verses of the oracle in 46:1–13 are a variation on the message of victory. They point back to 45:20–25 and forward to 46:3–4 and 9–13, the meaning of the message of victory for Israel. The address in 46:3, "remnant of the house of Israel" (found only here), corresponds to the expression "you survivors of the nations" (45:20). Those who come through a catastrophe share a common destiny. The three divisions in 46:1–13 are marked by three imperatives, "Hearken to me" (v. 3), "Remember the former things of old" (v. 9), and "Hearken to me" (v. 12). Verses 1–2 are a proclamation of victory that anticipates the fall of Babylon. The two high gods of the Babylonian Empire have collapsed; the statues of the gods have been carried away in the collapse of the empire. They were unable to save; they themselves had to be saved, to be transported away! In the hour of catastrophe we see what it means that the gods are tied to their images. In a profound play on words it is said by contrast that the God of Israel is the one who carries his people through the catastrophe. Israel experienced this in its history whenever that which God announced came true. So too they will now experience that this promised liberation will become reality.

Isaiah 48:1–17

The cycle of Cyrus oracles could be concluded with 46:1–13. Chapter 48:1–17 adds nothing to what has been said. It is a concluding summary and is to be read as a unit, contrary to what I said in my commentary. In the detailed contrast between the old and the new the prophet emphasizes that the saving action of God which is now proclaimed differs from that which was proclaimed earlier. Since he tacitly turns his attention to the doubters, the text resembles the disputation oracles. This is the reason for the repeated exhortations to listen. The new is based on God's works as creator, involving a work wrought by the Creator and Lord of history. Following the end of this text there is an exhortation to go forth from Babylon, contained in a song of praise that belongs to the cycle of Cyrus oracles (48:20–21). It is a call to liberation and it brings forth the response,

"The Lord has redeemed his servant Jacob!" The message of liberation includes the message that God will lead his people home, in allusion to the exodus from Egypt.

Yahweh's Judgment on the Peoples

These oracles are found only in Isaiah 41–44 and lead up to the Cyrus oracles in 44–45. They deal with Yahweh's claim to be god. Yahweh, the God of Israel, denies to the gods, primarily the gods of Babylon, the right to make this claim. Thus the oracles take the form of a judgment oracle: summons, presentation of the claim, arguments and counterarguments, presentation of witnesses, and verdict or the silence of the defendants.

Isaiah 41:1–5

In vs. 2–3 Yahweh advances the claim that as the Lord of history he had aroused Cyrus (cf. 41:25; 43:14). It is Yahweh alone who has announced this (41:21–22, 25, 26; 43:12; 44:7–8. Israel can bear testimony that Yahweh has brought to pass all that he foretold (43:10–13). In 44:6–8, 21–22 the words of judgment merge into words of deliverance for Israel. Here the demonstration of divine power is no longer, as elsewhere in the ancient world, shown in a simple display of power in war; it is shown by God's leading his people through history in such a way that his words and his deeds agree, that what he foretells comes to pass, that is, by the continuity of his works. In this respect the gods of Babylon have failed. The claim to deity on the basis of this principle means that there can be only one God (41:4, 26–27; 43:10–11, 13; 44:6). This claim becomes the basis of the certainty of the salvation that has been proclaimed, and this certainty attains central theological significance. If Yahweh alone is God, then he is also the sole Lord of history, who holds in his hand the fulfillment of that which has been foretold.

The Disputation Oracles

A distinction is to be made between two groups of these oracles. The first group is directed against the despair of the people and their persistent lamenting, as seen in the first major poem following the prologue (40:12–31), where the quarrel is found in vs. 27–31. Similarly in the first composition of the major group, chapters 49–52, salvation is announced in 49:14–26 in response to the threefold lament (49:14, 21, 24). This text was considered above among the proclamations of salvation. The lament and its refutation are integral parts of the text.

The second group contains oracles of God's judgment on his people (42:18–28; 43:22–28; 51:1–3). These oracles deny that God has forsaken his people. He had to punish them because of their sins, but that is not his final word.

Isaiah 40:12–31

In this larger composition the actual quarrel is found only in the final verses, 27–31. The questions in the preceding parts serve to call the people back to the praise of God's majesty. Chapter 40:27 contains an accusation that the people brought against God after the collapse of the state: "Why do you say, . . . 'My way is hid from the Lord'?" In answer the prophet tells the mourners to praise God. In this passage God's majesty, as praised in vs. 12–26, is summarized in v. 28, "The Lord is the everlasting God, the Creator. . . . He does not faint or grow weary, his understanding is unsearchable"; and God's goodness is praised in vs. 29–31, "He gives power to the faint." By so doing the prophet awakens the praise of God that had been silenced, and sets it in contrast to the despair and fatigue of the people.

Isaiah 49:14–26

This text, discussed above at p. 43, combines a proclamation of salvation with a dispute oracle. In response to the lament of the exiled people, salvation is proclaimed in such a way that the accusation brought against God, the lament of the people, and the lament against the foes are all contrasted with the prospect that God will be gracious to his people. Similarly in the dispute oracles in 42:18–25; 43:22–28; and 50:1–3 it is denied that God has forsaken his people. God had to punish his people because of their sins.

Isaiah 42:18–25

This unit bristles with problems. It is clear from the many questions in vs. 19ab, 23, 24a that the text is a dispute oracle. But the conclusion is missing. Perhaps these verses are intended as an introduction to 43:1–7. Yahweh addresses his people as blind and deaf, because in all that they have experienced with Yahweh they have learned nothing. But now that God has brought judgment on them they bewail their misery. They accuse God of having forsaken them. There was "none to rescue" them. If they had not been deaf and blind they would have had to "attend and listen for the time to come" (v. 23). They would have had to stop and think, "Was it not the Lord against whom we sinned?" (v. 24). But they did not take it to heart, and here the text breaks off. Chapter 43:1–7 begins, "But now thus says the Lord . . . ."

Isaiah 43:22–28

Yahweh here rejects the accusation that Israel makes in v. 28:

> Therefore I profaned the princes of the sanctuary,
> I delivered Jacob to utter destruction
> and Israel to reviling.

Israel bases this accusation on the claim that it has served Yahweh faithfully through its offerings and sacrifices. But Yahweh rejects even that claim. In the center of this oracle we find the reversal of the argument with which Israel justifies its accusation of God: "[You have not really served me.] But you have burdened me with your sins, you have wearied me with your iniquities" (v. 24b). (On the wordplay with *'abad,* meaning either "burdened" or "worshiped," compare 46:1–2; and on both passages see my book *The Parables of Jesus in the Light of the Old Testament,* 1990.)

Here Deutero-Isaiah is clearly referring to the cultic denunciation which the prophets of judgment had called down on the inauthentic worship that had brought judgment on itself. But the goal of God's rejection is not the confirmation of his judgment on Israel. God wants to make it known that he has forgiven his people and is now favorable to them again. Thus this dispute oracle is also in the service of the proclamation of salvation.

Isaiah 50:1–3

This passage begins with a question that resembles an oracle of judgment and plunges into the middle of the issue: "Where is your mother's bill of divorce, with which I put her away?" It responds to the complaint that God has rejected Israel, with whom he had made a covenant, the same complaint as that which lies behind 40:27 (cf. Ps. 44:13). God's response does not deny the fact of rejection, but stresses that God had to do this (cf. 43:28). Israel's sins have called forth God's judgment. The complainant is silent in the face of God's reply. Verse 1 has already indicated Yahweh's readiness to be gracious again to his people, and 2b deals with the other complaint, that God was powerless to help, by affirming God's power as Creator (as in 40:12–26, 28). The Creator is able to bring about vast changes (Ps. 107:33). Israel can therefore be certain that this God can bring about their release.

The Songs of Praise

The songs of praise that are found throughout Deutero-Isaiah's proclamation include 40:9–11; 42:10–13; 44:23; 45:8; 48:20–21; 49:13; 51:3 (fragment); 52:7–12; 54:1–2. Already at the end of the prologue, 40:9–11, there are hints of the songs to come. Often they stand at the end of a section, as in 44:23; 48:21; 52:9–10. This in itself makes their function clear. They are the answer of those to whom the prophet's proclamation is addressed and who accept it, that is, they are a choral response. They speak the language of worship of the Psalms, and are themselves short psalms. In contrast to the psalms of praise in the Psalter, Deutero-Isaiah created his own forms of the songs of praise. They are, first, an imperative call to praise or to rejoicing, and second, a basis for praise in the perfect, stating that Yahweh has come.

The difference is that in the Psalms the imperative call to praise is followed by descriptive praise, but here by declarative (narrative) praise. Declarative praise, though in the perfect tense, does not describe something that has already taken place, but speaks of an event that is proclaimed as if it had already taken place. It is the same perfect that in the prologue introduces the message, "Cry to her that her warfare is ended, that her iniquity is pardoned" (Isa. 40:2b; cf. 40:9–11).

Praise in the Perfect

All these texts consist of announcements of salvation. The perfect (or present) anticipates an event that lies yet in the future and proclaims that it will happen. In all these texts without exception the event that awakens jubilation is the deliverance of Israel from exile. The artistry and the theological profundity of these "proclamations" is that this historical event as such is never identified unambiguously. That which is proclaimed (in the perfect) is for the most part God's turning once again to his people.

49:13 "For the Lord has comforted his people,
   and will have compassion on his afflicted."
 40:2 " . . . that her warfare is ended,
   that her iniquity is pardoned."
 51:3 "For the Lord will comfort Zion;
   he will comfort all her waste places."

In these three passages it is a personal transaction that forms the basis for the call to rejoicing and praise; it is the act in which God turns again to his people, not a historical event.
 The same is true of three texts that contain the verb *ga'al*:

44:23 "For the Lord has redeemed Jacob,
   and will be glorified in Israel."
48:20f. " 'The Lord has redeemed his servant Jacob!' . . .
  He led them through the deserts;
   he made water flow for them from the rock."
 52:9f. "For the Lord has comforted his people,
   he has redeemed Jerusalem."

The verb *ga'al*, which has its origin in family law, indicates a personal turning to someone, as is seen especially in the parallelism of "comforted" and "redeemed" in 52:9–10.

The one remaining text is 45:8, "I the Lord have created it." This is a general, abstract expression that really does not refer to a historical event.

In this way the reasons in the perfect tense for the calls to joy and to praise are protected from the misunderstanding that they are mere predictions. That which here summons the people to praise, jubilation, and rejoicing is something that happens with God, and thus cannot be defined in historical terms: God has returned to his people. That is truly an event in the perfect tense; it has already happened.

In two places what has happened is portrayed in the perfect as a battle and victory:

> 42:13   "The Lord goes forth like a mighty man . . .
>   he shows himself mighty against his foes."
> 52:10   "The Lord has bared his holy arm
>   before the eyes of all the nations."

This is, however, a reminder of the time of the wars of Yahweh and by no means necessarily indicates an act of war in the present.

Praise in the Imperative

It strikes the reader at first glance that the passages in the imperative are in every respect more fully developed, and almost always longer, than those in the perfect. Deutero-Isaiah must have been particularly concerned with these passages, probably because they are a conscious extension of the imperative calls to praise in the Psalms. Closely related to these passages are the imperatives in which those addressed are called to praise or rejoicing, joined by the peoples of all the earth, as in 52:10.

> 42:10–13   "Sing to the Lord a new song,
>   his praise from the end of the earth! . . .
>   Let them give glory to the Lord,
>   and declare his praise in the coastlands."
> 48:20–21   "Declare this with a shout of joy, proclaim it,
>   send it forth to the end of the earth;
>   say . . . ."
>   51:3   "Joy and gladness will be found in her,
>   thanksgiving and the voice of song."

52:9–10 "Break forth together into singing,
    you waste places of Jerusalem;
for . . . "

The call to the "waste places of Jerusalem" marks the transition to the next group. It could literally mean the ruins of the buildings, but it could also refer in a general sense to all that survived the catastrophe. In this case the ruins and the surviving persons are seen as one.

All Creation Is Called to Praise

42:10b "Let the sea roar and all that fills it,
    the coastlands and their inhabitants.
42:11 Let the desert and its cities lift up their voice,
    the villages that Kedar inhabits;
let the inhabitants of Sela sing for joy,
    let them shout from the top of the mountains."
44:23 "Sing, O heavens . . . ,
    shout, O depths of the earth;
break forth into singing, O mountains,
    O forest, and every tree in it!"
49:13 "Sing for joy, O heavens, and exult, O earth;
    break forth, O mountains, into singing!"
45:8 "Shower, O heavens, from above,
    and let the skies rain down righteousness;
let the earth open, that salvation may sprout forth,
    and . . . righteousness . . . spring up also."
55:12 "The mountains and the hills before you
    shall break forth into singing,
and all the trees of the field shall clap their hands."

Without doubt, the continuation of the call to praise, which always tends to expand, moves here with these imperatives out to the created world and into that world, as we see happening in Israel's psalms of praise (e.g., Psalm 148). The difference is that in the Psalms the call to the creation is descriptive praise, while here it is declarative (narrative) praise. The created world is to join in the joyful praise, because Yahweh has turned again to his people. This is closely related to the "new," that the proclaimed liberation of Israel is made possible by God the Creator, who after the catastrophe remains Lord of creation and Lord of

history (40:12–31; 44:24–45:7; 48:12–15; 51:12–16).
Here what is said of God as Savior and of God as Creator are
quite close. The combination of the call to praise with God's
saving action in the perfect tense is already found in the
formula *baruk yhwh* ("blessed be Yahweh, who has . . . ") in
early prose texts such as 1 Samuel 25:32, 33. Thus in Isaiah
42:10, 11 we find humans and the created world mentioned
together, and in 45:8 the showers of blessing are included in
the praise of God.

In all these passages we encounter a function of the Hebrew imperative that is distinctive and whose meaning is
not yet fully recognized. This is the use of the imperative
within the proclamation of salvation, in which, on the usual
understanding of the function of the imperative, it has no
place and makes no sense. It is far removed from the function of a command, as suggested by the term "imperative."
Rather these calls to praise are in sharp distinction to any
sort of command. It is necessary to reach a new understanding and definition of the functions of the so-called imperative in the Old Testament in terms of their context so that
the proper meanings of these functions can be identified
and distinguished from one another. (On this issue see the
festschrift for Alfons Deissler, *Der Weg zum Menschen,*
1989, 13–27, "Bedeutung und Funktion des Imperativs in
den Geschichtsbüchern des Alten Testaments.")

The Individual Motifs

The Motifs of Assurance of Salvation

In exploring the individual motifs of assurance of salvation it is necessary to distinguish between two differing
groups. The first group is always constant and its main features do not change: introduction; address with terms in
apposition; words of reassurance; basis of reassurance
(nominal forms); basis of reassurance (verbal forms):

> Terms in apposition to Yahweh, the speaker: Self-identification
> (as in 43:1a; 51:13)
> Terms in apposition to Israel, the one addressed: Looking
> back to God's former deeds (as in 41:8–9, 13, 14a; 43:1b;
> 44:2b; 51:12–13)

Words of reassurance (41:10, 13, 14a; 43:1b; 51:12–13)
Basis of reassurance (nominal): (41:13, 14b; 43:1b, 3, 5; 54:4a, 5; 51:12–13)
Basis of reassurance (verbal): (41:13, 14b; 43:1b; 54:6; 51:14 [future])

The two categories of basis for reassurance can always be distinguished, but the language remains general. They never include a concrete historical statement, because the assurance of salvation was originally directed to individuals. This is seen above all in the nominal category: "I am with you" (41:10a; 43:2, 5), with the variants "I am your God" (41:10a, 13a), "your Redeemer" (41:14; 54:5), "your Savior" (43:3). All these statements have as their basis the promise that God is with, or remains with, the people. They are first encountered in the patriarchal narratives, where they are without doubt directed to individuals (see my book *The Promises to the Fathers*, 1980, 130–133). They are found particularly in the promise to go with an individual as he sets out on a journey. But they are also found in many places in varied contexts throughout the old Testament. The verbal reassurance, by contrast, is not so limited: e.g., "I have redeemed you" (43:1b). See also 41:10, 13, 14. Only in the words of address and terms in apposition to them is it said unambiguously, insofar as God's earlier saving deeds are involved, that these promises of salvation are addressed to the people.

Thus we see that the first part of the assurance of salvation, the core of the statement, that this was not originally a statement addressed to the people. Already in the first sentence of the message, "Comfort, comfort my people," the people are addressed as an individual. The assurance of salvation intensifies the message by concentrating it on the narrow, intense range of the life of an individual human being, who is rescued from his plight by the message. Only in this limited scope is the assurance of salvation in the perfect tense possible and meaningful.

In the second, future part of the statement, the situation is different. To be sure, it is intended as the sequel to the part that is in the present or the perfect tense, but it clearly bears on the future of the people in the wider historical context of the nations. Therefore it speaks of concrete

events and agrees with the proclamation of future salvation
wherever this is preceded by an oracle of salvation. In this
part too we meet only motifs which are found also in independent proclamations of salvation.

The individual motifs of the proclamation of salvation and
the secondary forms can be structured according to the sequence of events that are found in the proclamation of
Deutero-Isaiah as a whole, so that the proclamation of deliverance can be placed in the total context of the history of
God's dealings with his people Israel (see above, pp. 39ff.):
God's earlier saving deeds; the apostasy of the people; God's
judgment on his people; the lament of the people from the
depths of their suffering; God's return to his people; deliverance, assembly and return; God's blessing; the future that is
open to the nations. The motifs are as follows.

1. God's earlier saving deeds for his people

At the beginning of each oracle these are referred to by
terms in apposition to Yahweh, the subject, and Israel, the
object. Yahweh has chosen Israel (41:8, 9; 44:1; 43:10, 18;
45:4; 49:7); he created Israel (43:1–7, 15–16, 20–21; 44:2,
21, 24); he is their redeemer (44:6, 24). He brought deliverance to Israel at the beginning of their history (41:8–9;
43:16–17); we see the former things (43:18 and elsewhere,
51:9–10); he remains true to Israel and accessible to them
(49:7, 15; 43:10).

2. Israel's apostasy and Yahweh's judgment

50:1–3   "Behold, for your iniquities you were sold . . . "
43:24   "You have wearied me with your iniquities . . . "
43:28   "Therefore . . .
         I delivered Jacob to utter destruction . . . "
42:24   "Who gave up Jacob to the spoiler,
         and Israel to the robbers?
         Was it not the Lord, against whom we have
            sinned . . . ?"

3. The suffering that Yahweh had to bring on his people

42:14   "For a long time I have held my peace,
         I have kept still and restrained myself."

> 51:17 "You who have drunk at the hand of the Lord
> the cup of his wrath . . . "
>
> 51:19–20 "These two things have befallen you:
> devastation and destruction, famine and sword. . . .
> Your sons . . . lie at the head of every street . . . ,
> full of the wrath of the Lord."
>
> 49:7 " . . . one deeply despised, abhorred by the
> nations,
> the servant of rulers."

4. The lament motifs

The proclamation of salvation often begins after the introduction (which may be missing) with a lament or allusion to a lament. It gives expression to the situation in which the proclamation is made. It is always a lament of the people, or a part of such a lament, while the oracle itself presupposes an individual lament. The lament of the people corresponds to the proclamation, which in turn presupposes the distress of the people. It is usually not a sorrowful description of the situation of the exiles in Babylon, but consists almost entirely of motifs derived from the traditional lamentation of the people, as we find it in the Psalms. This is especially clear in 49:14–26, where the three parts of the message begin with motifs of the three parts of the lament: Accusation against God (v. 14), first-person plural lament (v. 21), lament about the foes (v. 24). This example shows that the three parts of the lament served the author as elements of his composition and that beginning the oracle of salvation with a lament was deliberate.

The accusation against God (40:27; 42:14; 49:14; 51:17; 54:7a, 8a). Because in these statements the accusation is only alluded to, its wording is often changed into a statement made by God.

The first-person plural lament (40:6–8; 41:17a; 42:22; 49:7, 21; 51:17b–21; 54:4b).

The lament about the foes: This has almost disappeared and is only hinted at in 42:22; 49:7, 24. Only one passage, 51:17b–21, is more detailed, and it is the only passage that portrays in context the situation after the catastrophe. Therefore it closely resembles the songs of lament. Laments from other situations could be transferred to the situation

following the catastrophe, such as the lament in drought
(41:17), the lament over human frailty (40:6–8), over childlessness (49:21) or widowhood (54:4). Often the lament includes Yahweh's anger and his judgments that have brought
the suffering (42:14; 51:17, 20; 54:7a, 8a).

In terms of tradition history, beginning a proclamation of
salvation with lament (or allusion to a lament of the people)
means that the prophet is expressing the situation in which
he is addressing his hearers by using their own words. For
them lament is the language of suffering. The laments of the
people, of which we have echoes here, are recognized by
those who hear them. This shows how in Deutero-Isaiah
prophecy and worship come together. We know the great
significance which the acts of lamentation held after the
catastrophe. This is also indicated by the similarity between
the extended lament in Isaiah 51:17b–20 and the psalms of
lament. The major poem in 40:1–31, in which the comfort
of v. 1 builds toward the lament in v. 27, corresponds to the
structure of the proclamation of salvation in its use of the
lament.

5. God turns again to his people

Another point of correspondence between the proclamation of salvation and the psalms of lament is that in both of
these forms the pleas and petitions addressed to God are
always in two parts—the petition for God to turn again to
his people, and for God to intervene. Thus in the proclamations of salvation God's turning again to his people is a particularly important motif. It brings the lament to an end,
and this is often mentioned or hinted at as in 51:22, "I have
taken from your hand the cup of staggering" (see also
41:17; 49:15; 54:7–8). God's turning again to his people
always implies his forgiveness, and sometimes it is expressed (40:1–2; 43:25; 44:21–22).

This begins with God hearing the cries of his people as in
41:17: "I the Lord will answer them." See also 49:8. In the
other passages the hearing is implied; instead of "pledge of
salvation" we might say "pledge of a hearing." This element also confirms the connection between the oracle of
salvation and the prayer psalm. God turns again to his peo-

ple because of his compassion for them: "With everlasting love I will have compassion on you" (54:8; cf. 49:13; 52:9). Because God is moved with pity, he comforts the people (40:1–2; 49:13; 51:3, 12). This pity which God shows to his people is not a divine attribute, but is rather an action, the pity which is expressed at the sight of suffering. This corresponds to the accounts of healing in the New Testament. Jesus sees those who are suffering, and he is "moved with pity." It is the same compassion that we find in the praise of God in the Psalms, and which turns the lament into praise (e.g., Psalm 103).

God's turning again to his people is expressed in a variety of metaphors: The cries of a woman in travail that announce the coming birth (42:14; 49:15); "Behold, I have taken from your hand the cup of staggering" (51:22); the wife is taken back again (49:16; 55:5–6); "He gives power to the faint" (40:29–31); "even . . . to gray hairs I will carry you" (46:4). The figures of speech reinforce the nature of God's turning again to his people as an event.

6. God's intervention, the liberation

When God turns again to his people, his intervention follows. It involves several motifs: The intervention as such— God has acted (44:23), has created (45:8)—and an epiphany, "Behold your God!" (40:9). He intervenes as a warrior, a heroic figure (42:13; 55:5–6, 9–10).

There is an astonishingly large number of ways for expressing liberation, or deliverance, or redemption. Although the same historical event is being referred to, its description is never stereotyped. In many of the statements involved, liberation is only implied, and often the verb is transformed into a title for God, e.g., "your Redeemer." The most important and most frequently used verb is *ga'al,* "redeem" (43:1, 14; 44:22, 23; 48:20; 49:26; 52:3; 54:5). That the verb *ga'al* receives particular emphasis in Deutero-Isaiah's proclamation of salvation is due at least in part to its origin. The *go'el* was originally the one who looses, who redeems (see the article *ga'al* in *THAT* I). Other verbs also refer to the same event: release (51:4); help (41:13); hold (41:13); call by name (43:1); carry and save

(46:4); set the exiles free (45:13); leads you in the way you should go (48:17); sends to Babylon (43:14). The call to go forth sometimes takes the place of the act of liberation (48:20; 49:9; cf. 40:2).

Indirect expressions, allusions, comparisons all presuppose the proclamation of liberation (40:27–31; 41:17–20; 42:16–17; 44:24–25; 45:7). This is something "new" (43:19); it is the release of a prisoner (51:14); the loosing of bonds from a captive's neck (52:2); the calling of a bird of prey from the east (46:11); the giving of Egypt as a ransom (43:3); the bringing of salvation to Zion (46:13). The great variety of these statements, which all say the same thing, make it clear that this motif of "liberation" is the heart of the message of salvation. Any of the other motifs could be omitted, but this could not. It must at least be implicit in the text. This makes clearer the relationship of this motif to the proclamation of salvation. The part that points to the future and corresponds to the parts of the proclamation that follow, is separate from the part in the perfect and present tenses with its motif of "liberation" and the various other verbs, especially "redeem."

7. The defeat of the enemy

There are only a few passages that announce God's intervention against the oppressors. They generally use traditional language such as "I will contend with those who contend with you" (49:25; cf. Ps. 35:1). See also 42:13 (cf. 52:9–10); 41:11–12 and its development in vs. 15–16; 51:22–23. Several passages speak of the results of the defeat of the enemy: "Those who swallowed you up will be far away" (49:19–20); " . . . for there shall no more come into you the uncircumcised and the unclean" (52:10). The song of victory in 46:1–4 relates only to the gods of Babylon. In Deutero-Isaiah we find, instead of the destruction of Israel's oppressors, the commission to Cyrus to liberate the exiles of Israel. Then in the oracles of judgment the lawsuit takes the place of military action. In this context we also find that Deutero-Isaiah combines the proclamation of the fall of Babylon with his invitation to those of other nations who have escaped. This would not have been possible if Israel itself had been the victor.

8. The gathering together and return, the preparation of the way, protection along the way

While the proclamation of liberation says nothing about the specific circumstances, the proclamation of the gathering of the people and their return points to a unique, unmistakable event, the return of the Israelites from Babylonian exile. No other group of texts in the Old Testament sets forth so effectively the historical significance of the exile and return as do the many texts containing this one motif of the proclamation of salvation, and they are found not only in Deutero-Isaiah but also in a large number of other oracles. In addition, in many passages in Deutero-Isaiah and elsewhere these events are seen as parallel to the exodus from Egypt at the dawn of the nation's history. These parallels contributed greatly to the picture of Israel's history as a unity; see especially 51:9–10.

The gathering of the people is followed by the departure, the journey, the arrival. The gathering is portrayed in 43:5, "I will bring your offspring from the east . . ." (see also 49:12, 22). The departure, "For you shall go out in joy" (55:12), and the call to depart, "Rouse yourself, rouse yourself . . ." (51:17; see also 48:20; 52:5). Yahweh himself prepares the way for them: "I will make a way in the wilderness" (43:19; also 42:16; 49:11; cf. 40:3–5). He transforms the wilderness with water and vegetation (41:18–19; 43:19–20; 48:21; 55:13) and with food (49:9–10; 51:14; 55:12–13) amid the rejoicing of all nature. He goes with them on the way (42:14–17; 48:20–21) and protects them from all danger (43:2).

In all this God dealt with Israel on the way through the wilderness just as he had dealt with them after the deliverance from Egypt (51:9–10). They arrive back in Jerusalem, "And the ransomed of the Lord shall return, and come to Zion with singing" (51:11; cf. 49:18). The nations will bring Israel's sons and daughters home (49:22).

9. Restoration

Only a few passages contain this motif (44:26; 45:13; 49:8, 16–17). The restoration of the city of Jerusalem is proclaimed in two of the Cyrus oracles. The first is in

44:24–28, in the self-predication of God, "who says . . . of Jerusalem, 'She shall be built,' and of the temple, 'Your foundation shall be laid' " (v. 28). The second is in 45:13, where God says of Cyrus, "He shall build my city and set my exiles free." This motif is found elsewhere only in 49:16–17. The restoration appears only as a consequence of liberation in 49:8: "To establish the land, to apportion the desolate heritages."

Promise of Blessing

In the structure of Isaiah 40–55 the proclamation of salvation (or assurance of salvation) is followed by the promise of blessing, or depiction of blessing, which in origin is different from the proclamation of salvation and goes back to the earliest history of the people. The connection between the two, and the sequence in which promise of blessing follows on deliverance was already there for Deutero-Isaiah's use in the promise of the exodus in Deuteronomy 30:1–10, where we find deliverance in vs. 3–5a and blessing in 5b. Blessing constitutes the final section of 54:1–55:5, and the last of the promises of salvation ends with a promise of blessing (44:3–5). In the foreword to his book *Die prophetischen Heilserwartungen im Alten Testament* (1965), S. Herrmann speaks of deliverance and blessing as the content of the promise: " . . . in a series of promises . . . in which the God of Israel promises his people deliverance and blessing" (p. 1).

Isaiah 54:1–10 (17)

Both this passage and 55:1–5 begin with a cry of invitation. In chapter 54 it is a cry to the "barren one" (1a) with the promise of many children (1b). From the outset blessing and posterity belong together. In vs. 2–3 the same promise is restated in other words. The call to rejoice (v. 1) is resumed in v. 4a in words of reassurance, "Fear not." This is followed, however, not by assurance of salvation in the strict sense, but by allusions to it. By means of the broadly developed motif "God turns again to his people," the section that begins with v. 4 brings together the promise of blessing and the proclamation of salvation that preceded it.

In 4b–5 we have the basis for the call "Fear not" in the assurance that the abandoned wife will be taken back. In vs. 7–8 we find the same motif of acceptance after a period in which God had forsaken the people and hidden himself from them. With emphasis he says, "With great compassion I will gather you" (v. 7). The message is reinforced in vs. 9–10 by a metaphor of blessing chosen from the world of nature. The promise of a "covenant of peace" that God swears to keep corresponds to God's promise after the flood, "While the earth remains . . . " (Gen. 8:22). God's consistent activity in blessing is in accord with the permanent laws of the world of nature.

Isaiah 54:11–17

The description of Jerusalem's magnificent splendor in gold and precious stones (vs. 11–13) does not fit this context. It reminds us of the language of Trito-Isaiah and seems out of place here. While vs. 14–17 could follow directly on v. 10, the beginning of the passage is unclear. In this text also we are dealing with a state of well-being. Zion is assured of peace and security. K. Elliger holds that chapters 54 and 55 are from Trito-Isaiah. While this may be true of 54:11–13 it is less certain for 54:14–17. But it is not possible to deny the passages in 54:1–10 and 55:1–5 to Deutero-Isaiah. Elliger's ascription of 54–55 to Trito-Isaiah still leaves unclear why 54:11–13 is so different from its context.

Isaiah 55:1–5

This section also begins with a cry of invitation, with imperatives in vs. 1–3a that follow on those in 54:1–4. The imperatives introduce a proclamation of salvation (3b–5), with a twofold "Behold!" that emphasizes the relationship between vs. 4 and 5. The initial call to hear is expanded through a metaphor of satisfaction and delight (v. 2), in the language of blessing. The repeated call to come and buy is in imitation of the cries of vendors in the marketplace. The prophet then adds to the proclamation of deliverance the assurance that the fullness of God's blessing awaits them (vs. 3b–5). Harking back to the promise of a covenant with

David, God will now establish with his people an enduring
covenant like the one with David, a covenant of blessing.
But it is not a new "Davidic covenant" nor a "Messiah" that
is promised here. The promises to David are now transferred to the people, as the theme is developed in vs. 4–5.
Yahweh makes David "a witness to the peoples" by that
which he had done for David. In addition the new deliverance of Israel will bring about peace (cf. 45:20–25). The
promise is not that other peoples will be conquered, but
that through them the nation will grow (cf. 54:1–6). In all
this Yahweh will exalt Israel, but in a new way that differs
from that of David's time. Israel will be a witness (v. 4) to
the wonderful acts of Yahweh.

The Fulfillment of the Proclamation

Deutero-Isaiah stresses in various passages that those
things which had been proclaimed earlier, both judgment
and salvation, have come true: "Behold, the former things
have come to pass" (42:9). See also 44:26; 46:10; 48:3, 5.
Yahweh now reminds his people of the "former things" that
he proclaimed through his messengers (44:26), the judgment that the prophets proclaimed before the catastrophe,
as he now announces "new things": "New things I now
declare" (42:9; see also 48:6; 43:12; 44:8; 45:19, 21;
46:10). Chapter 48:15 refers directly to Cyrus: "I, even I,
have spoken and called him." It is denied that the gods of
Babylon had anything to do with this, especially in light of
the catastrophe that had befallen Babylon (41:27, 29; 43:9;
44:7; 48:14). Deutero-Isaiah said this in an hour in history
when it seemed that Yahweh had failed and been proven
impotent. In answer Deutero-Isaiah said that Yahweh's
lordship over history is proven in that even beyond the catastrophe of his own people that which he had proclaimed
had come true and thus provided historic continuity (46:1–
4). The fulfillment of the proclamations made earlier enables God's people to have unconditional trust in their God
and to rely on his word (55:10–11). Only in this way is a
"history of God with his people" possible. This is seen in
the Deuteronomic history, in which the reference to the
fulfillment of earlier promises is an important motif (see
above, pp. 32ff.).

The Worship Motifs

The basis of the worship motifs in the proclamation of Deutero-Isaiah is that both the assurances of salvation and the proclamations of salvation are related to the laments of the people and of the individual as these are collected in the Psalter, and thus to a worship tradition in Israel. In part the oracles of salvation are specific answers to such laments. Now since it is the case that in the Psalter lament and praise of God are related to each other in a variety of ways—for example, the psalms of lament lead to a vow of praise—it was easy for the proclamations of salvation to become combined with praise of God, and this in various ways. But since in terms of form criticism these worship motifs belong in the context of the psalms of lament and praise, they will be sketched here only briefly.

1. The assurance of salvation is not originally a prophetic form of speech, but has its origin in worship (J. Begrich, ZAW 52, 1934, 81–92) as God's word in response to laments of the individual (cf. Lam. 3:37).

2. In a large number of motifs the lament of the people is a component of Deutero-Isaiah's proclamation of salvation.

3. In Deutero-Isaiah's proclamation the frequent use of descriptive praise of God (hymnic elements), especially in 40:12–31, has the specific function of answering the charge that the God of Israel had failed and had abandoned his people, answering it by bringing vividly before the eyes of the exiles the greatness and majesty of their God, the Creator and the Lord of history. The same function is served by the many terms in apposition to Yahweh, which in their content are praise of God.

4. The closeness to worship is seen most clearly in the songs of praise found together with Deutero-Isaiah's proclamations of salvation, from the conclusion of the prologue to the final words in 55:12–13. Their purpose is to serve as a response to and an affirmation of God's acts of redemption announced in the proclamation of salvation, a response that rings out beyond the circle of those liberated and reaches to the nations and to the whole of creation.

The relationship of the prophetic proclamation of salvation to lament and praise of God illustrates the relationship between the prophetic movement that was nearing its end and the exilic and postexilic worship of God through the word. In Deutero-Isaiah there is no trace of a resumption of the sacrificial cult after the return from exile. But just as, after the destruction of the temple, lamentation continued as a part of worship and was a basis of Deutero-Isaiah's proclamation, so the prophet in his proclamation continued the praise of God as found in the Psalms, praise that in the worship services of those who had returned to their own land would continue to be offered, both as praise from those whom Yahweh had liberated and as praise of the Creator and Lord of history.

Deutero-Isaiah's proclamation is at basic points normative for the proclamations in the oracles of salvation of Group 1 in the subsequent period. First, the salvation announced for Israel is open to the people of all nations. The destruction of other peoples is no longer proclaimed as a prerequisite for Israel's salvation, in contrast to the oracles of Group 2. Second, and related to this, the regaining of political power and influence is not proclaimed. That was not a part of the salvation that was being announced. This is also supported by the striking fact that among the many oracles against the nations in the Old Testament there are none against the Persian Empire.

3

Isaiah 1–39

In the investigation of the oracles of salvation in Isaiah 1–39 we must distinguish between those found in the context of a narrative and those which are transmitted in collections of the prophet's words. This is the same distinction that holds for the transmission of all the prophetic messages: Before Amos the words of the prophets were preserved only in the context of narratives. The Elijah and Elisha traditions mark the transition, and from Amos on almost all such messages are preserved in collections. In the case of prophetic messages transmitted in a narrative context, there is the advantage that the exegesis of the messages is made appreciably easier through the study of the context in which they were given. This also includes the question of whether the message could have been spoken by the prophet to whom it is ascribed. This criterion has especial importance for the oracles of salvation. Thus it is not only possible to begin with the text of those oracles in Isaiah 1–39 that have been transmitted in a narrative context, that is, the texts in chapters 7–8 and 36–39, but it is methodologically correct to do so. This includes, as a matter of course, the words of Isaiah transmitted in 1 Kings.

Oracles in Narrative Contexts

Oracles in Chapters 7 and 8

Isaiah 7:1–17

This section is an announcement of deliverance from trouble. In defining and interpreting the passage I follow Wildberger in all the major points. He says, "We are here in the fortunate position of being able to give a precise date to a prophetic message" (*Jesaja*, BKAT, vol. X/1, 2nd ed., 1980, 273). According to him the account was recorded soon after the war of 735/34 B.C.

That the introduction in Isaiah 7:1 agrees with 2 Kings 16:5 means that "the prophetic books were read together with the historical books" (Wildberger, p. 269). First the approach of the enemy is reported and then the reaction to it (v. 2). This is followed by the twofold commission to the prophet in the style of a messenger, "Go . . . and say" (v. 3). He is then commanded to deliver an oracle of salvation:

> Take heed, be quiet, do not fear, and do not let your heart be faint because of these two smoldering stumps of firebrands . . . . Because Syria, with Ephraim . . . , has devised evil against you . . . , thus says the Lord God:
> It shall not stand,
>   and it shall not come to pass.
> For the head of Syria is Damascus . . . .
> If you will not believe,
>   surely you shall not be established." (Isa. 7:4–9)

In vs. 11–12 a sign is offered to Ahaz, but he rejects it. To this Isaiah replies, "Therefore the Lord himself will give you a sign" (vs. 13–16). This sign, however it may be interpreted, confirms the fulfillment of the prophet's oracle of salvation. But since the king has rejected the sign, and with it the oracle, there follows in v. 17 an announcement of judgment on the king, and a judgment on Judah's future.

This passage contains a well-documented oracle of the prophet Isaiah, as is almost universally acknowledged in current scholarship. Several distinctive features of the oracle should be noted. First, it fits the situation in which it is given. The fixed form of an oracle of salvation is indicated in

v. 4, but vs. 5–9 speak only of the situation, and the oracle says only that the plan of the enemy (vs. 5–6) will not succeed (v. 7). In vs. 8–9 an explanation is given, in which that which is meant is not made explicit: The true "head" is Yahweh. You will survive only if you trust him. The same idea is expressed in the name Immanuel.

Thus the oracle is formulated here in terms of the situation, which is similar to that in Jeremiah 32. Such oracles always announce deliverance from a present danger. Therefore they are always found in the form of a narrative, and the danger from which deliverance is announced must first be reported. This is confirmed in Isaiah 36:12–20 in the speech of the Assyrian commander who is besieging Jerusalem and addresses the inhabitants of the city in order to convince them to surrender. In this speech a proclamation of Yahweh's deliverance of Jerusalem is cited with negative omens. It agrees with that which happened later.

This type of salvation oracle—the announcement of deliverance from a threatening situation that has just been described—can be identified by the characteristic feature that the announcement and the occurrence of what has been announced take place within definite limits of time and space, so that both can be reported in the same context. This is fundamentally different from another type of oracle in which the announcement and its fulfillment are widely separated, perhaps by decades. This type of oracle becomes detached from the situation in which it was given and becomes independent of it. It is no longer an element in a narrative.

This difference agrees with that between two types of promises to the patriarchs (see my book *The Promises to the Fathers*, 1980). In the first type the promise is given in a perilous situation that has just been described, and its fulfillment can be recounted in the same context. The distance between the two is limited, as, for example, in the promise of a son. In the other type the promise is fulfilled only after a long lapse of time, as in the promise of the land. It is not possible to report the two together. The first type belongs to an older stage of tradition, and the second to a younger stage. On the basis of this contrast it is easy to understand that Isaiah's proclamations of salvation which were restricted in time and space were transmitted in a narrative context.

This distinction also accounts for the fact that oracles of salvation given in a situation clearly defined in time and space are often accompanied by a sign. The sign has the function of corroborating the context of the proclamation and its fulfillment. Thus it always has its significance only in the limited time frame of that context. This is the case in the giving of the name of the child "Immanuel" as the sign in 7:14, 16 (v. 15 is a later addition), in the parallel passage in 8:1–4, and in the story of King Hezekiah's illness in 38:5 (vs. 7–8 are a textually corrupt addition). Note that the parallel in 2 Kings 20:5 reports a sign that was to be fulfilled more quickly: "Behold, I will heal you; on the third day you shall go up to the house of the Lord." All these signs emphasize the brief lapse of time. It is clear that in situations involving a longer time period the signs lose their significance.

Oracles in Chapters 36–38

Isaiah 36:12–20

In a speech to the soldiers defending Jerusalem, the commander of the Assyrian forces quotes a message that says Yahweh will rescue Jerusalem, and then seeks to refute that promise (v. 15). He contrasts it to the definite proclamation of the Assyrian king, "Thus says the king of Assyria . . . " in carefully wrought language that resembles the prophetic oracles of salvation. Even though this may be a later reconstruction of the speech, it still shows that proclamations of deliverance in the name of a god were known at that time and were often given.

Isaiah 37:1–7

These verses contain an oracle of Isaiah's, a proclamation of deliverance from the threatening situation that has been depicted in 36:12–20. On hearing the report, the king rends his clothes and goes to the temple (v. 1). In this way a lament of the people is introduced, one verse of which is quoted in v. 3. At the same time the king sends for the prophet Isaiah and asks him to intercede with Yahweh for the people and the city (vs. 2, 4). Thus here Isaiah performs the same function that Amos is reported to have performed in the time of drought (Amos 7:4–6). The answer that is given to the king speaks directly to the situation: "Do not be afraid because of the words that you have heard" (v. 6b). "Behold, I will put a spirit in him, so that he shall hear a rumor, and return to his own land" (v. 7; 7b is a later addition). This proclamation of deliverance, with no literary form, arising directly out of the situation, and speaking to it, corresponds precisely to that in chapter 7. There follows in vs. 9b–20 a deuteronomistic retelling of this account.

Isaiah 37:30–32

These verses contain the sign given to Hezekiah. They do not fit after vs. 21–29 but presuppose a message of salvation that was given earlier. Verse 30, "And this shall be the sign for you . . . ," probably fits with the proclamation of deliverance in 6b, 7a, since it agrees with the sign given with the oracle in chapter 7 (cf. Jeremiah 32). Verses 31–32 are a promise to the remnant and were added later.

Isaiah 38:1–8

This account, concerning Hezekiah's illness, deals with an oracle of salvation for an individual, just as Hezekiah's psalm in vs. 9–20 is the psalm of an individual. In the historical books there are several accounts of a prophet or a man of God being consulted by a sick king (e.g., 2 Kings 1:2). Because Isaiah 38 closely resembles these accounts and because what Isaiah says and does is so close to what a man of God such as Elijah or Elisha said and did, we may assume that we have here an old and reliable tradition. In any case, an older narrative has been considerably expanded here. The parallels, however, do not permit us to reconstruct that narrative.

The report of the healing is followed in vs. 9–20 by Hezekiah's psalm (compare the psalm of Hannah in 1 Samuel 2). The sign in vs. 7–8 belongs to Hezekiah's request for a sign in v. 22. The insertion of the psalm moved vs. 21–22 from their original place.

The oracle of salvation to an individual in chapter 38 and the oracles in chapters 7–8 and 36–37, which announce the deliverance of Jerusalem from danger, demonstrate that the prophet Isaiah spoke not only messages of judgment but messages of salvation as well.

Oracles Not in Narrative Contexts

A distinction must be drawn between independent oracles that are in themselves recognizable as such (e.g., Isa. 9:1–6 and 35:1–10), and oracles that were added to Isaiah's oracles of judgment. They consist of only one, two, or at the most three lines and are often clearly related to the oracles of judgment to which they were added. These two groups represent differing processes of expansion. They did not develop in the same time period or in the same communities. Nonetheless in terms of the future salvation promised in them they are quite similar. And we find in both the same introductory formula, "In that day." This leads to the assumption that both groups have a similar history of transmission. But both groups are clearly distinguishable from the oracles of Isaiah in narrative contexts, which proclaim deliverance from a present danger, in a limited framework of time and space. The combination of an oracle of salvation with a sign is found in the latter group but never in the former.

The promises of salvation added to Isaiah's oracles of judgment presuppose a lapse of time since the issuing of those oracles (because there was now access to the written texts). Thus the promises of salvation point to a different situation from that of the oracles of judgment, different because the judgment announced by Isaiah had now taken place. In the oracles of salvation that judgment is often mentioned. The changed situation that resulted from the judgment required that the continuation of God's activity on Israel's behalf, which could now be only for their well-being, be taken up in the book of Isaiah only in conjunction with Isaiah's prophecies of judgment. This was also required by the use in worship of the book of Isaiah, as is clearly seen in chapter 12.

If in what they say about future salvation the independent oracles of salvation largely agree with the oracles added to the messages of judgment, then it can be said of both that they arose out of the same necessity, the necessity of proclaiming the continuance of God's activity with his people after judgment had come upon them. This is the same necessity that is shown on a larger scale by the addition of Isaiah 40–66 to Isaiah 1–39. It is only that here the solution took another form. Three stages can be distinguished. The first occurred when individual messages of salvation were added to individual messages of judgment. This probably took place while the Isaiah tradition still consisted of individual collections. At the second stage independent oracles of salvation were added at the conclusion of the small collections. The final stage saw the combining of Isaiah 1–39 and the collections of words of salvation, 40–55 and 56–66.

God's Constancy with His People: The Proclamation of Deliverance in Independent Oracles of Salvation

These texts fall into three groups. Those of the first group are proclamations of salvation in two parts: God turns again to his people, and God restores them (or in the second part, a description of their new well-being). They are 29:22–24; 30:18–26; and 33:17–24. Those of the second group are almost totally descriptions of their new state, and God's turning to them again is implicit or only hinted at. They are 4:2–6; 32:15–20; and 29:17–21. The third group is proclamation of liberation, with the sequence of liberation, gathering together, returning home. It consists of one text (11:11–16), but another text resembles it (35:1–10).

Proclamations of Salvation in Two Parts

Isaiah 29:22–24

This text consists of two parts: In vs. 22–23a we see God returning to his people and intervening for them; vs. 23b–24 depict the restoration of the saving relationship with God. In the middle of the passage is the proclamation of God's intervention for his people's salvation: Jacob will see "the work of my hands in his midst" (23a). This is preceded by God's return to his people in v. 22b, which also signifies God's forgiveness: "Jacob shall no more be ashamed." But this new return of God to his people is a continuance of his earlier saving grace toward them: "The God of the house of Jacob, Abraham's redeemer" (29:22, JB). Yahweh is now again the savior of Israel, just as he was with his people from the beginning. If Israel will now see "the work of my hands in his midst" (v. 23) he will respond to this work of God with praise and by sanctifying his name. This praise of God that is not freed from the pain of those who have been humiliated will also bring about a change of heart among those who "err in spirit," and they "will accept instruction."

Isaiah 30:18–26

This passage also consists of two parts. Verses 18–21, 26b describe God's return to his people, and vs. 22–25a describe restoration and blessing. The first part is connected to the preceding word of judgment against Israel (vs. 13–17) by the transition in v. 18, "Therefore the Lord waits to be gracious to you . . . ." Verse 18, however, could be an independent message of salvation and as such a supplement to 13–17, ending as it does with a psalm, "For the Lord is a God of justice; blessed are all those who wait for him." Verses 19–21 contain a sequence of events that are typical of such oracles: God's earlier saving deeds, implied in 20b–21; the sin of the people and God's punishment, 20a; God returns to his people again, vs. 19, 26b; and they respond in obedience, vs. 21b–22. In all this God's return to his people precedes their restoration, as is expressed again in the conclusion in v. 26b. The similarity of this passage to Deutero-Isaiah is particularly clear in the words of comfort in v. 19 and in the metaphor taken from the language of the Psalms, "the bread of adversity and the water of affliction," v. 20a (cf. Ps. 80:6 [5]). The reference to Yahweh as "your teacher" (twice in v. 20) occurs only here in the Old Testament. God is the one who shows the way. His new presence, he "will not hide himself any more," is proclaimed so that his people can be certain of the road they are to travel.

In the second part, after the proclamation that the worship of idols will be eliminated (v. 22), there is a full description of the new blessing that is coming (vs. 23–25a). Here the oracle provides an example of how both blessing and God's deliverance of his people are part of God's gracious presence with his people. Verses 25b and 26a are a later apocalyptic addition.

Isaiah 33:17–24

This is a proclamation of salvation in two parts. Verses 17–19 (20) announce that God is again favorable, and vs. (20) 21–24 portray the restoration and the resultant prosperity. There are a number of textual difficulties. Verses 21b and 23a belong together and are an addition, a gloss to v. 21a, which they did not understand. Through the error that introduced this gloss into the text, v. 22 (which belongs at the end) became misplaced. W. Eichrodt himself saw clearly that v. 22 belongs at the end of the passage. A further argument for this is that 33:17–24 is one of the oracles of salvation in which, as in 35:1–6, the proclamation of salvation constitutes the framework. Also the title of king for Yahweh in v. 17 and v. 22 is consciously designed to be a part of the framework.

Verses 17–19 (20) are marked by the key word "see." Verse 17: "Your eyes will see the king . . . , behold a land that stretches afar." Verse 19: "You will see no more the insolent people." Verse 20: "Look upon Zion. . . . Your eyes will see Jerusalem." This key word calls to mind the sayings of the "seers," and shows how they appeared again in the later oracles of salvation. Proclamation and portrayal merge. Moreover this composition is so carefully thought out that the oracle reveals poetic power. "King" and "Zion" are clearly coordinated, as are the tradition of the King and of Zion in Psalm 132. Of course in v. 17 "king" refers to Yahweh (cf. v. 22), but behind v. 17 there stands the concept of the audience of an earthly king, "the king in his beauty," as in Psalm 45. Verse 22 is in the language of the Psalms.

The second part, 33:(20) 21–24, begins with the announcement that God is again favorable to his people—the King has come into his city, and this is followed by the restoration, which is presented here only by describing the new state. Verse 20 provides the transition between part one and part two. It belongs to vs. 17–19 insofar as Zion is the city of the King, and to vs. 21–24 insofar as security is one of the motifs of the restoration. Here too we can detect the influence of the sayings of the seers. The dark

picture of the time of occupation by a foreign army (vs. 18–
19) is followed in vs. 20–24 by a picture of the future of
Jerusalem, safe and secure under God's protection. In a particularly beautiful and poetic fantasy Jerusalem is compared
to a tent "whose stakes will never be plucked up, nor will
any of its cords be broken" (20b), an allusion to the exile,
when the people were driven from their homes. "Look
upon Zion, the city of our appointed feasts!" Only when
there is peace, when the city is free again, can there be
joyful feasts. Festival, peace, and joy belong together here,
as so often elsewhere. The city is "a place of broad rivers
and streams" (v. 21), signifying fertile land and abundance
of water, but also a reminder of the stream in the city of
God (Psalm 46). Those who are sick become well again (vs.
23b, 24a), and "the people who dwell there will be forgiven their iniquity" (v. 24b). The relationship between
God and the people is again whole. In v. 23b (following an
emendation in *BHS*), "The blind and the lame divide spoil"
combines two motifs. One is that the blind see again and the
lame walk. The other is that joy reigns when spoil is taken.
The combination assumes both as well known, and so the
passage must be relatively late.

The conclusion in 33:22 is praise of God the King (all
three terms, judge, ruler, king refer to the king), combined
with the proclamation that God comes as king (v. 17) in
order to help his people. But v. 22b can also be translated,
"He is the one who helps us" (*hu' yoshi'enu*). Then the
sentence would be an expression of trust, that is, the language of the Psalms. It is probably intended that both
meanings be in play here. The boundary between proclamation (a speaker addresses the group) and expectation
(the group is the subject) is fluid. In these late oracles of
salvation the proclamation of a messenger shades over into
the expression of expectation, of the community's trust.

Texts Where God's Return to His People
Is Only Hinted at or Implied

Isaiah 4:2–6

The distinctive feature of texts in this group is that it is
not possible to separate them into two parts. The entire text

speaks of the future state of salvation. The expression in v. 3, "He who is left in Zion," and the whole of v. 4 presuppose that God has again become gracious to Israel after the coming of judgment. Since this text cannot be divided into two parts, it is simply a heaping up of motifs of salvation.

It is because of this heaping together of motifs that the introduction takes on greater significance: "In that day . . . " Here it can only be understood as a clue that all to whom the message is directed will understand. It is the day on which the great turning point is reached, the day of which all the well-known proclamations of salvation speak. On that day "the branch of the Lord shall be beautiful and glorious, and the fruit of the land shall be the pride and glory of the survivors of Israel" (4:2). Here too two motifs are combined. The parallelism of "the branch of the Lord" and "the fruit of the land" is a promise of blessing. But this is combined with another motif: The blessing of God will (once again) lead to "pride and glory," a motif that we encounter in Trito-Isaiah. Verse 3 adds to this the promise of life, a life of security. "Holy" means here inviolate. "Every one who has been recorded for life" is thus secure.

But the subject of the sentence in v. 3, "he who is left in Zion and remains in Jerusalem" (in v. 2, "the survivors of Israel") points forward to v. 4. It is those who have been rescued from the judgment of God and are still living. The transition from this judgment to God's renewed favor for his people is clearly expressed in v. 5. The Lord will come and rule over the whole of Mount Zion and those who gather there. This then is the day that is proclaimed in v. 2 in the introduction, the day of Yahweh's return to Zion to be once more favorable to his people. The text then continues, "A cloud by day, and smoke and the shining of a flaming fire by night," pointing to God's mode of being present with his people in ancient times. And this is now transferred to the future blessing of God's people. This is the way God will be present on Mount Zion, as the one who guides and protects his people. The judgment that has taken place (v. 4) is understood as a time of cleansing and purging of those who have survived. We have here echoes of the language of Ezekiel and the Priestly Document. The supplements to the oracles of salvation "grew out of the liturgical usage of the prophetic writings in the gatherings of the community in the period of the second temple" (H. Wildberger, BKAT, vol. X/1, 154). O. Kaiser, in his commentary (p. 92), writes, "This passage dates from the later Persian period . . . or early Hellenistic times."

Isaiah 32:15-20

Here too the turning point in the life of the people is only implied. Verse 15a refers to the power for new life that comes from God (see also Isa. 44:3 and Ezek. 37:6). No trace remains of a proclamation of deliverance. Verses 15b–20 portray the prosperity that was to be brought about by the coming of the Spirit from on high. To him belongs the blessing that transforms the desert into a fruitful garden, to him belong justice and righteousness, which in turn bring in peace and security. This is a typical and beautiful poetic description of well-being. The text also shows how the proclamation rouses expectation. These are the words of a community living in expectancy. This oracle probably arose as a contrast to the message of judgment in 32:9–14. A community which knew Israel's guilt, and which knew that judgment was justified, now receives a word of salvation: that the time of judgment is limited and that God will bring new blessing and prosperity.

Isaiah 29:17-21

Only verses 17–19 belong here. They correspond to the portrayal of blessing with which 32:15–20 begins. Then vs. 18–19 speak of the healing of the blind and the deaf and the transformed relationship with God. Verse 20 adds a different motif—blessing for the pious. On v. 19, destruction of those who are evil, see below. The proclamation in v. 18, "In that day the deaf shall hear the words of a book" point to a later age in which the "book" had taken the place of the oral word in worship.

Proclamation of Liberation

Isaiah 11:1–16 and 35:1–10 describe deliverance in the sequence of liberation, gathering of the people, return of the people.

Isaiah 11:11-16

"The Lord will extend his hand yet a second time to re-cover the remnant which is left of his people" (11). He will gather those Israelites that have been scattered, he will dry up the sea and make a road for the remnant, as he did in the exodus from Egypt. Following the first return from exile, a second, later return is awaited, in which the Jewish diaspora will return from many lands.

In contrast to the preceding texts this passage proclaims the liberation of the remnant in the three acts mentioned, with reference to the deliverance from Egypt, "a second time." As then, a road will be prepared for their return. In v. 13 there is a motif of the restoration—the reunification of the northern and southern tribes. The announcement of the subjugation of the neighboring peoples in v. 14 is a supplement.

Isaiah 35:1-10

We have here a call for the desert to rejoice and bloom. They will see the glory of Yahweh! Water will flow in the desert, grass and reeds will grow, and a holy road will be there, on which those whom Yahweh has redeemed will return to Zion with joy.

This passage is quite similar to the proclamation of Deutero-Isaiah, especially the call to rejoicing, grounded in the announcement that Yahweh is coming, vs. 1-4, in a beautiful parallelism of the verses: the call to rejoice corresponds to the extended call of reassurance, and the basis given in 2b corresponds to that in 4b. The distinctive literary form grew out of the combination of prophecy of salvation with praise of God as found in the Psalms. It was developed by Deutero-Isaiah and imitated here (see Wildberger, BKAT, vol. X/3, on this passage). This borrowing is evidence of the continuation of the proclamation of Deutero-Isaiah. The text could be included with the oracles of salvation in two parts—vs. 1-4 and 8-9—but as a whole it is characterized by the proclamation of deliverance: God comes to rescue (1-4), the way of the return through the desert (8-9), the return to Zion (v. 10). The whole text moves somewhat in the direction of a depiction of blessing.

In vs. 1–2 we have the glory of Lebanon, in 5–6a the healing of the sick, in 6b–7 the transformation of the wilderness, in 9a the absence of wild animals. This illustrates the transition from proclamation to the description of the state of well-being and blessing.

Brief Supplements with Only One Motif

These passages resemble the collections of brief oracles of salvation containing only one motif that are found in Jeremiah 31:23–40. The passages to be examined here are 1:25–26; 10:20–21; 28:5–6; 37:31–32; 14:1–2; 17:7–8; 7:21–22. In addition, 16:4b–5; 11:10; 18:7; and 16:1 are discussed in the following section, on the expansion of a motif into an oracle.

What these passages have in common is that they are not much more than a direct reaction to the word of judgment to which they are appended. They say little more than "Some day it will be different!"

Isaiah 10:20–21

> In that day the remnant of Israel and the survivors of the house of Jacob will no more lean upon him that smote them, but will lean upon the Lord, the Holy One of Israel, in truth. A remnant will return, the remnant of Jacob, to the mighty God.

This short supplement does not follow an existing structure, but grew out of the expectation of a change for the better. We are justified here in speaking of the expectation of salvation. Isaiah had brought against Judah the accusation that they had relied on the great powers instead of relying on God (9:12a). In contrast to that, the speaker here says, "Some day it will be different." The time is more precisely identified in 20a, "remnant . . . survivors." This recognizes that God has judged Judah. What is proclaimed here will no longer be anticipated for the entire people and state of Judah, but only for those who have survived this judgment. Verse 21 says this quite explicitly. The return to God which is expected of this remnant includes also the acknowledgment of Isaiah's complaint against them: Now they will no longer "lean upon him that smote them, but will lean upon the Lord, the Holy One of Israel, in truth" (20). It is probable that such short, spontaneous oracles are older than the texts that precede them.

Isaiah 28:5–6

In that day the Lord of hosts will be a crown of glory,
    and a diadem of beauty, to the remnant of his people;
and a spirit of justice to him who sits in judgment,
    and strength to those who turn back the battle at the gate.

This brief supplement has in common with 10:20–21 that deliverance is anticipated for the remnant, and that it is a spontaneous reaction to an oracle of judgment from Yahweh (28:1–4). "The proud crown of the drunkards of Ephraim" (28:1) to whom the message of woe is addressed, served to aggrandize the powerful rulers who trusted to their own might. The judgment has come upon them. The one speaking here announces a time of well-being in which Yahweh alone will be honored by the remnant who survive the judgment. Verse 6 supplements the well-known features of the portrayal of salvation, probably presupposing the promise to the king, but "democratizing" it. Yahweh will give to those who sit in judgment the spirit of justice and to those who defend the city the spirit of power.

Isaiah 37:31–32 (=2 Kings 19:30–31)

And the surviving remnant of the house of Judah shall again take root downward, and bear fruit upward; for out of Jerusalem shall go forth a remnant, and out of Mount Zion a band of survivors. The zeal of the Lord of hosts will accomplish this.

This oracle explicitly deals with the remnant that has survived the catastrophe and promises them new life, growth, and expansion. The final sentence refers to God's once again returning to his people, and the descriptions of the remnant to the preceding judgment of God. This supplement too can be reduced to one sentence: Someday it will be different! It is expanded into an independent unit through a parallelism of sentences in which two things are compared (cf. Isaiah 54). The final statement, "The zeal of the Lord of hosts will accomplish this," does not have the form of a proclamation but of an expectation, a firm hope. It is an allegorical interpretation of the sign given to Hezekiah (Isa. 37:30 = 2 Kings 19:29) and thus shows itself to be a late addition.

Isaiah 14:1–2

The Lord will have compassion on Jacob and will again choose Israel, and will set them in their own land, and aliens will join them and will cleave to the house of Jacob. And the peoples will take them and bring them to their place, and the house of Israel will possess them in the Lord's land as male and female slaves; they will take captive those who were their captors, and rule over those who oppressed them.

This supplementary oracle is a composite. God will turn again to his people; the wording is similar to 11:11. The final sentence in v. 1 announces the peaceful inclusion of "aliens" in Israel, somewhat similarly to Isaiah 45. Verse 2 announces the conquest of other peoples by Israel, who enslave their enemies and so pay them back. This is clearly in contrast to 1b and can only be an addition, much like 11:14. Here a new group are speaking, and the message is the same as that of the second group of oracles (destruction of the foes—liberation of Israel).

Isaiah 17:7–8

In that day men will regard their Maker, and their eyes will look to the Holy One of Israel; they will not have regard for the altars, the work of their hands, and they will not look to what their own fingers have made, either the Asherim or the altars of incense.

This supplement, which resembles the first group of oracles, follows a message of judgment on Damascus and Israel (17:1–6). Here the unifying motif is that of a reaction to God's return to his people, but it is only hinted at: "their eyes will look to the Holy One of Israel" (v. 7; cf. 31:1). Israel will once again turn to her God and reject the false gods (cf. 30:22; 2:18, 20; 31:7).

Isaiah 7:21–22

> In that day a man will keep alive a young cow and two sheep; and because of the abundance of milk which they give, he will eat curds; for every one that is left in the land will eat curds and honey.

The connection between this supplement and the others of this group is found in the introduction, which proclaims the coming of salvation, and the final sentence, "every one that is left in the land." These are those who have been rescued, who have survived, who are now promised a time of fertility and blessing. The depiction of blessing has taken the place of the proclamation of deliverance.

Isaiah 1:25–26

This is a supplement that clearly corresponds to the proclamation of judgment to which it has been added (1:21–24). The destructive judgment (v. 24) is turned into a refining judgment (25): "I will turn my hand against you and will smelt away your dross as with lye." This is a clear contrast to v. 22, "Your silver has become dross." Similarly this comparison corresponds to the message of judgment, which brought accusations against corrupt judges (21–23). In contrast it is promised, "I will restore your judges as at the first" (26). Building on the theme "righteousness," a two-line proclamation is added to this promise.

Isaiah 28:16–17

These verses were added later to the word of judgment in 28:14–19. The "precious cornerstone" (16) is contrasted to the "overwhelming scourge" (15). The meaning of 31:4–5, 8–9 is uncertain.

The majority of these supplements are introduced by the words, "In that day." This means the day in which Israel's fortunes take a turn for the better and God turns to them again, as Isaiah 14:1 expresses it. This is probably the origin of the expression. The brevity of the introduction is a result of the brevity of the supplement. It is found in Isaiah 4:2; 7:21; 10:20; 11:11; 17:7; 28:5. Israel's apostasy and God's judgment are not explicitly mentioned, but they are presupposed in 10:20–21 and 28:5–6 as the direct reaction to a message of judgment delivered by Isaiah. The authors of these supplements acknowledge the verdict that God has pronounced on his people. God's return to his people is mentioned only in 14:1, but it is implicit in the other passages, e.g., 7:21. Also in 37:31–32 the new time of prosperity and growth promised to Israel presupposes that God has turned again to his people. The proclamation of deliverance is implicit in the terms "remnant" and "survivors," which occur frequently in this group of texts (7:22; 10:21, 22; 28:5; 37:31, 32). Those who after the catastrophe speak of future salvation were aware that they were no longer the old people of Israel, but were the survivors who owe their existence to Yahweh's compassion (14:1; 37:32). Only as changed persons can they belong to this remnant (10:20–21; 17:7–8; 28:5–6). A remnant will repent. An echo of this is found in the gloss in Genesis 45:7b: "to preserve for you a remnant on earth, and to keep alive for you many survivors."

Expansion of a Motif Into an Oracle

In addition to the possibility of an oracle of salvation existing in the brief form of a supplement to another text, it was also possible for an individual motif to be expanded into an independent oracle. In terms of form criticism, this corresponds to the expansion of an individual psalm motif into a whole psalm, for example, Psalm 23. Such expansions are found in the proclamation of the coming of a king who will reign in peace and that of aliens and distant peoples turning to Israel. Both are found as individual motifs. Thus we may conclude that the expansion of the motif into an oracle represents a later stage of tradition history.

The Promise of a King

Isaiah 9:2–7

The concluding statement in v. 7b conclusively marks this oracle as a proclamation, a position with which Wildberger is in agreement. Through the motif of a time of enduring peace the proclamation of Israel's liberation from a long period of oppression is combined with the promise of the birth of a king of peace. Both of these ideas proclaim such an era of peace. This presupposes a long period of darkness and oppression, as described in many late oracles. Here, however, the change is brought about, not by the destruction of the nation's foes, but by the birth of a royal child. This oracle cannot have been pronounced by Isaiah, because he was not speaking in a time of prolonged oppression of Israel-Judah. Thus it is similar to other oracles of a late period.

Albrecht Alt attempted to read 9:1 as poetry, but it can only be read as prose, and its content shows that it is not a suitable introduction to vs. 2–7. Above all, 9:1 speaks of the northern provinces, and 9:2–7 of David's throne (as H. W. Wolff and others also note). Chapter 9:1 can be considered a gloss which proclaims something unique, that an area of the kingdom of Israel is promised deliverance from its oppression, followed by a time of well-being.

Isaiah 9:2–7

This passage is a literary unit, but it brings together several motifs that have a separate tradition history. As the parallel passages show, the announcement of the birth of a savior king, as in vs. 6–7, comes from an independent tradition. The message (or proclamation) of liberation is also an independent tradition. That the author of 2–7 combined the two is clear from the final sentence, "The zeal of the Lord of hosts will do this," which is an appropriate conclusion to 2–5, but not to 6–7. That vs. 2–5 are composite is shown by the change between 2 and 3–4, and between 3–4 and 5. The two middle verses, 3–4, are a psalm of declarative (narrative) praise sung by those who have been liberated. It praises God for liberation from slavery (v. 4) and for the joy that this has brought (v. 3). It is praise of God that points to the future, as Mowinckel wrote, "so that they already rejoice in anticipation of the coming victory and prosperity" (*He That Cometh*, 104). Verse 2 speaks of "the people" in the third person and is not part of the psalm of praise that addresses God. This verse serves as an introduction, and its function is to set the stage for the proclamation. This is characteristic of Trito-Isaiah, and the similarity to Isaiah 60:1–3 is unmistakable. Moreover the contrast of light and darkness is characteristic of Trito-Isaiah. Verse 5 concludes the first part (vs. 2–5), but it seems isolated, and the *ki* at the beginning of the sentence does not fit well with the *ki* in v. 4.

The composite structure of 9:2–7 confirms that it is an oracle from a late period. Because v. 2 so clearly resembles Trito-Isaiah the oracle probably dates from his time. The language of the eighth-century prophet Isaiah is very different from what we have here. On vs. 6–7, see Mowinckel (pp. 104–110). On the basis of the background of the passage in the history of religion, he shows that vs. 6–7 constitute an originally independent tradition.

Isaiah 11:1–9

Wildberger accepts this passage as being from Isaiah, but the argument of Mowinckel and others is convincing. The metaphor of the stump and the roots means that the tree has been cut down and only the stump is left, and thus that the Davidic dynasty has been overthrown. Mowinckel writes,

> But the fact cannot be ignored that both here and in Job 14:8 the word *geza'* means the stump of a tree which has been felled, from which a new shoot is to issue, and that Jesse's family tree is here regarded as hewn down, with only the stump remaining. . . . Thus the passage presupposes the fall of the monarchy. (*He That Cometh,* 17)

Thus this proclamation of a royal savior belongs to the oracles of the exilic or postexilic period.

The oracle consists of two independent parts. Verses 1–5 belong to the motif, "proclamation of a savior king." Verses 6–9 depict a time of blessing, that of peace within the animal world in the time of security. This also hints at peace between humans and animals. This section presupposes a transformation that involves not only history but also the natural world, and thus peace and well-being in a transcendent realm. Thus this description moves toward apocalyptic, but that is not the case in the first part, vs. 1–5. In 3b–4 another motif is in play, the fate of the righteous and the unrighteous. It has been inserted between vs. 3a and 5, which belong together. Literally 11:1–9 can be considered a unit, but it is composed of motifs from different sources. If we assume literary unity, then the insertion of the motif of the righteous and the unrighteous and their fate provides a convincing argument for its origin in the postexilic period.

This passage makes clear that the late oracles of salvation are to a large degree composite compositions. The motif "proclamation of a savior king," as found in differing texts, can be supplemented by various motifs, such at that of peace among the animals and the fate of the righteous and the unrighteous. We then must ask whether these motifs once existed as separate units, or were found from the beginning only in composite units, that is, collections of motifs. For the motif "the fate of the righteous and the unrighteous," the answer is clear. It is a motif in the late wisdom literature, where it was an independent unit in the form of a proverb. This motif was always inserted secondarily in proclamations of deliverance, for it was originally foreign to them.

Isaiah 32:1–5

This oracle consists of two major parts: the proclamation of the reign of a righteous king and princes (1–2), and the state of well-being which the king brings about (3–5). In the latter section we have the healing of the sick—eyes and ears are opened and tongues are loosed (3); the mind of the rash will learn judgment (4a); and fools will no longer be called noble, as the government will be just (5). Verses 6–8, which draw the contrast between fools and the noble, are a supplementary addition.

Most exegetes regard the text as postexilic. Several features of the structure point in this direction. The proclamation is limited to vs.. 1–2. Verses 1, 3–5 are purely a portrayal of deliverance and blessing, in which motifs are heaped up without any recognizable context, as Mowinckel observed, adding, "The passage is not primarily a prophecy" (p. 17). It is striking that the "reign in righteousness" is not developed, and at the end of v. 5 it is only hinted at. All the emphasis is placed on the description of blessing. It is also striking that 4a, "The mind of the rash will have good judgment," is inserted into the motif "healing of the sick" (vs. 3–4).

The following two texts, 16:4b–5 and 11:10, belong, on the basis of their form, to the supplementary oracles with only one motif.

Isaiah 16:4b–5

These words, quoted below, are a supplement to 16:1–4a, an oracle concerning Moab:

> When the oppressor is no more,
>   and destruction has ceased,
> and he who tramples under foot
>   has vanished from the land,
> then a throne will be established in steadfast love
>   and on it will sit in faithfulness
>   in the tent of David
> one who judges and seeks justice
>   and is swift to do righteousness.

This proclamation of a savior king is a unit, in which each statement is in its place and is an essential part of the proclamation. There are two parts: looking back to the time of oppression, and proclamation of a just and enduring kingship. From this structure we see that it is not really an event that is being proclaimed, although the formula, "a throne will be established," could be taken in that sense, but we look from one condition (that of oppression) to another, transformed condition. The relationship is thus not that of moment of peril—moment of deliverance, as in Isaiah 7–8, but ongoing peril—ongoing prosperity and security. The throne that is to be established and the permanence that it is to enjoy are indications of this continuity. Kings and kingship are not seen here in their political function, but as the guarantee of security and justice. The oracle is not formulated as a prophetic word, but it is simply stated that it will be thus, without the formula "on that day," or something similar. The indication of the time frame is given in "When the oppressor is no more." This is not spoken by God. In fact, there is no indication that it is God who brings about this transformation. Thus it cannot be understood as a prophetic proclamation. It is rather the expression of a hope, a wish, a longing for a change.

Isaiah 11:10

In that day the root of Jesse shall stand as an ensign to the peoples; him shall the nations seek, and his dwellings shall be glorious.

This is an independent supplement with its own introduction. Verses 11–16 begin with a new introduction. The meaning is not clear, but what is clear is that in that time peoples will seek out the "root of Jesse," probably the king of the time of salvation. The phrase "shall stand as an ensign to the peoples" probably means that the king of that time will be seen by the people from a distance and will be honored. He points the direction in which the people shall go. The final clause, "and his dwellings shall be glorious" (*wehayetah menuhato kabod*) can scarcely refer to the king, because in late oracles it always refers to the people. The meaning is that the people will have a glorious place to dwell. Then we must ask if the "root of Jesse" could have here another meaning, that of the people of that time of well-being. In that case this oracle would be a variant of the motif "pilgrimage to Zion." If, however, the root of Jesse means the king of that time, then there is a merging of the two motifs, king of the time of salvation, and pilgrimage to Zion.

These four texts have only two motifs in common: the coming of a king (9:6a; 11:1; 32:1; 16:5), and that he will be a just king who establishes right (9:7b; 11:3–5; 32:1, 5; 16:5b). These two motifs are the heart of all these texts; everything else is an expansion. The expansions include the idea that this king will bring in an era of permanent peace. He is hailed as a king of peace in the two larger poems, 9:2–7 and 11:1–9. The description of the time of peace which the king inaugurates varies greatly in these oracles. All the motifs which we find here are also found in other oracles. In 32:1–5 we have security and blessing, healing of the sick, and good judgment; in 11:1–9, peace in the animal kingdom and a whole relationship to God; in 9:2–7, destruction of the weapons of war and eternal peace.

In all these texts, however, the historical motifs of the prophetic proclamation are missing: God's turning again to his people, liberation, etc. The place of the proclaimed deliverance is taken here by a reign that brings salvation and well-being, including often the birth of a king. The motifs are derived from the royal theology and the royal ritual. All the texts are more the expression of an expectation than they are a proclamation. In all of them the role of the king in international affairs is missing, in contrast to Psalms 2 and 110. This signifies a moving away from the concept of kingship in the period from David to the exile. There are also passages with apocalyptic features (peace among the animals, 11:6–9).

Pilgrimage and Peace Among the Nations

Isaiah 2:1–4 (5)

The structure of this passage is to be understood as follows. The heading in v. 1 is not meant only for vs. 2–4, but for a collection of oracles of Isaiah, and it is a redactional addition. The introduction, "in the latter days," marks a clear boundary between the present and that which will happen in the end time. Everything will be different then. For this reason the text is not really the proclamation of an event but the depiction of a situation. It is closer to being the word of a seer than that of a prophet.

The description that follows is in three parts: The Temple Mount will be different, the worship of God will be different, and the relationship among the nations will be different. We see here three realms: creation (the mountains), history, and worship. These three are intended to designate the entirety of the present world of reality. Everything will be transformed. To speak in this way of everything, including the world of nature and world history, is typical of apocalyptic. The future is spoken of in such a way that everything that belongs to present reality is included. This excludes the possibility that these words were spoken by Isaiah. To say that would be to say that Isaiah, the prophet of the eighth century B.C., was an apocalyptist. (For the dating of the passage, see O. Kaiser, *Isaiah 1–12, A Commentary*, OTL, 2nd ed., 1983.)

The exalting of Zion above *all* the mountains, and the coming of *all* peoples to it are two sides of the same transformation. Both emphasize the universal aspect, and both through their hyperbole point us beyond the conditions of

present reality. In v. 3 the call issued by the nations themselves to join the procession to Zion (as in Psalm 122) is
motivated by their goal, not to offer sacrifices, but to receive instruction. That all the nations await the word of
Yahweh means that this instruction is not a Torah which
Israel alone possesses in distinction from all the nations, but
instruction that is normative for all nations. It no longer has
the function of separating the nations, but of bringing them
together. In v. 4 we see that the result of this teaching for
all the nations is that wars cease among them. Of course
there will continue to be conflicts between nations, but
they will be settled when God gives judgment. God will no
longer be partial to his own people, but he will pronounce
judgment between Israel and its foes. Both the teaching
that God imparts to all the nations and the regulating of the
conflicts among them by God's law will be possible only in a
transformed world in the end time. But it is not God's will
to move in the direction of separating out the people of
God with the law that they alone have, nor to move in the
direction of continual warfare among the nations.

Isaiah 18:7

> At that time gifts will be brought to the Lord of hosts
>> from a people tall and smooth,
>>> from a people feared near and far,
>> a nation mighty and conquering,
>>> whose land the rivers divide,
> to Mount Zion, the place of the name of the Lord of hosts.

Here is another expression of the motif of the worship the
peoples give to God on Zion, an addition to an oracle about
Cush (18:1–6), which takes up the description of the people in v. 2, and is therefore clearly identifiable as an addition. This worship offered by the nations has Akkadian and
Egyptian parallels (Wildberger). There is a prophetic parallel in Zephaniah 3:9–10; and in the Psalms, parallels are
found in 68:30–32; 72:9–11; 45:1–3 (for the king). We
should note a difference. In Isaiah 18:7 and parallels, the
motif is only that of worshiping, but in Isaiah 2:1–4 and
Micah 4:1–3 the peoples themselves are drawn into participation in God's saving deeds. In terms of tradition history

the situation here is like that of the proclamation of the savior king: the earlier stage is the brief supplement to the word of judgment, the later stage is the expansion to an independent, detailed oracle.

Isaiah 16:1

In a oracle about Moab (16:1–5) this verse is parallel to 18:7:

They have sent lambs
　　to the ruler of the land, from Sela, by way of the desert,
　　to the mount of the daughter of Zion.

Isaiah 11:10

This verse is a supplement to 11:1–9 and probably is a mixed form, involving the motifs of pilgrimage to Zion and worship of the king of the time of well-being (see above, p. 89).

Isaiah 19:19–25

[19]In that day there will be an altar to the Lord in the midst of the land of Egypt, and a pillar to the Lord at its border. [20]It will be a sign and a witness to the Lord of hosts in the land of Egypt; when they cry to the Lord because of oppressors he will send them a savior, and will defend and deliver them. [21]And the Lord will make himself known to the Egyptians; and the Egyptians will know the Lord in that day and worship with sacrifice and burnt offering, and they will make vows to the Lord and perform them. [22]And the Lord will smite Egypt, smiting and healing, and they will return to the Lord, and he will heed their supplications and heal them.

[23]In that day there will be a highway from Egypt to Assyria, and the Assyrian will come into Egypt, and the Egyptian into Assyria, and the Egyptians will worship with the Assyrians.

[24]In that day Israel will be the third with Egypt and Assyria, a blessing in the midst of the earth, whom the Lord of hosts has blessed, saying, "Blessed be Egypt my people, and Assyria the work of my hands, and Israel my heritage."

This text too is a message of salvation added to an oracle about the nation of Egypt. But in contrast to the other supplementary oracles, the salvation proclaimed here concerns Egypt (and Assyria) together with Israel—God blesses all three. This one oracle, 19:19–25, has the weight of a little prophetic book. Its significance for the later history of prophecy has still scarcely been evaluated properly. In the boldness and concentration of what is said here it is unique, thought out down to the last word. As for its structure, the first part, vs. 19–22, deals with the relationship with God and worship of God, and the second, 23–25, with history. In theological language, the first part deals with salvation and the second with God's blessing.

The distinctive message of this oracle is that both God's power to save and power to bless are no longer meant only for Israel, but for all peoples. This is one of the most powerful evidences of the use of daring universalistic language about God to be found in late Israelite history. It is a parallel to Isaiah 2:1–4 in that this oracle too, in both its parts, speaks of humanity's common relationship to God and of peace among the nations. It follows from this agreement in content that both are to be counted among the late oracles of salvation. (Wildberger holds that only 19:19–25 is late, and ascribes Isaiah 2:1–4 to the prophet Isaiah.)

Summary: Pilgrimage and Peace Among the Nations

The relationship of the short texts (16:1; 18:7; 11:10) to the two more extensive texts is that the short texts (supplements to oracles on the nations) represent an earlier form, and the more extensive ones a later form. The basis of the oracles is the old and widespread motif, found widely outside Israel as well, of guests or pilgrims who come from distant places bringing gifts to kings or sacrifices to sanctuaries, as did the "wise men from the East." This motif becomes a feature of the description of the time of salvation in these short texts.

In Isaiah 2:1–4 (Micah 4:1–4) and Isaiah 19:19–25 the motif is transformed, in that the relationship between Israel and the nations becomes completely different. Israel and the nations will live together in peace, and they will share a common relationship to God. The feature of peace among the nations connects this group of oracles with that of the future savior king. There must be a reason for this transformation of an old motif. It became possible through the proclamation of Deutero-Isaiah, especially in 45:20–25, where the "survivors of the nations" are invited to come to Yahweh. Thus the two longer oracles are witness to the fact that the trailblazing message of Deutero-Isaiah was heard and carried forward.

Both oracles portray the future transformation in a comprehensive manner. It embraces the created world (mountains and highways), history (peace), and the relationship to God (pilgrimage to Zion and altars in Egypt). They also have in common that Israel's privileged position is abolished. If the peoples go on pilgrimage to Zion in order to receive God's instruction, it follows that the Torah is not the exclusive possession of Israel. In chapter 19 what God says (vs. 19–21) and what God does (vs. 23–25) includes Egypt and Assyria as well. Both texts are not really proclamation but description. Since the transformation affects the whole world of reality, both texts represent a movement toward apocalyptic (see above, p. 84). But since both arose out of prophecy (that of Deutero-Isaiah), they are intended as the word for their hearers in the present. Both texts therefore represent a further development of an already existing motif of the portrayal of salvation (18:7; 16:1; 10:2), but not of prophetic oracles in the strict sense. That they developed late is shown by their closeness to apocalyptic.

Summary of the Motifs

Motifs of God's turning to his people and of liberation

The motif of deliverance leads the way. In Isaiah 29:22a, there is the remembrance of God's early acts of deliverance: "Thus says the Lord, who redeemed Abraham, concerning the house of Jacob . . . " There is also the remembrance of the rescue from Egypt: "Yet a second time . . . " (11:11, 15–16); "A cloud by day, and smoke and the shining of a flaming fire by night" (4:5); "The Lord . . . will again choose Israel" (14:1).

The apostasy is presupposed in 4:4: "when the Lord shall

have washed away the filth of the daughters of Zion." It is
implied in 29:22b; 10:20f.; 17:8. Israel's apostasy resulted
in God's judgment (4:4): "By a breath of judgment and by a
breath of devastation" (my trans.). This judgment is alluded
to in 30:20a: "And though the Lord give you the bread of
adversity and the water of affliction." There is an explicit
portrayal of the time of terror in 33:18–17, and also 9:1, 3;
16:4b–5; 30:26b.

In the midst of the terror of the judgment, lament breaks
forth. This is spoken of only in one text (30:19):

> Yea, O people in Zion who dwell in Jerusalem; you shall
> weep no more. He will surely be gracious to you at the sound
> of your cry; when he hears it, he will answer you.

But the portrayal of the terror in 33:18–19 can also be regarded as lament.

God's turning again to his people is assumed or proclaimed in all the texts, but in very different ways, and often
in quite general expressions. It is expressed in language that
closely resembles that of the Psalms (Isa. 30:18–26, beginning "Nevertheless" to show the contrast to the preceding
proclamation of judgment):

> Nevertheless the Lord waits to be gracious to you;
> > therefore he exalts himself to show mercy to you.
> For the Lord is a God of justice;
> > blessed are all those who wait for him.

The final sentence is in the language of the Psalms.
God comes to help his people:

> Say to those who are of a fearful heart,
> > "Be strong, fear not!
> Behold, your God will come with vengeance,
> with the recompense of God.
> > He will come and save you." (35:4)

This constitutes the basis for the call to jubilation in 35:1–
3. God's coming is expressed in quite general terms in
11:11: " . . . to recover the remnant which is left of his
people." It is only implied in 29:22: "Jacob shall no more
be ashamed" (cf. 30:19). In 4:5–6 this coming is not expressed, but it is implied in Yahweh's new presence on Zion
(cf. 32:15; 28:5f.; 14:1). It implies or presupposes forgive-

ness. This is expressed with particular clarity in the metaphor of washing or cleansing in 4:4. Compare this with
33:24, where the passage concludes, "The people who
dwell there will be forgiven their iniquity."

It is striking that the center of all these texts, the liberation that is proclaimed, is more often hinted at than expressed, especially in view of the fact that in another group
of oracles of salvation, *only* liberation is proclaimed. This is
seen in the following examples:

> 29:23   "For when [Jacob] sees . . . the work of my hands in
>   his midst . . ."
> 30:26b " . . . in the day when the Lord binds up the hurt of
>   his people, and heals the wounds inflicted by his
>   blow."

This comparison combines the judgment with God's turning
to his people, which leads to "healing." In 35:3–4, "Behold, your God . . . will come and save you" is the language
of an epiphany. Chapter 33:17–24 is similar. The statement, "The Lord will extend his hand yet a second time to
recover the remnant which is left of his people" (11:11),
can mean God's turning to his people just as well as it can
mean the act of deliverance. That act is only alluded to in
4:2, "the survivors of Israel" (cf. 35:8f.). The expressions
"survivors," or "remnant," etc., take their meaning especially in the context of the short supplementary oracles,
where they are often found: Those who have been saved
out of the catastrophe. There is a unique, poetic, and lovely
paraphrase in 30:20b–21. In an allusion to the lament
"How long wilt thou hide thy face from me?" (Ps. 13:1), we
read:

> Your Teacher will not hide himself any more, but your eyes
> shall see your Teacher. And your ears shall hear a word be-
> hind you, saying, "This is the way, walk in it."

By "teacher" is meant the one who shows the way, who
leads absolutely, whose instruction leads to life.

The strikingly indirect or only allusive language of the
proclamation of liberation was used because the proclamations before the return from exile were to serve the proclamation of salvation in a wider sense long after the return
had taken place; therefore general expressions and allusions

were appropriate. In some texts the proclamation of deliverance is followed by the anticipated reaction in praise of God by those rescued. Thus in 29:23b we read, "They will sanctify my name." In 30:18b the praise of God is expressed in God's attributes: "For the Lord is a God of justice; blessed are all those who wait for him." In 35:1–10, in the style of Deutero-Isaiah, the call to the created world to rejoice is combined with praise of God and placed at the beginning, vs. 1–2, and in 6b–7. Praise of God provides the conclusion of 33:17–24, "The Lord is our ruler" (v. 22; this verse is to be read at the end of the passage). In 9:3, "Thou hast increased its joy . . . " is also anticipated joy.

In contrast to the adumbration or paraphrase of deliverance in the oracles in two parts is the proclamation of deliverance in the sequence of deliverance, gathering together, leading back home, which is clearly and unambiguously a reference to deliverance from exile. It is found only seldom in the book of Isaiah, once in 11:11–16 and alluded to in 35:1–10. In both passages the highway on which the exiles return is developed in clear detail (35:8–10; 11:12, 15, 16).

Motifs of Restoration, Blessing, and Salvation

Blessing

In 4:2–3 and 30:23–26, a portrayal of blessing follows God's turning again to his people. "Is it not yet a very little while until Lebanon shall be turned into a fruitful field" (29:17a). Similar passages include 32:15b; 30:23, 25; 35:1–2, 6b–7; 33:21. "And the surviving remnant of the house of Judah shall again take root downward . . . " (37:31–32; see also 7:21–22).

A new relationship with God, inward change

"Those who murmur will accept instruction" (29:24b; cf. 32:4). Those whom God has chosen for survival in Jerusalem will be called holy (4:3). "But your eyes shall see your Teacher . . . , your ears shall hear" (30:20b–21a; cf. 29:19). The worship of idols will cease (2:18, 20; 17:7–8; 30:22; 31:7); they "will no more lean upon him that smote them, but will lean upon the Lord, the Holy One of Israel"

(10:20). "The Lord . . . will again choose Israel" (14:1; cf.
17:7). "The earth shall be full of the knowledge of the
Lord" (11:9).

Justice and righteousness

> Then justice will dwell in the wilderness,
>   and righteousness abide in the fruitful field.
> And the effect of righteousness will be peace,
>   and the result of righteousness,
>   quietness and trust for ever. (32:16–18)

> . . . and a spirit of justice to him who sits
>   in judgment. (28:6a)

This is seen especially in the royal oracles:

> Behold, a king will reign in righteousness. (32:1a)

> . . . to establish [his kingdom], and to uphold it
> with justice and with righteousness.
>   (9:7; cf. 11:3–5; 16:5)

> He shall judge between the nations. (2:4)

Security, quiet, and safety

> For over all the glory there will be a canopy
> and a pavilion (4:5b; 33:20)

> The effect of righteousness will be peace,
>   and . . . quietness and trust for ever.
> My people will abide in a peaceful habitation,
>   in secure dwellings and in quiet resting places.
>   (32:17–18; cf. v. 20; 11:10b; 14:30, 32; 16:5;
>   32:20; 33:6a)

> The Lord . . . will set them in their own land. (14:1)

> . . . a hiding place from the wind,
>   a covert from the tempest. (32:2)

Peace

> For every boot . . . and every garment . . .
>   will be burned. (9:5)

> For to us a child is born, . . .
>   and his name will be called . . .
>   Prince of Peace. (9:6)

> Of the increase of his government and of peace
>   there will be no end. (9:7)

> They shall beat their swords into plowshares . . . ;
>   nation shall not lift up sword against nation,
>   neither shall they learn war any more. (2:4)

We see peace in the animal world in 11:6–9, and peace among the nations in 19:18–25. The celebration of festivals is a feature of peace:

> Look upon Zion, the city of our appointed feasts! (33:20)

> And the effect of righteousness will be peace,
>   and the result of righteousness,
>   quietness and trust for ever.
> My people will abide in a peaceful habitation. (32:17–18a)

All these passages belong together, and what is meant by "peace" can be understood only by viewing them together.

Healing of the sick

It should be noted that this feature of salvation does *not* include the promise of political greatness, military victory over Israel's enemies, political expansion, or political fame. These features are completely lacking. By contrast a new promise is given—the sick will be healed (32:3–4).

> Then the eyes of the blind shall be opened,
>   and the ears of the deaf unstopped;
> then shall the lame man leap like a hart,
>   and the tongue of the dumb sing for joy. (35:5–6)

> Even the lame will take the prey.
> And no inhabitant will say, "I am sick." (33:23b–24a)

> In that day the deaf shall hear
>   the words of a book,
> and out of their gloom and darkness
>   the eyes of the blind shall see. (29:18)

This promise is found in Deutero-Isaiah, and nowhere in

the earlier writings. It is the other side of the rejection of
political might and greatness. The healing of precisely these
infirmities as a part of the work of Jesus has its roots in this
promise.

Motifs in Later Expansions

In the oracles that arose through the expansion of individual motifs we find motifs which are absent from all the traditions of the major groups of oracles, and which have their
origin in various other traditions. These include the statements in the royal oracles which are a part of the kingly
ritual, such as the birth of the king (9:6–7; 11:1) and the
equipping of the royal savior (11:2). They also include the
traditions of the mountain of God in the passages concerning
the pilgrimage of the nations to Zion (2:1–3; 18:7; 16:1) and
the highways that bind the nations together (19:19–25).

The union of distant foreigners with Israel, their pilgrim-
ages, and peace among the nations: The nations make their
pilgrimage to Israel (2:1–4). Gifts are brought to Mount
Zion (18:7), and lambs are sent as gifts (16:1). There is a
highway from Egypt to Assyria (11:10?; 19:19–25).

In only a few texts is the proclamation of salvation identical with that of deliverance, as it is in Deutero-Isaiah. In
most of the texts there are still echoes of deliverance, but
the emphasis is placed on God's turning again to his people.
The proclamation of deliverance (liberation) becomes a
more general proclamation which no longer pertains only
to an historical event. Thus it is all the more surprising that
the motifs of the proclamation of liberation are still found or
at least have their echo. We find the remembrance of God's
earlier saving deeds, the apostasy of Israel and God's judgment, lament, and the depiction of liberation. This is a sure
sign that the epoch-making significance of liberation from
Babylonian exile, together with its proclamation by
Deutero-Isaiah, long continued to play a profound role in
the postexilic period.

In reference to the motifs of blessing, restoration, and
portrayal of salvation we should note that, just as in
Deutero-Isaiah, God's acts of blessing follow and are the
consequence of his act of deliverance. Again we can observe a distinct change in that in these oracles the events of

the restoration are obscured (the rebuilding of the city and the temple are not encountered at all, but already lie in the past) and in their place we find chiefly the portrayal of a state of well-being and peace. Political and military motifs are absent. Never is there a proclamation of an increase of political power, of revenge on one's enemies, or their destruction. The king of that age is a king of peace.

Excursus on the Oracles of Salvation in Isaiah 24–27

Isaiah 24–27, the little Isaiah apocalypse, is a late insertion into the book of Isaiah. This complex of texts is strikingly different from the exilic and postexilic oracles, whose history is not continued here, though they find a quite weak echo.

These chapters contain oracles of woe and judgment on the earth and its peoples, and by contrast, a collection of songs (mostly songs of praise) which are distant reminders of Deutero-Isaiah. But they contain, and this is the striking difference, very few oracles that resemble those of the exilic and postexilic periods. Only a single text is really similar, 27:12–13. It is a clear statement of the proclamation of the gathering of the people and their return and is a sign of the lively power which this motif possessed. The questionable text 27:6–9 should also be mentioned: "In days to come . . . Israel shall blossom. . . . Has he smitten them as he smote those who smote them?" This oracle is at least reminiscent of the exilic and postexilic oracles.

Chapter 25:6–8 is apocalyptic, an oracle of universal salvation like 19:19–25. By contrast, 26:7–11 combines the proclamation of salvation with the nonprophetic motif of the fate of the ungodly and the fate of the pious.

4

The Minor Prophets

Introduction: The Texts

Oracles of salvation in *Amos*. Amos 9:8b–15 is a late addition to the book. It consists of three units, 8b–10; 11–12; 13–15, and is a small collection of oracles of salvation. Within the book of Amos there is a proclamation of conditional salvation in the form of paraenesis: 5:4–6, 14, 15. The book does not contain any other messages of salvation.

Oracles of salvation in *Hosea*. The first of three groups found here consists of oracles of hope addressed to Israel, following message of judgment. These include independent units (2:1–3; 3:1–5; 2:16–25; 14:2–9), the brief supplement in 11:10–11, and the original form of 2:1–3 (see H. W. Wolff in BKAT, vol. XIV/1 on this passage). In addition there are conditional oracles with exhortations (10:12; 12:7–10).

The second group consists of oracles to Judah, following messages of judgment on Israel (1:7; 4:15; 12:1b; 6:11?).

Third, a supplementary message of salvation with only one motif: That God is again favorable to his people (11:8–9).

Oracles of salvation in *Micah*. Chapters 1–3 are a clearly defined block of oracles of judgment, interrupted only once by a message of hope (2:12–13). There is a second group of oracles of judgment in 6:1–16; 7:1–6. Chapters 4 and 5 are a collection of oracles of salvation, and 7:7–20 contains parts of a psalm closely related to the oracles of salvation

(7:11–12 is such an oracle). There are independent messages of salvation in 2:12–13; 4:6–8; 4:9–12, 14; 5:9–13; 7:11–12; and then a message about the royal savior (5:1–3) and one concerning the pilgrimage of the nations (4:1–4, 5). Short supplements in two parts, describing the destruction of the foes, are found in 4:13; 5:4–5a; 5:7; 5:8, 14.

Oracles of salvation in *Nahum*. Distinct oracles of salvation addressed to Judah are 1:9 (10) (added to the psalm in 1:2–8); 1:12–13; and 2:1–3. The book contains only these words of hope, which together could constitute one oracle. In 2:4–3:14 there are no oracles of salvation.

The book of *Habakkuk* contains no prophetic oracles of salvation, although 2:1–4 could be considered to be one. In the song of lament that runs through the whole book (1:2–4, 12–13; 2:1–4; 3:18–19), the words of hope function as God's answer to the prophet. The answer in 2:4 is introduced by vs. 1–3, but in the place where a word from God is expected we have a variant on the fate of the righteous and the wicked (cf. Job 4:12–17).

The book of *Zephaniah* contains three parts: messages of judgment on Judah (1:1–2:3 and 3:1–8); messages concerning the nations (2:4–15); and oracles of salvation (3:9–20). In the first part, 2:3 is a conditional word of salvation added to the preceding passage at a later date. In part two, added to the oracles of judgment on Philistia and Moab are two brief statements (vs. 7 and 9b) that promise that the land will be given to the remnant of the people of Judah. At the beginning of part three (3:9–20), vs. 9–10, properly the conclusion of the messages concerning the nations (but separated from them by 3:1–8), contain a message of universal salvation, which promises a transformation of the nations and their inclusion in the worship which Israel offers to God. In the remainder of part three we find the cleansing of Israel (11–13), praise of God for what he will do (14–18a), and the change in Israel's fortunes (18b–20).

The book of *Joel* contains (in 1:1–2:27) two laments of the people over a plague of locusts and (in 2:28–3:21) the proclamation of God's judgment on the nations (the final judgment). Two oracles of salvation are given as God's answer (2:18–20 and 2:21–27), and there is a proclamation of conditional salvation in 2:12–14. The oracles in 2:28–3:21 are for the most part twofold messages of destruction of the foes and salvation for Israel (2:28–32; 3:1–3, 9–14, 15–17, 18–21). They are in part connected with descriptions of God's blessing (2:19a, 21–26, 2:28–29; 3:18, 21), which tend to become apocalyptic events (2:28–32; 3:1–3, 9–14, 15).

These texts cannot be called oracles of salvation in the strict sense. No turning point, no deliverance is proclaimed. Nor is there any restoration of a healing relationship with God. Many statements were borrowed from earlier prophets but removed from their context.

The little book of *Obadiah* contains proverbial sayings against Edom (vs. 1–14, 15b). Verses 15a, 16–21 are a supplement that extends God's judgment on Edom to encompass the day of Yahweh's judgment over all the nations. This is a composite composition that can be divided into 15a, 16–17 and 18–21. The former is a twofold proclamation of destruction of the enemy and deliverance of Israel, transferred to the day of Yahweh's judgment on the nations. Verse 18 is an independent saying that announced Edom's forthcoming destruction at the hands of Judah, expanded in 19–21 to include Judah's occupation of the territory of Edom.

In the book of *Jonah*, the conditional proclamation is presupposed in the didactic tale in 3:7–10.

In *Haggai* there are proclamations of salvation in 2:6–9, in reference to the building of the temple, and in 2:20–23 to the choice of Zerubbabel as king. This indicates that cultic and court prophecy were alive again. Both are combined here with apocalyptic elements. The message to Zerubbabel is a twofold proclamation. The promise of salvation is conditional on the rebuilding of the temple. The exhortation is strengthened by the promise that God will be with them (1:13; 2:4–5).

In *Zechariah* 1–8 we find a preponderance of visions, which marks the transition from prophecy to apocalyptic. The messages directed to Israel in chapters 1–6 involve eight visions, which are closely related to the proclamation of salvation. For example, the vision of the four horses in 1:7–11 is followed by the lament of the angel (13–14) and by an oracle in vs. 14–17 as the answer to the lament. The following visions are also all related to motifs of the oracles of salvation.

The visions (6:9–8:22) are followed by a series of supple-

ments or additions, which are in part fragmentary (e.g.,
8:7–8). Verses 14–15 (and 4–6?) are probably an oracle
that belongs with the seventh vision.

Oracles of salvation in Zechariah 1–8 are 1:(12) 14–17;
2:10–17 (without vs. 12–13); (8:4–6?); 8:7–8, 14, 15; 8:9–
13; 8:20–23; and a supplement on the destruction of the
enemy (2:12–13). In the section that deals with the question of fasting (7:1–14 and 8:18–19), the answer in vs.
18–19 is a conditional proclamation of salvation. Further
examples are found in 1:1–6; 3:6–7; 16:15b.

In Zechariah 9–14 there are four divisions of oracles.
First, the proclamation of liberation, the return home, and
the reestablishment of Israel (9:11–12; 10:6b–7; 10:8–12).
Second, proclamation of a cleansing (12:10a; 13:1–2, 3–6;
13:8–9; 14:20–21). All these passages announce a transformation of human beings for the coming time of peace and
prosperity. Third, the promise of a king (9:9–10). And
fourth, judgment on the nations, a twofold proclamation
(9:13–16; 10:3–6a; 12:1–8; 14:1–19, to which may be
added Mal. 3:19–21).

Oracles of Liberation, Gathering, and Leading Home

All the texts in this group presuppose the collapse of 587
B.C. and the exile.

Hosea 11:10–11

> 10They shall go after the Lord,
>   he will roar like a lion;
> yea, he will roar,
>   and his sons shall come trembling from the west;
> 11they shall come trembling like birds from Egypt,
>   and like doves form the land of Assyria;
>   and I will return them to their homes, says the Lord.

This oracle proclaims that the gathering together of the
Israelites and their return home is the deed of Yahweh. It is
in three parts: Yahweh roars, his sons respond to his call; he
takes them home and lets them live in their own houses.
This announces an occurrence that takes place in a sequence of three acts. That Yahweh roars like a lion can only

mean that he reveals himself as the mighty and powerful one, who through the display of his might makes the return possible. The precondition for the return is his gathering together those who have been scattered (v. 11a). These events are generally found together in oracles of this group. The final statement, "and I will return them to their homes," marks the transition from an event to a state or condition. Living in houses after the exile involves security and permanence.

Micah 2:12–13

> [12]I will surely gather all of you, O Jacob,
>   I will gather the remnant of Israel;
>   I will set them together
>   like sheep in a fold, like a flock in its pasture,
>   a noisy multitude of men.
> [13]He who opens the breach will go up before them;
>   they will break through and pass the gate,
>   going out by it.
>   Their king will pass on before them,
>   the Lord at their head.

This oracle follows a complex of words of judgment and is a proclamation of deliverance. It proclaims the gathering of those scattered in exile (v. 12), their liberation through the one "who opens the breach," and their return to freedom through the gate (v. 13). Marching before them is Yahweh their King (cf. Isa. 40:10–11). This event in Israel's history unfolds in stages. The similarity to Second Isaiah is obvious. The addition of this oracle to a group of Micah's words of judgment can only mean that after the judgment which Micah announced has taken place, God's history with his people still continues.

Micah 4:9–5:1

The following lines are excerpts; I have reconstructed the text here.

> [9]Why do you cry aloud . . .
>   like a woman in travail? . . .
>   [There is] no king . . .

Your counselor [has] perished . . .
¹⁰Now you shall go forth from the city . . . ;
    you shall go to Babylon.
There you shall be rescued . . .
    from the hand of your enemies.
¹¹Many nations are . . . saying,
    "Let her be profaned." . . .
¹²They do not know the thoughts of the Lord . . . ,
    that he has gathered them as sheaves to the
    threshing floor.
¹³Arise and thresh,
    O daughter of Zion . . . ;
you shall beat in pieces many peoples.

⁵:¹Gash yourself . . . [cf. NJB note; JPSV].
Now you are walled about with a wall;
with a rod they strike upon the cheek
    the ruler of Israel.

This text proclaims liberation and gathering together out of exile, with references to the preceding history in the fall of Jerusalem and the road into exile. This is recounted in order to explain the whole sequence of events as based on God's plan.

Verses 9–10a. The city of Jerusalem is asked why it cries out in pain, and the answer is implied in the question—the people have lost their leaders. The imperative "gash yourself" in 5:1 continues the imperatives in 4:10. The victims cry out because the city is under siege, the king is slain, and the inhabitants must leave the city and go into exile in Babylon. The text is strongly reminiscent of the songs of Lament (cf. Lam. 4:19ff.). The ceremonies of lamentation after the fall of Jerusalem were shaped by the remembrances of what happened then. Lamentations 5:22 voices the question about the future: "Or hast thou utterly rejected us? Art thou exceedingly angry with us?" Reflection on this question is seen in vs. 11–12. The troubles were caused by the nations that intended to destroy Jerusalem, but they did not know that in God's plan justice and redemption were united in both the collapse and the new beginning. This reflection on the judgment is placed in the framework of the proclamation of deliverance: "There the Lord will redeem you from the hand of your enemies." He will gather them like sheaves on the threshing floor.

This unusual message of salvation shows that there is a close connection with the lament of the people after the fall of Jerusalem. The proclamation of salvation is not possible without an affirmation of the preceding history and an acknowledgment that God's judgment leaves open the possibility that he will turn again to this people. This gives an indication of how this group of oracles came into being. They originated in the circle of those who in their grief wondered about the possibility for a continuation of God's history with his people. Expectation and annunciation can no longer be clearly distinguished in these oracles. This oracle can be dated with certainty, because in it the memory of the fall of Jerusalem is still vivid and its resemblance to the psalms of lament is unmistakable. But then also the messages of salvation that were proclaimed soon after the catastrophe were handed on through generations with little change. Thus it is understandable that they remained anonymous and were added as supplements to the oracles of the prophets of judgment.

Micah 7:11–12

> [11]A day for the building of your walls!
>   In that day the boundary shall be far extended.
> [12]In that day they will come to you,
>   from Assyria to Egypt,
>   and from Egypt to the River,
>   from sea to sea and from mountain to mountain.

This text could be either a fragment or an independent unit. Although the subject "a day" has no predicate, it is possible to understand "day" as a predicate. The sentence could be read as a proclamation of salvation that is introduced in the sense of "And it will come to pass on that day," or something similar. The oracle contains the motifs of this groups of oracles: gathering together those who have been scattered and leading them home. To this, v. 11 adds restoration: building of the walls and extending of the boundaries.

Micah 4:6–8

> ⁶In that day, says the Lord,
>> I will assemble the lame
> and gather those who have been driven away,
>> and those whom I have afflicted;
> ⁷and the lame I will make the remnant;
>> and those who were cast off, a strong nation;
> and the Lord will reign over them in Mount Zion
>> from this time forth and for evermore.
> ⁸And you, O tower of the flock,
>> hill of the daughter of Zion,
> to you shall it come,
>> the former dominion shall come,
>> the kingdom of the daughter of Jerusalem.

This text begins with the announcement of the gathering of the exiles and then follows, in what may be an addition, a looking back to God's judgment on Israel. Thus far it is an event that is only proclaimed; but vs. 7–8 announce the restoration. God will make the remnant a mighty people (restoration) and Yahweh will reign as king on Mount Zion. In v. 8, possibly an addition, the restoration of the Davidic kingdom in Jerusalem is announced.

The four texts from Micah have in common that they proclaim an event, the return from exile. Compare 4:9–12 and its looking back to the fall of Jerusalem. In all four texts the return follows the gathering together (2:12; 4:6; 4:12b; 7:12). It is a unified group, the origins of which must be as early as the exile. In addition there are some additional oracles with the motif liberation–gathering–return.

Zephaniah 3:18b–20

> "Behold, at that time I will deal
>> with all your oppressors (19a).
> I will remove disaster from you,
>> so that you will not bear reproach for it (18b).
> And I will save the lame
>> and gather the outcast (19b) . . . ,
> when I restore your fortunes
>> before your eyes," says the Lord (20b).

At the midpoint we have the proclamation of the rescue of those who were slain and those paralyzed and the gathering of those who were scattered (19b). That is the central motif of this group, but somewhat altered. First, God will put an end to those who oppress Israel (19a). Special emphasis is placed on the announcement that the honor of the people will be restored (18b, 20a). The conclusion in 20b could also serve as the introduction. In it Yahweh announces the turning point in his people's destiny, another proclamation of salvation from the time of exile. It is possible that there was a special group of these oracles to which 20b served as either introduction or conclusion. In this connection see the excursus on the expression *shub shebut* (below, pp. 259ff.).

Zechariah 8:7-8, 14, 15 (perhaps also vs. 4-6)

Introduction: "Thus says the Lord of Hosts" (7a). Then the announcement of rescue from exile, gathering together, and return (7b-8a). Restoration of the sacred relationship between God and people (covenant formula; 8b). A look back to the time of apostasy and the judgment, and God's turning again to his people. This was perhaps followed by 14-15, a promise of blessing.

This announcement of salvation corresponds to Group 1 in the book of Isaiah, with the same motifs: apostasy of the people, God's judgment on them, God's turning to this people again, salvation from exile, gathering, leading home, the sacred relationship to God, and perhaps, in conclusion, the promise of blessing.

Zechariah 9:11-12

> [11]As for you also, because of the blood
>   of my covenant with you,
>   I will set your captives free from the waterless pit.
> [12]Return to your stronghold, O prisoners of hope;
>   today I declare that I will restore to you double.

This is an oracle of salvation to the prisoners in Babylon, announcing release from captivity. "Because of the blood of my covenant with you" probably refers to the ceremony in which the covenant was established and implies that God is once again attentive to his people. "Waterless pit" is the language of the Psalms. That this brief oracle contains two expressions related to worship is an indication that this is where the oracle was used. Liberation is followed by the return of the prisoners. The motif of the gathering is missing. They will receive double repayment for all they suffered in captivity (cf. Isaiah 40), the motif of restoration.

Zechariah 10:6b–7

6bI will bring them back because I have compassion on them,
  and they shall be as though I had not rejected them;
    for I am the Lord their God and I will answer them.
7Then Ephraim shall become like a mighty warrior,
  and their hearts shall be glad as with wine.
 Their children shall see it and rejoice,
  their hearts shall exult in the Lord.

This oracle emphasizes God's return to his people. He has mercy on them (6a), he is their God and hears their cries of pain (6b). Because of his mercy, he leads them home and restores them. The act of liberation brings a response of joy and praise from those freed. Compare Second Isaiah.

Zechariah 10:8–12

Another proclamation of salvation that points clearly to the time of the exile. The sequence of events is as follows: God has freed the people; he summons them to gather together (8a); he brings them back from Egypt and Assyria to their homeland (10a). They pass through rivers on their journey (11a). In order to liberate his people, God shows them how powerful he is by humiliating Assyria and Egypt. He will restore his people and increase their numbers (8b) so that they need more space to live in (10b).

The special feature of this oracle is the remembrance of the time of exile (v. 9). It can have originated only in a time of looking back to the exile, and it accepts the recognition of the political catastrophe as God's judgment. God "scattered them among the nations," but this scattering, as of

seed, will be followed by a harvest. In exile they held fast to
the God who brought judgment on them (9b), and their
relationship with God held firm. Thus they can now say that
God is bringing them back home, and this return reminds
them of the road to the promised land at the dawn of their
history (11). Only here is it mentioned that those returning
from exile come as families: "They return with the children
whom they have brought up there" (9c, my trans.). Here
the custodian of the tradition is thinking that in the children
to whom it has been given to live in their own homeland
there is a continuation of the history which the parents
taught to their children while in exile. This is a fundamental
feature of the tradition implied in this looking back.

Verses 11b and 12 are a later addition, and 11a should be
read between 10a and 10b.

Zechariah 2:6–13

> [6]Ho! ho! Flee from the land of the north, says the Lord; for I
> have spread you abroad as the four winds of the heavens. . . .
> [7]Ho! Escape to Zion, you who dwell with the daughter of
> Babylon. [8]For thus said the Lord of hosts . . . [about] the na-
> tions who plundered you . . . : [9]"Behold, I will shake my
> hand over them, and they shall become plunder for those
> who served them. . . . [10]Sing and rejoice, O daughter of Zion;
> for lo, I come and I will dwell in the midst of you, says the
> Lord. [11]And many nations shall join themselves to the Lord in
> that day and shall be my people. . . . [12]And the Lord will in-
> herit Judah as his portion in the holy land, and will again
> choose Jerusalem."
>
> [13]Be silent, all flesh, before the Lord; for he has roused
> himself from his holy dwelling.

This oracle is quite similar to those of Second Isaiah.
There is a long sequence of imperatives, with the reasons
for them in vs. 6–7, that are almost word-for-word the same
as Isaiah 48:20, and also a call to rejoicing (as in Zeph.
3:14). But the sequence of sentences is jumbled. The basis
of the call to flight in 6–7 is followed in Isaiah 48:20b by
"The Lord has redeemed his servant David." Here, however, in vs. 12–13 we have a proclamation of the destruction of Israel's foes, which could belong to Group 2 of the

oracles. The announcement, with Yahweh as subject in 10b, "I will dwell in the midst of you," does not fit this context. Instead, as a parallel sentence, v. 13 should follow: "Be silent, all flesh." Verses 11–12 interrupt the sequence. See above, pp. 90f.

God's Return to His People; Restoration and Blessing

The following passages are oracles of salvation in two parts. They differ from the oracles discussed previously in that liberation, gathering, and leading home are not mentioned. The whole emphasis is on Yahweh's once again being there for his people. As a consequence, they are restored and blessed.

Hosea 1:10–2:1

The promise of increase in number in v. 10 is continued in v. 11b, the original introduction. Several things will happen: They will receive new names, indicating that God is gracious to them once more (vs. 10b, 11); reunification of Judah and Israel (11a); the name Jezreel is changed from a curse into a blessing (11b); continuation of the new names (2:1).

Hosea 1:10–2:1 can only be understood as a late addition to 1:2–9. Here we find the promise that God will once again be gracious to his people. The prophet Hosea's words of judgment are supplemented in a later and different situation by an oracle of salvation in which the unfavorable names are transformed into names of blessing. The original form of this addition read as follows:

> It will be that instead of saying to them . . . , one will say, "sons of the living God." Say to your brothers, "My people, . . . you have received grace," for great shall be the day of Jezreel.

This addition, complete in itself, with a single motif— God's return to his people, was then expanded into an oracle in two parts through the addition of two motifs of restoration: increase in numbers and reunification. While the motif of the original supplement grew directly out of the proclamation of the prophet Hosea, the two expansions have nothing to do with Hosea's specific message. But through them the supplement became an oracle in two parts: God's return to his people and their restoration. The present confused sequence of the statements can probably be explained as the result of the addition of the supplementary material.

Hosea 2:14–23

This passage consists of an oracle in two motifs, the second of which has two subdivisions: First, God will take Israel back to its beginnings (14–15); second, their relationship with God will then be whole again (16–20), and they will receive God's blessing (21–23). Verse 23b returns to the message of 2:1.

In contrast to 1:10–2:1, Hosea 2:14–23 is a coherent, carefully constructed unit. Even though the three parts have separate introductions (vs. 14, 16, 21), it is clear that they belong together, in that each part begins not with a name but with a pronoun, as does v. 23 also. It is an oracle in two parts, the second of which, the restoration, moves into a depiction of the time of restoration in the form of a proclamation. Because God is again present with his people and takes them back to their origins (14–15), the restoration of the relationships (16–20) is made possible, both the relation of Israel to God (16–17) and that of God to Israel (18–20, 23b). The promise of blessing is loosely connected (18, 21–23). The oracle as a whole is closely related to Hosea's prophecy of judgment.

Verses 14–15. God speaks tenderly to Israel; cf. Isaiah 40:2. The promise to give back her vineyards (15) relates to 2:9, the removal of the vineyards. The promise to "make the valley of Achor a door of hope" refers to past destruction (*'akar* means making something taboo), just as Jezreel was to be restored (1:10). "And there she shall answer as in the days of her youth" (2:15) relates to 10:11; "when she came out of the land of Egypt" involves the motif of contrast between then and now, so frequently used by Hosea, and points back to God's earlier saving deeds.

Verses 16–17. Compare "no longer will you call me 'My Baal' " with 2:2–13; verse 17 contains the frequent motif of the elimination of idolatry in the time of salvation.

In vs. 18–23 the mutuality of the relationship with God is emphasized in the covenant (18), marriage (19–20), the change of name (23a), and the covenant formula (23b). All of this is closely related to Hosea's message of judgment.

In vs. 18–20 and 21–23 the description of the time of salvation includes the motif of blessing. The covenant is extended to the created world—the animals in 18a, and the vegetation in 21–22. In addition, peace is promised among human beings (18b), and weapons and war itself will be abolished. Especial emphasis is placed on the permanence of the coming age of salvation: "Betroth you to me for ever" (19a); "lie down in safety" (18b); "sow him for myself in the land" (23a). The conclusion of the oracle in v. 23, "my people—my God," expresses once again that here the decisive factor is the relationship with God. God is once again there for his people.

In the oracles typical of this group, peace among the nations and the end of war are promised, as in Isaiah chapters 2, 9, and 11. Likewise, in the entire group of oracles, there is never any mention of enemies.

Hosea 14:1–8

In verse 1–2a we have a call to return to Yahweh, followed by a remembrance of Israel's apostasy. Verse 2a, "take with you words," calls for confession of guilt and a promise of better behavior, not sacrifices and offerings. In 2b–3 we have a confession of guilt, a petition, and a vow of praise, followed by a promise of repentance—no more service of Assyria or of idols. Then 4–7 brings God's answer. First, God is present to them again: "I will heal their faithlessness; I will love them freely, for my anger has turned from them" (v. 4). "They shall return and dwell beneath my shadow" (7a), and plant grain and vineyards (7b). Ephraim renounces idols (8a). Yahweh has seen the acts of repentance (8b) and will be like dew for Israel, so that they will blossom like the lily (v. 5) and their shoots will spread out (6a). Yahweh says, "I am like an evergreen cypress, from me comes your fruit" (8b).

The oracle proper is found in vs. 4–8. The introduction in vs. 1–4 marks it as God's answer to a lament of the people (2b–4), and 1–2a is the call to lament. These verses recall the previous history: the apostasy of the people (1b), God's judgment on them (4b), and the lament of the people in their misery, together with the plea for forgiveness and help (2b–3).

The turning point in this oracle is God's return to his people (4ab), which is reinforced by its repetition in 8b. The previous history alluded to in the lament makes it clear that the same sequence is intended here as that found in the oracles of Group 1. The use of "stumble" (*kashal*) in v. 1 [2 Heb.] is a clear reference to the debacle of 587 B.C., but the work of liberation, which grew out of God's returning to his people, is included in that return. God's return is followed in 7a and 7b by "They shall return and dwell beneath my shadow, they shall flourish as a garden, they shall blossom as the vine." Then in 8a the motif of the end of idolatry follows immediately. It is to be clearly distinguished from the promises of blessing in 5–6, 8b, which speak a quite different language because they have a different origin. The sequence of the motifs of God's return, restoration, promise of blessing, takes differing forms in these oracles.

Amos 9:11–12 (12a is a gloss)

> [11]"In that day I will raise up
>   the booth of David that is fallen
>   and repair its breaches,
>   and raise up its ruins,
>   and rebuild it as in the days of old;
> [12]that they may possess the remnant of Edom
>   and all the nations who are called by my name,"
>   says the Lord who does this.

Verses 11 and 12 form a unit complete in itself. It is introduced in v. 11 by "In that day," and is concluded in v. 12 by "says the Lord." In this way this unit is a good illustration that such oracles of salvation that are appended to oracles of judgment can be very brief, but despite their brevity, independent entities. And also v. 12a shows that even such short units can themselves have additions.

This oracle announces in metaphorical language that in the future God will act to restore the ruined city of Jerusalem. It speaks of two interconnected events—the fall of the city of David and its future rebuilding. The former event preceeds the latter; they are two points on the line of the history of Israel, which is the history of God's activity with his people. The certainty that this reconstruction will take place is confirmed by the final statement, thus "says the Lord who does this." On the special force of the introduction in this context see pp. 77 and 149, and on the gloss in v. 12a, cf. p. 208.

Amos 9:13–15

[13]"Behold, the days are coming," says the Lord,
  "when the plowman shall overtake the reaper
  and the treader of grapes him who sows the seed;
the mountains shall drip sweet wine,
  and the hills shall flow with it.
[14]I will restore the fortunes of my people Israel,
  and they shall rebuild the ruined cities and inhabit them;
they shall plant vineyards and drink their wine,
  and they shall make gardens and eat their fruit.
[15]I will plant them upon their land,
  and they shall never again be plucked up
out of the land which I have given them,"
  says the Lord your God.

These verses too comprise a unit complete in itself, with the opening words, "says the Lord," and the closing formula, "says the Lord your God." It consists of a depiction of a time of blessing (13b), the proclamation of a change of fortune (14a), and the rebuilding of the city, which makes possible the planting of vineyards and the laying out of gardens. As a result of these events, the people will inhabit the cities, drink the wine, and eat the fruit. These statements affirm that the goal of the restoration is God's blessing on the people. The conclusion is a promise of permanence, expressed in a metaphor that builds on v. 14: "I will plant them upon their land" (cf. Ps. 80:8). It is reinforced by the promise that they will "never again be plucked up out of the land" which God has given them. This calls to mind the promise of the land at the beginning of Israel's history, and the exile as God's judgment (cf. Jer. 1:10).

Like verses 11–12, this oracle announces the rebuilding

(v. 14) but goes further in promising permanence, not only in the final verse, v. 15, but also in v. 14. This oracle demonstrates how the proclamation of an event (recon-struction) moves without interruption into proclamation of a permanent state of well-being which then comes to char-acterize its own group of oracles of salvation. On the other hand, the description in v. 13 is not original to the procla-mation of salvation, even though it is similar to it at many points. We see this in that while v. 13 speaks of fields and vineyards and their fruits, it does so in a manner that con-trasts with 14b. In the latter verse they are the factors that make the whole life possible, but in the former they repre-sent affluence and abundance (cf. the seer's oracles in Numbers 22–24 and Gen. 49:11f. and 25f.). We also see it in that the depiction in vs. 13 does not fit well as the opening statement, while 14 would more suitably follow on 13a.

Hosea 11:8–9

8How can I give you up, O Ephraim!
   How can I hand you over, O Israel!
How can I make you like Admah!
   How can I treat you like Zeboiim!
My heart recoils within me,
   my compassion grows warm and tender.
9I will not execute my fierce anger,
   I will not again destroy Ephraim;
for I am God and not man,
   the Holy One in your midst,
   and I will not come to destroy.

This oracle is a gloss, consisting of the one motif of God's turning again to Israel and his determination not to let Ephraim (Israel) be destroyed again (*'ashub*). Thus it may be termed an announcement of forbearance (cf. Amos 9:8b–9). The basis of this decision is God's compassion for his people. The oracle reminds us of Psalm 103. Here, as in the psalm, we read that God must be angry and pronounce judgment (9a), but he will not always deal with the people in anger (9b). No reason is given for this compassion; it is simply God's nature to be compassionate.

Zechariah 1:(12–13), 14–17

¹²Then the angel of the Lord said, "O Lord of hosts, how long wilt thou have no mercy on Jerusalem and the cities of Judah, against which thou hast had indignation these seventy years?" ¹³And the Lord answered gracious and comforting words to the angel who talked with me. ¹⁴ . . . "Thus says the Lord of hosts: I am exceedingly jealous for Jerusalem and for Zion. ¹⁵And I am very angry with the nations that . . . . ¹⁶Therefore, thus says the Lord, I have returned to Jerusalem with compassion; my house shall be built in it, says the Lord of hosts, and the measuring line shall be stretched out over Jerusalem. ¹⁷ . . . Thus says the Lord of hosts: My cities shall again overflow with prosperity, and the Lord will again comfort Zion and again choose Jerusalem."

This proclamation of salvation is closely connected with the first vision (1:7–13), and thus it is to be understood as a proclamation of deliverance out of a time of trouble. The vision of the four horses ends with a lament of the people (v. 12), which an angel presents in God's presence. The number "these seventy years" dates the lament in the time of the Babylonian exile. God's answer, given in "gracious and comforting words," reminds us of Isaiah 40:1–11, and the whole oracle is similar to the style of Second Isaiah. The use of the perfect tense in 14b is similar to the form of a message of assurance—God's anger with his people is now past, and the exile is to be understood as God's judgment. Special emphasis is placed on God's returning to his people (vs. 13, 14b, 16a, 17b, all of which are to be taken as pointing to the future). God's wrath is now directed against Israel's enemies (15). The part of the proclamation that deals with the future (16b) announces the rebuilding of the temple and the city of Jerusalem. This promise of restoration, followed by a new introduction (17a), leads into a brief promise of blessing. In 17b, perhaps based on the addition of 17a, God's return in mercy to his people is affirmed again.

Nahum 1:9, 12–13; 1:15–2:2

The text is damaged, and the sequence of the verses is uncertain. Verse 1:9 contains a question addressed to the weary and the doubting (cf. Isa. 40:28).

1:12a   The foes will surely be defeated.
  12b   Looking back to the judgment. God announces the end.
  13   Proclamation of liberation (yoke and bonds broken).
  15   The call to joy
  15b   The enemy will attack no more; he is crushed.
  2:2a   Yahweh restores Israel's glory, which had been destroyed (2b) (from the preceding lament of the people).

If we leave aside the question of the original sequence of sentences in Nahum 1–2, it is clear that we have in the above verses fragments of an oracle of salvation, with the motifs in the correct sequence.

Nahum 1:9 makes reference to v. 8, with which the acrostic psalm breaks off. Verse 9 promises that God will intervene in the near future for his people, to whom the psalm refers in the epiphany. In that case, v. 9 is a question addressed to the doubting people in order to give them courage, like Isaiah 40:28 in the same situation. The expected lament of the people is heard in 2:2b. The lament because of the foes is found in 1:12.

Nahum 1:12–13. In the midst of the oracle we find the proclamation of deliverance, vs. 12b, 13, deliverance that is seen as due to God's return to his people after judgment has been rendered: "Though I have afflicted you, I will afflict you no more." As in Second Isaiah, this liberation is the result of God's forgiveness. The verb used here, *'innah*, is found only in exilic and postexilic texts.

Nahum 1:15–2:2

The call to rejoicing at the beginning of the passage is almost identical with Isaiah 52:7a, and the call to rejoice in the religious feasts is close to Isaiah 52:1b. These similarities can only be due to an intentional agreement with the joyous message of Second Isaiah. The reason for the joy is the announcement of restoration, as in vs. 12–13. As for the foes, Israel is free from them, and as for Israel, Yahweh will restore all of Israel's ancient splendor. These two parts, 1:12–13 and 1:15–2:2, are so clearly related to each other that there can be no doubt that they belong together.

1:12–13   Return of God and liberation
  12a   the foes; 12b   Israel

1:15–2:2   Return of God and restoration
1:15   the foes; 2:2   Israel

Zephaniah 3:14–18a

14   The call to Israel to rejoice.
15   The reason: Yahweh has returned, liberated the people, and now reigns as king.
16–18a   God is near—rejoice!

The imperatives in 14 and 16 tie the sections 14–15 and 16–18a closely together. In Second Isaiah also the call to rejoice is combined with the cry, "Do not fear." These verses in Zephaniah are parallel to the earlier songs of praise in Second Isaiah, and the reasons for the shouts are also parallel: The punishment is rescinded; God has returned to his people. In Zechariah 8:5–13 the times past are contrasted to those that are to come (v. 10). God returns to his people (v. 11) and pours out blessings upon them (v. 12). Once again Israel will become a blessing and will be respected among the nations.

Expansion of a Motif Into an Oracle of Salvation

The following group differs from those previously considered in that it consists of oracles in which a single motif has been expanded into an independent proclamation of salvation. These motifs are found as individual members of an oracle of Group 1. Thus they are expansions that presuppose the existence of the proclamations of salvation in Group 1. They differ from proclamations in that only in them do we encounter apocalyptic features, or features that resemble apocalyptic writings.

In the traditional Christian interpretation, the meaning of the so-called Messianic prophecies has been greatly overemphasized. It can be seen that little has changed in this area, even down to the present, by looking at W. Werner's book *Eschatologische Texte in Jesaja 1–39* (1982). There in the chapter titled "Die Messianischen Weissagungen" these prophecies cover a broad range. In reality the promise of a savior king is found in only a small group of oracles in the prophetic books. As a later development they can be

explained and evaluated only on the basis of the total corpus of oracles of salvation.

The Promise of a King Who Brings Salvation

The concluding verse in the proclamation of salvation in
Micah 4:6–8 (see above, pp. 108f.) reads,

> And you, O tower of the flock,
>   hill of the daughter of Zion,
> to you shall it come,
>   the former dominion shall come,
>   the kingdom of the daughter of Jerusalem.

This is one of a group of oracles in which individual features of the restoration could be added almost at will. Here
it is the restoration of the Davidic dynasty in Jerusalem that
is announced. This announcement in structured in two different texts (in widely differing ways) as an independent
proclamation, in one by the use of the old David tradition
and in the other through the old motif of kingship.

Micah 5:2–4 (6)

> [2]But you, O Bethlehem Ephrathah,
>   who are little to be among the clans of Judah,
> from you shall come forth for me
>   one who is to be ruler in Israel,
> whose origin is from of old,
>   from ancient days.
> [3]Therefore he shall give them up until the time
>   when she who is in travail has brought forth;
> then the rest of his brethren shall return
>   to the people of Israel.
> And he shall stand and feed his flock
>   in the strength of the Lord,
>   in the majesty of the name of the Lord his God.
> And they shall dwell secure,
> [5a]and this shall be peace,
>   [4c]for now he shall be great
>   to the ends of the earth.
> [5][When the Assyrian comes into our land
>   and treads upon our soil,

then we will raise against him seven shepherds
    and eight princes of men;
⁶they shall rule the land of Assyria with the sword,
    and the land of Nimrod with the drawn sword;]
and he [RSV emends to "they"] shall deliver us
      from the Assyrian
    when he comes into our land
    and treads within our border.

The promise of a king can be traced back to the seer's oracle in Numbers 24:16–17, where it has the same structure as here: origin, manifestation, work, and it became a part of the David tradition. Origin is described in v. 2, manifestation and work in v. 3. Proclamation and description cannot be separated; the king will appear at an unspecified future time.

In verse 2, as in an oracle, it is a seer, not Yahweh who is speaking. "But you, O Bethlehem Ephrathah . . . " is a rhetorical address to a city, and it transmits a message about the city, as is often the case in the Old Testament. The king's place of origin is important. He comes from a small clan, like Saul and David, but it is a royal clan that goes back to primordial time. Its origin antedates the dynasty, which perished in the collapse of the Judean state (cf. Isa. 11:1).

Verse 3 is an addition that is significant for the history of the oracles of salvation. In the promise of a royal savior the time of his coming is left open, as in the seer's prophecy in Numbers 24:16–17. The addition of v. 3 is intended to correct that lack and to do so in a precise reference to the history which is characteristic of the oracles in Group 1. So it adds that the birth of the king can come only after God's judgment on his people and the return of the remnant from exile. It is in effect a parenthetical remark.

Verses 4, 6b. Verse 4a continues 2b. His origin—his appearance. He exercises his authority ("feeds his flock" as in the ancient designation of the king as shepherd) "in the strength of the Lord." This is a reference to the charismatic leaders, in contrast to the kings before the exile who were disobedient to God. In 4b the text is broken. In any case it means that the rule of this king will bring security and peace. As in the Royal Psalms, kingship includes greatness and worldwide power (cf. Zech. 9:10). He is the king who saves, who rescues from "Assyria," the foe from the north (v. 6b).

Verses 5–6a are a quite different addition. In contrast to the promise of a king, it announces the destruction of the foes. It belongs to the two-part proclamations of Group 2.

Zechariah 9:9–10

Here we find a quite different expression of the promise of a king:

> [9]Rejoice greatly, O daughter of Zion!
>   Shout aloud, O daughter of Jerusalem!
> Lo, your king comes to you;
>   triumphant and victorious is he,
> humble and riding on an ass,
>   on a colt the foal of an ass.
> [10]I will cut off the chariot from Ephraim
>   and the war horse from Jerusalem;
> and the battle bow shall be cut off,
>   and he shall command peace to the nations;
> his dominion shall be from sea to sea,
>   and from the River to the ends of the earth.

This promise takes the form of a proclamation of the triumphal entry of a king and reflects a number of models, especially Isaiah 52:9–10 and 40:1–11. The depiction of this king's glory resembles Isaiah 9:2–7 and 11:1–9. That he is a king of peace is expressed more clearly here than in Micah 5:2–6. He eliminates all weapons and chariots. Thus the office of king has been thoroughly transformed. In contrast to the majority of prophecies (especially Haggai-Zechariah) that speak of the expectation of a future king who will restore the greatness and power of Israel and triumph over his enemies, this oracle expresses the opposite—this king will reign in peace.

The expansion of another motif of the oracles of Group 1 deals with the nations.

Zechariah 2:6–12

> [11]And many nations shall join themselves to the Lord in that day, and shall be my people.

Zephaniah 3:9–10

This is a supplement at the conclusion of a collection of oracles about the nations.

> ⁹Yea, at that time I will change the speech of the peoples
> to a pure speech,
> that all of them may call on the name of the Lord
> and serve him with one accord.
> ¹⁰From beyond the rivers of Ethiopia
> my suppliants, the daughters of my dispersed ones,
> shall bring my offering.

Micah 4:1–4 (5)

For this passage, compare the exegesis of Isaiah 2:2–3, above, pp. 90f.

1b–2 Pilgrimage of the nations to Zion
3–4 Promise of enduring peace, concluding with "The mouth of the Lord of hosts has spoken."
5 "For all peoples walk, each in the name of its god, but we will walk in the name of the Lord our God for ever and ever." (See also Zech. 8:20–23)

The manner in which this expansion came about can be clearly discerned. A procession is depicted in Micah 7:12: "In that day they will come to you from . . . " and in Zephaniah 3:10, "From beyond the rivers of Ethiopia my suppliants . . . shall bring my offering." In Micah 4:1–4 nothing further happens except that a procession sets out for Zion (cf. Psalm 122). Thus the natural result is that when all the nations hear the word of God that issues from Zion they will be able to live in peace with each other and wars will cease.

Now, however, the lines of the procession become a pilgrimage of all people to Zion, Mount Zion is raised higher than all other mountains, the cosmos is transformed beyond the limitations of present reality, and the oracle approaches apocalyptic discourse.

The circle in which Isaiah 2 and Micah 4 arose was probably only a small opposition group. They had special interest in worship, but were not a group of priests, because for priests the sanctity of the cultic places and practices was of supreme importance. The heathen were not permitted to enter the temple. That we are dealing with a lay group is also seen in the connection ,with the psalms in which nations and their kings were called to render praise. The realization of this call to the nations to praise Yahweh could not fail to usher in the time of salvation. We may surmise that it was a group of temple singers among whom these oracles originated. Verse 5, an obvious gloss which shows that there were those for whom this universalism appeared dangerous, indicates that the preceding verses originated in a lay group. It is the same universalism that also found expression in Micah 5:7:

> Then the remnant of Jacob shall be
>   in the midst of many peoples
> like dew from the Lord,
>   like showers upon the grass,
> which tarry not for men
>   nor wait for the sons of men.

It was further developed in Isaiah 19:19–25 (see above, pp. 92f.).

In Zechariah 14:16–19 we find a grotesque contrast to this universal receptivity for the nations, where it is proclaimed that the remaining foreigners in Jerusalem will take part in the Feast of Booths, but under duress. Those who do not participate will be punished. That oracle belongs to Group 2.

Zechariah 13:1-2

This passage, with an appendix in vs. 3–6, can be included in these expansions of a motif, if it is not a fragment. Verses 1–2 unite the motif of the forgiveness of sins with the elimination of idolatry and the false prophets. To this is added in vs. 3–6 a remarkable portrayal of the downfall of the false prophets:

> [1]On that day there shall be a fountain opened for the house of David and the inhabitants of Jerusalem to cleanse them from sin and uncleanness.
>
> [2] . . . I will cut off the names of the idols from the land . . . and also I will remove from the land the prophets and the unclean spirit.

Zechariah 13:8–9

These verses, the proclamation of a purification through a cleansing judgment, can be considered as an expansion of a motif:

> ⁸In the whole land, says the Lord,
>> two thirds shall be cut off and perish,
>> and one third shall be left alive.
> ⁹And I will put this third into the fire,
>> and refine them as one refines silver,
>> and test them as gold is tested.
> They will call on my name,
>> and I will answer them.
> I will say, "They are my people";
>> and they will say, "The Lord is my God."

This oracle stands strikingly in the middle between the motif of the restoration of the holy relationship with God and that of the separation between the pious and the sinners. How and by what means this separation, or the removal of the sinners, will be accomplished is not stated.

Amos 9:8b–10

This passage is similar:

> ⁸ᵇ . . . Except that I will not utterly destroy the house of Jacob,"
>> says the Lord.
> ⁹"For lo, I will command,
>> and shake the house of Israel among all the nations
> as one shakes with a sieve,
>> but no pebble shall fall upon the earth.
> ¹⁰All the sinners of my people shall die by the sword,
>> who say, 'Evil shall not overtake or meet us.' "

This is an addition designed to correct the message in vs. 7–8, which ends with the statement "and I will destroy it (Israel) from the surface of the ground." That statement is modified by the one that follows it—not all of Israel, but only the sinful. This is an oracle of salvation only in the sense of a limitation on the prophetic proclamation of judgment. That proclamation will apply only to sinners, that is, those who have not heeded the message of judgment given by the prophet. In addition, already in this passage we find the division between the just and the sinful.

Addendum: The Judah Glosses in the Book of Hosea

These consist in oracles addressed to Judah which are added to oracles of judgment against Israel.

> But I will have pity on the house of Judah, and I will deliver them by the Lord their God; I will not deliver them by bow, nor by sword, nor by war, nor by horses, nor by horsemen. (Hos. 1:7)

This statement follows a message of judgment against Israel, Hosea 1:2–6, and proclaims in contrast to that message the rescue of Israel through the compassion of Yahweh. Its context is the contrast in the preceding verses, and it tells that the judgment is limited to northern Israel, and that Judah will not be subject to it. Though the language is awkward (v. 7a speaks of Yahweh in both the first and the third person), the verse contrasts the help that God gives with that which comes through force of arms, and thus points to the time of the other proclamations of the end of wars.

Further Judah glosses are as follows: Hosea 6:11; 12:1b. The text of these messages is so corrupt and uncertain that we can only say that they too are Judah glosses and have the same or a similar intention as Hosea 1:7. The condition of the text confirms that they are glosses that stood in the margin and then were later inserted into the text. Hosea 1:7 suffices to show their meaning and intention. Since they were added to messages of judgment against northern Israel, we can be sure that in the course of the handing on of preexilic prophetic oracles in new situations these oracles of salvation came to be added to the text. If this is the case, the texts show that the messages of the prophet Hosea were handed on in Judah, and that there oracles of salvation were added to them.

Motifs of the Oracles

The motifs found in the proclamations of liberation that contain only a single element are to be distinguished from those of two elements that proclaim that God is again present to his people and will restore their fortunes.

Motifs That Proclaim Liberation

God's earlier saving deeds in retrospect

Texts that speak explicitly of God's saving deeds in the past are infrequent. Examples found in the book of Hosea are attached to the frequent references to history, such as 2:14–23, in v. 15b, "As in the days of her youth, as at the time when she came out of the land of Egypt." Allusions to God's earlier deeds are frequent, e.g., Amos 9:11–12: "and rebuild it as in the days of old" (11b). It is significant that in Amos 9:13–15, a text which portrays the future state of blessing, v. 15 alludes to the gift of the land: "the land which I have given them." More significant, however, is that the motif of God's return to his people in itself presupposes God's saving deeds.

Apostasy and God's Judgment

Israel's apostasy and God's judgment on them are assumed in the proclamation of liberation. They are often mentioned or alluded to: Hosea 14:1: "Return, O Israel, to the Lord your God, for you have stumbled because of your iniquity." (This is further developed in the confession of sin in v. 3.) Nahum 1:12b: "I have afflicted you . . . " (See also 2:2b); Zechariah 2:6b, "For I have spread you abroad as the four winds of the heavens" (cf. Micah 7:9). God's judgment is alluded to in Amos 9:11–12: "the booth of David that is fallen" (see also Amos 9:15; Hos. 11:8–9). In the style of a lament of the people, Micah 4:9–10 gives a vivid reminder of the fall of Jerusalem.

The lament

Lament as such is not a component of the oracles of salvation, but we encounter laments or their components so often in these texts that there must be a connection between them. In all oracle texts in which we find lament motifs, the oracle of salvation (that is, the proclamation of deliverance or of God's restoration of his people) is an answer to the lament. This is clear in that the prophets often announce God's answer to a lament of the people.

Joel 1–2. The book of Joel begins with a lament of the people, and this is followed by two answers from God: 2:18–20 and 2:21–27. Habakkuk also begins with such a lament. In Zechariah 1:12–17, an angel, representing the people, presents their lament to God, and this is followed by God's comforting answer, 1:14b–17—God has returned once more to his people. In Hosea 13:16–14:7 the call to return to God (1–2a) introduces a lament of the people, which is alluded to in 14:1b–2. God's reply follows in vs. 4–7. Nahum 1:2–8 is a psalm fragment in which 3b is a statement from a lament of the people. Micah 4:9–11 refers back to the lament in an allusion to the fall of Jerusalem. In several passages the oracle includes God's promise to hear the people: Zechariah 10:6b; Hosea 14:8; Zephaniah 3:17; Micah 7:7.

On the basis of the data we conclude that the oracles of salvation from the exilic and postexilic times are closely related to the laments of the "remnant." This close relationship to lament involves the aspect that often the answer—the oracle of salvation—closely resembles the language of worship.

God's return to his people (forgiveness)

Even at first glance it is evident that this motif is the most frequent in the oracles in the book of Hosea and that it is the most fully developed. This is clearly due to the fact that in Hosea's proclamation in the eighth century this motif had central importance, and it shows how closely the exilic and postexilic oracles of salvation were adapted to the prophetic messages that were at hand.

> Hosea 1:7 "But I will have pity on the house of Judah . . . "
> (Cf. 1:10–2:1; 2:14–23)
> 11:8–9 "How can I give you up, O Ephraim!
> How can I hand you over, O Israel! . . .
> My heart recoils within me,
> my compassion grows warm and tender."
> 14:5–6 [4–5] "I will heal their faithlessness;

> I will love them freely,
> for my anger has turned from them . . . "
> (See also Zeph. 3:18b–20; Amos 9:13–15)

In Zechariah 1:17b and 2:12 God's return is described as his choosing Israel anew. It is also proclaimed openly that Yahweh will once again be favorable to his people: "I have returned to Jerusalem with compassion" (Zech. 1:16; see also 1:17b; Nahum 1:12b; Zeph. 3:17b).

Liberation, gathering together, leading home

> I will surely gather all of you, O Jacob,
> I will gather the remnant of Israel. . . .
> He who opens the breach will go up before them;
> they will break through and pass the gate. (Micah 2:12–13)
> (See also Micah 4:6–8, 9–14; 7:11–12; Hos. 11:10–11a;
> Zeph. 3:18b–20; Zech. 2:6–13)

The group of four texts in Micah constitutes the heart of this motif, but it is found in numerous additional passages. In other texts it is reduced to the motif of leading home, or that of gathering together.

Anticipatory praise of God

> Sing aloud, O daughter of Zion;
> shout, O Israel! Rejoice and exult . . . !
> The Lord has taken away the judgments against you,
> he has cast out your enemies. . . .
> you shall fear evil no more. (Zeph. 3:14–15; cf. 16–18a)

We have here proclamations of salvation in the form of the hymns of praise in Second Isaiah, and similar to them in content. The same anticipatory praise is often found as a single motif, with echoes of Second Isaiah and frequent sentences that are the same, word for word, as in the earlier prophet.

> Sing and rejoice, O daughter of Zion; for lo, I come and I will dwell in the midst of you. (Zech. 2:10)
> (See also Zech. 9:9–10; Nahum 1:15; cf. Zech. 10:6b–7)

These oracles demonstrate that the entire group is later than Second Isaiah, but they also show that many of these oracles were consciously dependent on his message.

In this first list of motifs we find a context that they all have in common: the history of God's dealings with his people. This is seen in the frequent references to God's earlier saving deeds in history, in the acknowledgment of the guilt that has brought God's judgment on his people, and the dominant significance of the motif of God's again being gracious to them, which contains the recollection of the intact relationship with God before the apostasy. All this is seen most explicitly in the firmly fixed tradition of liberation, gathering again, and leading home, which points to an abbreviated—or stylized—narrative, and finally, the response of praise of God, as was found in the prior history of Israel.

The intimate connection with history distinguishes this first series of motifs from the following second series, in which the motifs are no longer found in a time sequence, but are presented together.

Motifs of Restoration and Promise of Blessing

In this second series of motifs two groups can be distinguished. The first is identified by the catchword "restoration." The arrival in the ancient homeland must be followed by reconstruction, the restoration of the conditions necessary for life. The other group is identified by the catchword "blessing."

In many ways the tradition was such that deliverance would be followed by blessing. The work of the God who saves is followed by God's bestowal of blessing. This was the testimony of the patriarchs. These accounts took their final form in the Pentateuch. Following their deliverance from Egypt the people needed God's blessing when they entered the land. This is shown by the way Deuteronomy follows on Exodus through Numbers; indeed it was already shown by the ancient Credo. That blessing and the promise of blessing have an origin different from that of proclamation and deliverance is made clear in that the statements that speak of blessing are placed before, within, or following the annunciation in a manner that is not organic to the material. Fertility and increase in number are the main forms in which God's blessing is promised.

In Joel 2:21–27 the promise of blessing has replaced the

proclamation of salvation. The cry in vs. 21, 23a, "Fear not, O land; be glad and rejoice . . . ," and the basis for the cry (21b, "for the Lord has done great things!") in the perfect tense have the same structure as the proclamation of promise in the words of Second Isaiah. In Second Isaiah, however, the statement in the perfect is based on Yahweh's actions in history, while here in Joel the basis of the blessing of fertility (vs. 22–24) is found in God's answer to the lament over a plague of grasshoppers.

Increase in numbers and fertility are promised in Zechariah 2:4; 6:12; 8:12; 10:8b, 10b. And Amos 9:13 reads,

"Behold, the days are coming," says the Lord,
"when the plowman shall overtake the reaper
and the treader of grapes him who sows the seed;
the mountains shall drip sweet wine, and all the hills
shall flow with it."
(See also Hos. 1:10; 2:21–22; Micah 7:11b)

Blessing brings well-being and abundance.

For the Lord is restoring the majesty of Jacob
as the majesty of Israel. (Nahum 2:2)
(See also Zech. 1:17; Hos. 14:5–6)

The other series of motifs is based on the situation in which these oracles are issued, the time following the return to the homeland that had been destroyed in the catastrophe. The restoration proclaimed in the oracles can be analyzed according to the conditions of a rich and full life.

First is the restoration of the city or cities, the temple, the farmland, and the vineyards.

And they shall rebuild the ruined cities and inhabit them;
they shall plant vineyards and drink their wine,
and they shall make gardens and eat their fruit. (Amos 9:14)

In that day I will raise up the booth of David that is fallen . . .
and rebuild it as in the days of old. (Amos 9:11)
(See also Micah 7:11–12; Zech. 1:16; Nahum 2:2; Hos. 14:7)

The reconstruction naturally follows directly on the return, beginning with the removal of the rubble. A wholesome life requires wholesome houses, the reconstruction of the city and of the temple, from which blessing flows out into the land. The transition from these events to stability is shown in the three statements in Amos 9:13–15. This restoration can also be announced in a promise: "Today I declare I will restore to you double" (Zech. 9:12b; cf. Isa. 40:2).

Second is the restoration of quiet, security, and peace (the social aspect).

> I will make you lie down in safety. (Hos. 2:18b)

> But they shall sit every man under his vine and under his
>   fig tree,
>   and none shall make them afraid. (Micah 4:4a)
>   (See also Micah 5:4; Nahum 1:15a; Zech. 3:10; 8:4–5)

Quiet and security are part of a happy life, so that it is possible to live without fear of a sudden attack by the enemy. In this connection the word "peace" is often used, e.g., "And this shall be peace" (Micah 5:5a), not from a political perspective, but from the perspective of the common people who wanted to lead their lives in peace and quiet. Peace also includes the celebration of festivals (Nahum 1:15).

Restoration of a right relationship with God. A healthy continuation of life could result only from a healthy relationship with God. Hosea 2:14–23 explictly announces a right relationship with God, a relationship that must once again be faithful, from Israel to God and from God to Israel.

> And I will betroth you to me for ever; I will betroth you to
> me in righteousness and in justice, in steadfast love, and in
> mercy. (Hos. 2:19)

In v. 23 the names that signified trouble were turned into names signifying wholeness. The restoration of a right relationship with God means that God once again reigns in his city and is present with his people. In the background here is Ezekiel's concept of the *kabod*, the glory of Yahweh, that had forsaken Jerusalem and the temple (Ezek. 10:18–19).

> I come and I will dwell in the midst of you, says the Lord.
> (Zech. 2:10)

> They shall return and dwell beneath my shadow. (Hos. 14:7a)
>   (See also Zech. 2:12; Joel 2:27; Micah 4:7b; Zeph.
>   3:15b, 17)

In these passages there is a tendency to ascribe a greater

importance to God's presence than to his act of returning to his people. This indicates a transition to the language of the cult. Yahweh is king, as in the Jerusalem psalms of the divine kingship. We see the covenant formula in Zechariah 13:9.

The aspects of restoration considered above involve that which is necessary for life in general. There are also announcements that relate specifically to Israel's history.

Reunification and restoration of honor

"And the people of Judah and the people of Israel shall be gathered together, and they shall appoint for themselves one head" (Hos. 1:11a). Restoration of honor is found in Zephaniah 3:18, 20; Joel 2:19, 23, 27.

Restoration of the kingdom

This promise is made in Micah 4:8; 5:2–6; Zechariah 9:9–10. The restoration of the kingdom that is proclaimed in these oracles is an isolated motif (Micah 4:8) or the expansion of a motif (5:2–6). It is not primarily concerned with that which is necessary for the life of the community, but with the restoration of something desirable and valuable out of the past. This means, as the texts show, not the kingdom in its role in international politics, but in its social function. It is concerned with right and justice, peace and security in the land. The king is the guarantee of peace, not the representative of political greatness and power.

Inclusion of other peoples

"And many nations shall join themselves to the Lord in that day" (Zech. 2:11a; see also Zeph. 3:9–10; Micah 4:1–4; 7:12). The inclusion of other peoples is found as an isolated motif or as an expansion (Zech. 8:20–23). This is not necessary for the life of the community. It is a motif that goes back to Israelite history in the time of David and Solomon. Even so, as in the restoration of the kingdom, this inclusion of other peoples is not meant in terms of political power for the subjugation and exploitation of these peoples. There is no trace of that in the texts. Instead, in all the texts what is meant is religious unity. This is expressed in the pilgrimage to Zion.

The end of war and peace among the nations

> I will not deliver them by bow, nor by sword, nor by war, nor by horses, nor by horsemen. (Hos. 1:7b)

> I will abolish the bow, the sword, and war from the land. (2:18b)

> I will cut off the chariot from Ephraim . . .
> and he shall command peace to the nations. (Zech. 9:10)

> He shall judge between many peoples . . .
> and they shall beat their swords into plowshares. (Micah 4:3)

Peace among the nations is found in Micah 5:7:

> Then the remnant of Jacob shall be
> in the midst of many peoples
> like dew from the Lord,
> like showers upon the grass,
> which tarry not for men
> nor wait for the sons of men.
> (Cf. Isa. 19:19–25)

These oracles are by no means proclamations of the final end of war, of universal peace among the nations, even though that is what they seem. They all refer to the then current situation of Israel during and after the exile, but they were later expanded in meaning. They are saying something specific and unequivocal—that the future salvation which Yahweh is bringing to Israel will not be achieved through political and military struggles (Hosea 1:7). This proclamation to Israel, which goes back to Second Isaiah, was later expanded into a vision of the end of all wars and the time of universal peace.

5

Jeremiah

The Collection of Oracles in Jeremiah 30–33

According to the introduction in 30:1–3 (4), this collection consists of two small collections (30:4–31:22 and 31:23–40) plus two supplements (32:36–44; 33:1–13 and 33:14–18, 19–22, 23–26). The oracles in the first collection announce liberation (two texts also announce restoration), and those in the second announce restoration, but only in a single motif. The distinction between the two collections must have been known to those who handed on the materials. They might have originally been two independent collections, the first of which represents an earlier stage.

Supplementary material was added to each collection. The prose account 32:1–35 was added only because of 32:15, because that verse corresponds in form to the oracles in 31:23–40. There follow two texts, 32:36–40 and 33:1–13, both of which are deuteronomistic and consist of two parts each. And finally there are the quite late royal oracles in 33:14–26. In addition there are twelve oracles outside the collection in chapters 30–33. Five of these are announcements in two parts (Yahweh's return to his people, and their restoration); three are similar to those collected in 31:23–40; and four are supplements to the oracles to the nations.

The Collection in Jeremiah 30:1–31:22

Jeremiah 30:1–3

These sentences constitute a two-part introduction to the collection in chapters 30–33 (W. Thiel, 1981, 20ff.). The command to Jeremiah (v. 2) to write down the oracles is part of the deuteronomistic introduction and corresponds to 36:2. Verse 3 summarizes the message of salvation:

> For behold, days are coming, says the Lord, when I will restore the fortunes of my people, Israel and Judah, says the Lord, and I will bring them back to the land which I gave to their fathers, and they shall take possession of it.

This introduction summarizes the oracles in four parts: introduction, God's return in grace, bringing the people back, and restoration (implied).

Jeremiah 30:4–9

4	Introduction to a collection of oracles.
5–7	Judgment on Israel; announcement of deliverance.
8–9	(Prose) Announcement of liberation and restoration.
8a	New introduction—"in that day."
8b	"I will break the yoke . . . burst their bonds."
8c	"Strangers shall no more make servants of them."
9	"They shall serve the Lord their God and David their king, whom I will raise up for them."

A poem about Yahweh's day of judgment on Israel (5–7a) is followed in a mere half verse (7b) by the announcement of deliverance. It has apparently been shortened by the prose supplement (8, 9) with its new introduction and the continuation of the announcement in the first person. The liberation is depicted in 8b (yoke, bonds), the end of foreign rule (8c), and their serving Yahweh the King (9). This describes the new state of well-being brought about by the liberation.

Jeremiah 30:10–11 (almost identical with 46:27–28)

The text, which has the form of an assurance of salvation and of the salvation oracle found in worship, resembles a lament.

10a Assurance: "Fear not."
11a Basis for the assurance (present tense) "I am with you."
10b, 11b Basis for the assurance (future tense) "I will save
. . . your offspring from . . . their captivity. Jacob shall
return and have quiet and ease." I will destroy your enemies, but only chastise you.

This oracle is in the tradition of Second Isaiah and presupposes that tradition. In his Isaiah commentary B. Duhm
called particular attention to this fact. In this oracle alone
there are five borrowings. Later exegetes have belittled this
relationship between Second Isaiah and Jeremiah 30–33 in
order to defend Jeremiah's authorship. The use of the oracles of worship for the proclamation of deliverance is found
in both collections. Verse 11b could be a later addition,
because the reflective language of that half verse departs
from the style of the assurance of salvation.

Jeremiah 30:12–17

12–14a (15) A lament transformed into interpersonal
address.
12–13 "Your hurt is incurable." 15a, a "why"
question.
14a Forsaken by everyone
14b, 15, 17a God's answer, supplemented by 16, 17a
14b, 15 Their suffering is punishment from God.
17a Announcement of healing.

The beginning (vs. 12–14a) reminds us of the language of
lament. Statements from a lament of an individual are transformed into a lament of the people, as in Second Isaiah. As
God's answer to the people the oracle speaks to Israel in the
second person.

The answer is in two parts. The first part (vs. 14b, 15)
gives the reason why Israel must suffer so greatly. Here the
"why" question is dealt with: "I have dealt you the blow of
an enemy. . . . Because your guilt is great . . . I have done
these things to you." This explanation is followed by the
second part of God's answer (17a): "For I will restore
health to you, and your wounds I will heal, says the Lord."
God's reminder to the people, that he had to punish them
severely, corresponds to the words of Second Isaiah's dis-

putes with them, in which we find the same sequence, e.g., Isaiah 42:18–25.

The casting of the oracle in terms of sickness and health corresponds to the language of the Psalms and shows a certain distancing from any direct, concrete proclamation of deliverance from exile. This distancing also corresponds to the argumentation that is concerned to explain the collapse of the nation as the inescapable judgment of God.

Verses 16, 17b are a later addition (so also B. Duhm). Verse 17a, "For I will restore health to you . . . " resumes the content of 15b and is the original conclusion of the oracle, as is shown by the final phrase, "says the Lord." The announcement in v. 16, "Therefore all who devour you shall be devoured . . . ; those who despoil you shall become a spoil" does not fit well in the context of 12–17. Since v. 15 stresses that the national collapse and exile were caused by Israel's great guilt, it is then scarcely appropriate to say that Israel's foes, God's instruments for this judgment, are to be destroyed (against V. Rudolph). The harsh language of the revenge motif in v. 16 introduces an alien note into the oracle in 12–17. There is also a question of the form. The statement "because they have called you an outcast . . . " is the reason for v. 16, not for 17a. Verse 17b belongs to the supplement, and when the supplement was moved from the margin into the text, 17b ended up in the wrong place. Verses 16–17a belong to the twofold proclamations: Destruction of the foes, salvation for Israel so that the twofold nature of the passage results from the insertion. (On 30:18–22 and 31:1–6 see below, pp. 150ff.)

Jeremiah 31:7–9

7   "Sing aloud with gladness for Jacob . . .
      'The Lord has saved his people . . . ' "
8   "Behold, I will bring them from the north country"
9   "With weeping they [went forth],
      and with consolations I will lead them back . . .
    for I am a father to Israel. . . . "

This poem has the same structure as Second Isaiah's songs of praise: Call to rejoice (v. 7); reason for joy, in the perfect tense (7b); proclamation, in the future tense (8–

9a); reason for joy, in the present tense (9b). The passage presents the unfolding of a series of events: Liberation, gathering the exiles together, and leading them home. The prehistory is alluded to in 9a, "With weeping they [went forth]" (cf. Ps. 126:5). The whole corresponds in every point to the message of Second Isaiah: Rescue of Israel, gathering them in from distant places, leading them home in joy on a plain path (Isa. 42:11), and the weakness of some of the returnees, led home by Yahweh. At the end we hear that God has turned again to his people, like a father to his children (cf. Ex. 4:22). This oracle does not include a motif of restoration.

Jeremiah 31:10–14

10–11	Announcement of liberation
10a	Call to the nations and distant shores to hear
10b–11	The news of Israel's liberation. The one who dispersed Israel now redeems, gathers, brings them back.
12–14	Restoration (Blessing)
12a	They return in joy to Zion, to Yahweh's blessing, i.e., to the source of blessing.
12b	Grain, wine, oil, sheep, cattle
12c	They languish no more; their life is like a well-watered garden.
13	Mourning is turned to rejoicing; both young and old are filled with joy.
14	The priests and the people enjoy God's goodness.

In this passage also the resemblance to Second Isaiah is obvious. As there, the message of Israel's liberation is proclaimed in the forum of the nations (Isa. 52:10). The description there of the liberation in three events is the same as in 31:7–9. Here too the preceding history, the judgment, is alluded to: "he who scattered Israel," and the earlier mourning: "they shall languish no more."

The second part, vs. 12–14, limits the description of the restoration to the one motif of blessing, which is much expanded. They return to Zion, from where Yahweh's blessing flows out over the land, people, and cattle.

Jeremiah 31:15–22

15–17   Lament and comfort
15   Rachel weeps for her lost children
16a, 17a   Words of comfort—don't weep, there is hope for
your future.
16b, 17b   Promise of a return to their homeland.
18–20   God turns again to his people
18   Yahweh hears their confession of sin and their
readiness to repent.
19   Expansion: I repented and was ashamed.
20   God turns again to them—I *must* have mercy
on them.
21   Exhortation to return home
22   Supplement: How long will you waver?

The structure of this oracle is determined by the lament
of the people and Yahweh's answer to that lament (cf.
30:12–17). The lament is personified in Rachel, the tribal
mother. In v. 15 in three lines we have Rachel's lament for
her lost children. There follows in vs. 16–17 (to be read in
the order 16a, 17a, 16b, 17b) God's answer, a word of comfort that promises the return of her children. In 17–18 we
see God's return to his people, which makes the liberation
possible. It results from Israel's confession of sin, as a part of
the lament of the people, and Israel's readiness to repent. It
is recognized that the destruction of Jerusalem was God's
judgment, "Thou hast chastened me . . . " (v. 18). God is
again gracious to Israel because of his unfathomable compassion: " . . . I *must* have mercy on him" (v. 20, my
trans.). "Is Ephraim my dear son?" (20a) calls to mind
Psalm 103, as well as Hosea 11:8–9. Verse 19, a prose expansion in the midst of this beautiful poem, is a supplement
that underlines the element of repentance.

In all these oracles the emphasis is on the announcement
of liberation.

30:10   "I will save you from afar,
and your offspring from the land of their captivity."
31:7b   "Say,
'The Lord has saved his people, the remnant of
Israel.' "

31:10b–11   "He who scattered Israel will gather him,
                   and will keep him as a shepherd keeps his
                   flock."
                 For the Lord has ransomed Jacob,
                   and has redeemed him from hands too strong
                   for him."
                 (See also 30:1–3; 31:15–22, 14b, 17b)

What is proclaimed in the introduction and all these passages is an event—a turn for the better for Israel. The original word of prophecy announced an event. The portrayal of a state of well-being was added later.

The Collection in 31:23–40

The group of texts in Jeremiah 31:23–40 (and 32:15) belong together in that all of them (except 31:35–37) speak of the restoration, while each of them contains only a single motif. The deliverance is presupposed in each, but in none of them is it developed. In reality these are not complete oracles, but resemble brief supplements. They are best understood as the responses of individual members of the community that heard the promises. These brief oracles with but one motif are in effect voices in the chorus of those who accept and affirm the proclamation of deliverance. The guardians of the tradition were fully justified in seeing in the oracles in Jeremiah 31:23–40 an independent collection with its own history of transmission and therefore preserving them.

Jeremiah 31:23–26

(23)   " . . . when I restore their fortunes"
  23   "Once more they shall use these words [of blessing] in
           the land of Judah and in its cities."
  24   It will once again be inhabited by farmers and shepherds.
  25   I will replenish every languishing soul.
           [26 is a supplement]

The basis of the oracle is a rite of blessing. A blessing is pronounced on the land, "in the land of Judah and in its cities": "The Lord bless you, O habitation of righteousness, O holy hill!" In exile the people remember these words that were spoken, and they affirm that the time will come when this blessing will once again be pronounced. Verse 24 adds that the land will be inhabited again, and farmers and shepherds will live in it once more. The final statement, v. 25, which like 23b is rhythmical, was also probably a part of the rite of blessing: "For I will satisfy the weary soul, and every languishing soul I will replenish."

This oracle is an especially beautiful and significant example of how during the exile the proclamation of salvation was brought together with the hopes and longings of these who had been exiled. Apart from the subordinate clause, "when I restore their fortunes," which does not even stand at the beginning of the oracle, this oracle is mainly an expression of hope and longing. It becomes a proclamation of salvation through the insertion of this distinctive clause. This is clear proof that such combinations had already been made during the exile. B. Duhm held that 31:23–26 was the "conclusion of the little book that began with 30:4." The verses that follow are only later supplements. What was said in the preceding oracles about restoration has now been completed, and a blessing can once again be pronounced on the land.

Jeremiah 31:27–28

27 "Behold, the days are coming, says the Lord, when I will sow the house of Israel and the house of Judah with the seed of man and the seed of beast.

28 And it shall come to pass that as I have watched over them to pluck up and break down, to overthrow, destroy, and bring evil, so I will watch over them to build and to plant, says the Lord."

The proclamation consists of only one motif from the portrayal of restoration—the motif of multiplying the people. It has an introduction, "Behold, the days are coming, says the Lord," and a paraphrase of Jeremiah 1:10 is added, which reinforces the promise of increase. The one speaking here has Jeremiah 1:10 before his eyes or in his ears at a time when the proclamation of judgment which had been entrusted to Jeremiah has been fulfilled. God had watched over his word and it has come to pass. But what has not been fulfilled is the promise of restoration given there, of building and planting. The speaker remembers this, and thus the words of Jeremiah can give him the authority to reaffirm that promise. He is not a prophet of salvation and makes no claim to be one. He says only that what the prophet Jeremiah had proclaimed will be fulfilled. Jeremiah 1:4–10 in its present form has been shaped by Deuteronomy (thus F. Ahuis, *Der klagende Gerichtsprophet*, 1982, 177–180). By this use of the account of Jeremiah's call to be a prophet, his ministry is portrayed from the deuteronomic point of view. Thus in Jeremiah 1:10 the plucking up precedes the planting; the proclamation of deliverance follows the judgment (so also 18:7–10; 24:6; 31:28; 31:38–40; 42:10; on the basic metaphor used here, see E. Rohland in R. Rendtorff and K. Koch, eds., *Studien zur Theologie der alttestamentlichen Überlieferungen*, 1961.

Jeremiah 31:29–30

29 "In those days they shall no longer say:
 'The fathers have eaten sour grapes.
 and the children's teeth are set on edge.'
30 But every one shall die for his own sin; each man who eats
 sour grapes, his teeth shall be set on edge."

Here too a single motif has been expressed as an oracle of salvation, but only the introduction is given. The author of this oracle took Ezekiel 18:2 and expressed it in the form of an oracle. The comment on Jeremiah 27–28 also applies here. The collection that includes Jeremiah 27–28 and 29–30 presupposes both a Jeremiah tradition and an Ezekiel tradition.

Jeremiah 31:31–34

Here a complete oracle of salvation is based on a single motif: the inner transformation of men and women in the age of salvation. This is a secondary motif that developed out of reflection on the restoration.

31a Introduction
31b I will make a new covenant with Israel and Judah.
32 It will not be like the one that they broke.

33 But in this covenant I will write my law upon their hearts.
34a No longer will anyone need to be taught, because they will all know God.
34b Forgiveness makes this new relationship with God possible.

This announcement of deliverance transcends present reality, and presents a reality that is radically changed. Where no one needs further instruction, tradition is at an end, and where everyone knows God, the humanity that according to Genesis 2–3 was created as fallible, no longer exists. The establishment of this new covenant is an event that lies beyond history.

The question of whether this oracle is directed to northern Israel or to Judah seems to me of no consequence. The Israel addressed here is the Israel that God led out of Egypt, and which broke the covenant. That is, all Israel. This oracle belongs to a later layer of tradition. Some scholars (S. Herrmann, W. Thiel) hold that it is deuteronomistic. Though this may be true of 32:37–44, and perhaps also of 33:1–13, it cannot be true of 31:31–34, for these oracles differ too much from each other. If Deuteronomy and the Deuteronomist regard the tradition as fundamental for the people of God, they would not formulate a promise according to which there will no longer be any tradition in the new covenant. The same holds also for the word of exhortation.

Jeremiah 31:35–37

35 "Thus says the Lord, who gives the sun for light by day and the fixed order of the moon and the stars for light by night, who stirs up the sea so that its waves roar—the Lord of hosts is his name:
36 'If this fixed order departs from before me, says the Lord, then shall the descendants of Israel cease from being a nation before me for ever.'
37 Thus says the Lord: 'If the heavens above can be measured, and the foundations of the earth below can be explored, then I will cast off all the descendants of Israel for all that they have done, says the Lord.' "

In this oracle a single motif of the proclamation of salvation is expanded into an independent oracle by being reinforced by an oath sworn by God. This is a motif of God's return in mercy to his people, and probably ran as follows: "I will never again reject the descendants of Israel because of all that they have done. They will never cease to be my people." This assurance of God's favor was reinforced by the statement that it is as firmly based as the order of creation itself. In order to validate this, the oracle is introduced by praise of God in terms of Genesis 1, a doxology similar to many of the oracles in Second Isaiah (v. 35b = Isa. 51:15). The whole oracle is expressed in the language of the Psalms. As long as the earth stands God will not cease to be present to his people. This is no longer a proclamation of deliverance in the strict sense, but is a reflective intensification of a motif. Here a member of the worshiping community expresses his confidence in God's abiding presence with his people. Reinforcement of a promise is always secondary to a simple promise. The statements of reinforcement in 33:14–26, especially vs. 19–22, are similar.

Jeremiah 31:38–40

38a Introduction, "Behold, the days are coming . . . "
38b–40a Proclamation of the reconstruction of the city of Jerusalem, with precise statement of its boundaries.
40b It will never again be destroyed.

The motif of proclamation of the rebuilding of the city is provided with an introduction and precise data on its boundaries. It reads, "Behold, the days are coming, says the Lord, when the city shall be rebuilt for the Lord from the tower of Hananel to the Corner Gate. . . . It shall not be uprooted or overthrown any more for ever." The boundaries show that the city of Jerusalem is meant and that the text dates from the postexilic period when the rebuilding of the city and its walls was an issue. Thus the oracles that had their origin during the exile retained their significance after the return. According to B. Duhm, the reference is to the expansion of greater Jerusalem, as in Zechariah 14.

Additional texts outside chapters 30–33 could also be included under the same type found in 31:23–40 (that is, 16:14–15 = 23:7–8; 16:19–21; 23:5–6 [cf. 33:14–16]), but it is better not to include them. 23:5–6 is a variant of

33:14–16 and belongs as such to the supplement in 33:14–24 (Royal Oracle). 23:7–8 (= 16:14–15), which in the Masoretic text follows 23:5–6, is not a true proclamation of salvation, but is rather a reflective reinforcement of the historical significance of the liberation from exile in Babylon, cast in the form of a proclamation of salvation. This oracle might at one time have formed the conclusion of a collection of oracles.

In this case the form of the language enables us to recognize the later alteration. The introduction, "Behold, the days are coming . . . " refers to something that was happening in these days (that is, in the future). That this is what was meant here is indicated by the conclusion. The reflective thought, "Men shall no longer say . . . , but [they will say] . . . " speaks of Yahweh in the third person, but 8b has the first person, "out of all the countries where I (RSV, "he") had driven them." It is clear that the initial expression, "Behold, the days are coming . . . " originally continued "I had driven them." This would then be an oracle of the same type as 30:1–31:22.

Jeremiah 16:19–20

This is a distinctively constructed oracle that begins with a confession of trust, thus illustrating the influence of the language of worship on the oracles of salvation, just as in other oracles doxologies were added to the motif of the other nations coming to Yahweh. The oracle is expanded through the traditional polemic against idolatry, which is often found in supplementary material. The conclusion includes a confessional formula, which is also a supplementary addition.

The three royal oracles in 33:14–26 are an addition to 31:23–40. (They are missing in the LXX.)

Jeremiah 33:14–18

14 Proclamation that an earlier promise will be fulfilled.
15 "I will cause a righteous Branch to spring forth for David."
16a Then Judah will be saved and Jerusalem will dwell securely.

16b The name of the city will be "The Lord is our righteousness [i.e., "salvation"]."

17 David will never lack an heir to the throne.

18 And never will there be a lack of Levitical priests.

Jeremiah 33:19–22

If you can break my covenant with the day and my covenant with the night, . . . then also my covenant with David my servant may be broken . . . and my covenant with the Levitical priests my ministers.

Jeremiah 33:23–26

24 Against the people who say that Yahweh has rejected his people:

25–26 Just as truly as I have created day and night and established the laws of heaven and earth, so surely will the descendants of Jacob and David never be totally destroyed.

26c "I will restore their fortunes, and will have mercy upon them."

In these three royal promises (which could also be seen as three parts of one oracle, for the final statement, "I will restore their fortunes," applies to all three) a motif has been expanded to form a new unit. In other passages the restoration of the monarchy is one motif among others, e.g., 30:18–21. The distinctive feature here is the addition of Levi—the priesthood receives the same promise given to the monarchy. The strong emphasis on unending duration is also distinctive (v. 17b; 18; 18–22). The assurance of permanence in vs. 25–26 agrees with 31:35–37, but is applied here to God's abiding presence with his people. The language indicates that these three parts are quite late.

A distinctive feature of the collection of oracles in 31:23–40 is the importance of the various introductions.

31:23–26 In this land they will once again say . . .

31:27–28 "Behold, the days are coming, says the Lord, when I will . . ."

So also chapters 31–34:

31:29–30   "In those days they shall no longer say . . . "
31:38–40   "Behold, the days are coming, says the Lord,
           when . . . "

The vague references to a time in the future are reminders that these oracles are derived from others that spoke of
a specific event in the future—deliverance from present
danger. That such oracles recurred in a later period is illu-
minating, as is the fact that they are no longer intended to
be authoritative proclamations, but rather expressions of
hope and expectation.

Expansion of a Motif to an Oracle

In 31:31–34 the motif of inner transformation is expanded into an independent oracle, just as that of God's
becoming gracious again is expanded in chapters 35–37. To
these we should add the three royal promises in 33:14–26,
and also 23:5–6.

Oracles in Two Parts: God's Return to His People, Restoration and Blessing

In the collection in chapters 30–33, oracles of salvation
in two parts are found in 30:18–22 and 31:1–6 and also in
32:36–44 and 33:1–13 (all are deuteronomistic). There are
also such oracles outside those chapters. They constitute a
third, independent type of salvation oracle in Jeremiah, and
most of them are somewhat longer.

Jeremiah 30:18–22

18a   A change in the nation's fortunes; God is again favorable.
18b   Rebuilding of the city and the palace.
19a   Joy and gladness return.
19b   Increase in numbers, honor.
20a   Strength of the community, more dear to God than ever
      before.
20b   (An addition: destruction of the foes)
21   A ruler from their midst who can approach God
22   They are my people, I am their God.

There are two parts to the oracle. Verse 18a corresponds
to the announcement of liberation in the group of oracles in

30:1–31:22, but the announcement is only alluded to here in a formalized statement which forms an inclusio, v. 18a and v. 22. The main emphasis of the oracle lies on the announcement of restoration, 18b–21. A quick sequence of individual elements portrays the restoration of the state of well-being that formerly existed. Thus this is a different type of oracle, in that here God is not primarily the one who rescues, but the one who guarantees the well-being of the people.

Jeremiah 31:1–6

1   Prose introduction: Yahweh is Israel's God, and Israel is his people (as in 30:22).

2–3   God returns to his people
(2) Those who escaped found grace in the wilderness through their merciful God (text uncertain). (3) "I have loved you with an everlasting love."

4–6   God restores his people
(4a) Reconstruction; (4b) the festivals are again celebrated; (5) vineyards and fields are again planted on the mountains of Samaria; (6) watchmen summon the people as pilgrims to Jerusalem.

This oracle has the same two parts: return and restoration. Verse 2 probably alludes to the escape from exile. The last part of the verse is unclear. Verse 3 expresses clearly God's loving return to the people. Verses 4–6 depict the restoration (but it is not clear how they are related to vs. 2–3) and are clearly parts of an oracle of salvation pertaining to northern Israel.

Was there a short "Book of Comfort" that contained Jeremiah's messages to those exiled from the northern Kingdom? Such a hypothesis was first advanced by P. Volz and later taken up by a number of other scholars. A group of oracles of hope which Jeremiah addressed to the exiles from northern Israel approximately a century after the fall of the Northern Kingdom would of necessity be quite different from the oracles of the exilic and postexilic period that were collected in chapters 30–33. This is not the case, except for a few of these oracles which are clearly addressed to northern Israel. In 30:18–22 the expression "tents of Jacob" does not necessarily refer to northern Israel, but the mention of city and palace in v. 18b could refer to Samaria. On the other hand, the promise in v. 21 of a ruler "from their midst" elsewhere always means the king in Jerusalem. In 31:1–6 there is a clear reference to the mountains of Samaria. The prose addition in v. 1 expands the message to include "all the families of Israel," but v. 6 promises the return to Zion of those making the pilgrimage to Jerusalem. The oracle in 31:15–22 addresses Ephraim and begins with the lament of Rachel, the ancestral mother of the northern tribes. Oracles addressed to northern Israel form the basis of these texts (with the possible exception of 30:18–22), but they have been conformed to the other oracles of this collection. We cannot identify the circumstances of their origin more precisely. Like many other prophetic messages to northern Israel, they were preserved and handed on in Judah. There are many reasons why they could scarcely have been spoken by Jeremiah, above all because according to the criterion of 28:9 he would be one of the false prophets. See the commentary of W. Rudolph (p. 174): "Those exiled from the northern kingdom did not return, but disappeared without trace."

To these passages must be added 33:37–44 and 33:1–13, both of which are deuteronomistic additions to chs. 30–33. They each contain two parts and are quite detailed. (There are also the additions in 33:14–24.)

Jeremiah 32:37–44

37	The ingathering and the return after judgment
38	They are my people, I am their God. (44b: I will bring about a change in their fortunes)
39–44	Restoration
37b	They will live securely
39	An inner change so that they will fear me (40b)
40a	I will make an eternal covenant with them
40b–41a	I will always do good to them
41b	I will establish them in this land
42–44a	Paraphrase of 32:15
44b	For I will restore their fortunes, says the Lord.

This is clearly a deuteronomistic oracle that adopts traditional motifs of salvation and, in part, expands them. (The expansion in v. 41b does not quite fit.) Verses 42–44 are a paraphrase of the symbolic action in 32:1–36, with the verbatim addition of 32:15.

The oracle is in two parts. The first is vs. 37–38, the announcement of the gathering and return of the people, with their liberation alluded to in the stereotyped expressions in v. 44b. This part marks the transition from the oracles in 30:1–31:22. The second part, restoration, vs. 39–44, is a random collection of motifs. For example, v. 37b, "and I will make them dwell in safety," would fit better with 41b, "and I will plant them in this land." Verse 39 is reminiscent of 31:31–34.

By repeating 32:15 in 42–44a, the Deuteronomist shows that he understood the meaning of these words of Jeremiah. He felt it was necessary to preserve the oracle untouched in the collection he had made.

Jeremiah 33:1–13

1–5	Introduction: The situation
6–7a	Liberation: "I will bring to it health . . . security. . . . I will restore the fortunes of Judah and . . . Israel"
7b–13	Restoration
7b	Restore them as they were at first.
8	Cleanse them from all guilt
9	They will give me glory before all the nations
10–11	Reconstruction, the voice of mirth and gladness, bridegroom and bride; thanks to the Lord of hosts; I will restore the fortunes of the land.
12–13	Pasture for the flocks, shepherds for the sheep.

The oracle contains deuteronomistic language at several points. Verses 6–7a announce the coming liberation, but describe it in terms of healing, and the phrase "restore the fortunes of" occurs in 7a and again in 11b. The description of restoration in 7b–13 adds one element to another—security, peace, reconstruction (vs. 10, 12f.), cleansing from guilt, praising God in the presence of all the nations—without indicating their interconnections. In vs. 10–13 the proclamation becomes a beautifully poetic description.

Oracles that portray God's return to his people and his restoration of their fortunes are also found outside the collection in Jeremiah 30–33.

Jeremiah 3:11–18

This passage is deuteronomistic, or else revised in the deuteronomistic style. Verses 11–13 contain a proclamation of salvation. They are connected with vs. 14–18 by the call to return (repent), but in this second passage God's return is not conditional, though the passage has been revised in deuteronomistic style, as for example in v. 17b. The oracle in vs. 14–18 is in two parts: 14a, b, liberation; and 15–18, restoration.

The proclamation of liberation and restoration in v. 14 is repeated in v. 18, together with the motif of reunification, and provides the framework for the oracle. Restoration includes the promise of "a shepherd (thus author; Heb. and RSV, shepherds) after my own heart" (v. 15); increase of population (implied; 16a); God's presence in Jerusalem, and no longer only in the ark (16b, 17a); pilgrimage of the nations to Jerusalem (17b); inner renewal (17b); reunification, with allusion to the promise of the land (18).

Jeremiah 23:(1–2) 3–4

1–2   "Woe to the shepherds"
3a   "I will gather the remnant of my flock . . . and I will bring them back"
3b   "And they shall be fruitful and multiply"
4a   "I will set shepherds over them who will care for them"
4b   "They shall fear no more . . . neither shall any be missing"

This brief oracle of salvation also has the two elements of liberation (only gathering and leading home are mentioned) and restoration. It is preceded by a judgment on the evil shepherds. Restoration contains the motifs of the promise of good shepherds; increase in numbers; security; assurance that they will never again be dispersed. The whole is a variant of Ezekiel 34. In 23:5–6 there is the promise of a king without a comparison of the king with the shepherds.

Jeremiah 50:4–8, 17–20

4–5a   Announcement of the return, sorrow, question of the way to Zion.

5b	Return to an everlasting covenant
6-7	Remembrance of their suffering, apostasy, and God's judgment
8	Exhortation to flee from Babylon
17-19	God's punishment of Babylon, Israel's return
20	Israel's guilt is forgiven

This passage is a late addition to a message of judgment against Babylon. It is not a true oracle of salvation, but a reflection of history, which uses the motifs of the salvation oracle. Its significance is that it shows how firmly fixed this form of salvation oracle was. Additional brief allusions to such oracles are found in chapter 51. Also to be included among the two-part oracles of salvation are the following: the part of the deuteronomistic reworking in 23:5-8 of the oracle of the two baskets of figs (24:1-10) and 29:12-14.

Summary: Oracles in Two Parts

God Is Again Gracious

In the majority of texts, the first part contains the proclamation of the turning point in Israel's destiny: Jeremiah 30:18-22; 31:1-6; and also 30:22; 32:38; 3:14-18. The difference between these oracles and those dominated by the proclamation of liberation is that in the latter the experience of liberation is remembered more vividly, while here the time elapsed is greater. The expression "restore the fortunes of my people" implies a greater time span. From this we may conclude that these oracles in two parts are later than those dominated by the proclamation of liberation.

Even here the proclamation of liberation, of gathering the people and leading them home, finds an echo: 32:27; 3:14; 23:3a; 50:4-8, 17-20. This however, is to be seen as the result of the deuteronomistic revision, which was very extensive and which expanded the previous oracles of salvation.

Restoration

The basic emphasis in the proclamation of restoration is that all will be again as it once used to be (33:7b). A frequent metaphor is that the wounds will be healed (33:6; 30:17a). That is to say, the proclamation does not refer to some bygone time of prosperity, nor some ideal period, nor some perfect age, but simply to the restoration of well-being after devastation, loss, suffering, captivity. This is the reason that no complete description of a restored state is intended. The proclamation lists only those things the lack of which was especially felt in the time of suffering. This does not require a systematic order. Sometimes one thing will be named, sometimes another, in a fully open and free sequence.

Restoration begins with the rebuilding of the cities and houses (30:18b; 31:4a; 33:7b, 10; 24:6b) and the cultivation of fields and vineyards (31:5). God's blessing and an increase in population are also a necessary part of the picture (30:19b; 32:42–44; 33:12–13, 3:16; 23:2b; 50:19b). Of especial importance is a life in safety and security (32:41b; 33:6b; 23:4b). Only in safety can people lead a joyful life (30:19a) and celebrate the feast days (31:4b; 33:10–11). Above all, the mutual relationship between God and his people must be whole again (30:20a): "You are my people, I am your God" (30:22; 32:38; 24:7a) in an eternal covenant (32:40a). God has forgiven his people (33:8; 50:20); he will not cease to do good for them (32:40b). He will hear them when they call to him (24:7a). Because of them, all the people of the earth will praise God (33:9).

On the other hand the Israelites will undergo an inward transformation: "I will give them a heart to know that I am the Lord" (24:7a); they will return to God with their whole heart (24:7b); they will once again fear him (32:39, 40). Their worship will be restored: the watchmen will call out to those who come in procession to Zion, that they should praise the Lord (31:6). There will no longer be any need for the ark of the covenant, because they will call Jerusalem the throne of Yahweh and all people will go there on pilgrimage (3:16–17). Then a ruler will arise from among them who will stand before the Lord (30:21). The Lord will give his people shepherds who will truly care for them (23:4). All the nations will go on pilgrimage to Jerusalem (3:17).

Supplements to the Oracles to the Nations
in Chapters 46–51

"Yet I will restore the fortunes of Moab in the latter days" (48:47). Amon (49:6) and Elam (49:39) are addressed in almost the same words, and Egypt (48:26) slightly differently.

This group of similar supplements belongs to the context of a later universalistic tendency, which can be seen also in Isaiah 19:19–25. Judgment on the peoples is not the last word that Yahweh will speak to them as the Lord of history. For them too there will come a turning point.

Oracles of Salvation in Narratives

This section is based on what was said about oracles of salvation in the book of Isaiah (see above, pp. 67–72).

Jeremiah 32:15

The collection of materials in 31:23–40 concludes with the oracle about the rebuilding of the city in vs. 38–40, but the redactor inserted at this point the account of the purchase of land (and some expansions) in the correct view that the oracle in the midst of the chapter (32:15) belongs to this group of oracles, or at least is closely related to them. The redactor regarded this statement from the mouth of Jeremiah as so important that he literally placed it at the end of this collection. But he also knew that the narrative was essential to its understanding.

> For thus says the Lord of hosts, the God of Israel: Houses and fields and vineyards shall again be bought in this land.

On the significance of this oracle in the mouth of Jeremiah, W. Thiel (p. 31) wrote, "In 32:6b–15 we have the oldest component of the chapter, an authentic autobiographical account. The prophet reports . . . . It is a very concise and calm oracle which explains what Jeremiah had done. He merely said that life in the land would continue, but under the perspective of imminent destruction it is an authentic promise." I agree with Thiel, but something essential must be added to our understanding of the oracle. It is an oracle of salvation, but it is not an annunciation of deliverance as are all the oracles in 30:1–31:22. The term "announcement of salvation" includes both deliverance and blessing. Often the announcement of deliverance is expanded by a promise of blessing. Here, however, we have only a promise of blessing. At this moment it was not the prophet's task, nor did he have the authority, to announce deliverance to those in the besieged city, as Isaiah did in chapter 7. Normal life will continue in the land, but in a land and in a city that have been conquered by the enemy.

Jeremiah 29: The Letter

In the same way Jeremiah wrote chapter 29 to the exiles in Babylon denouncing the false prophets there who were proclaiming that the enemy would soon be destroyed. Here as in chapter 31 the prophet does not announce in the name of Yahweh that deliverance will come soon as a result of the destruction of the enemy, as the false prophets promise in vs. 8–9.

15   "You have said, 'The Lord has raised up prophets for us in Babylon,'—

8   Thus says the Lord of hosts . . . : Do not let your prophets and your diviners who are among you deceive you, and do not listen to the dreams which they dream,

9   for it is a lie which they are prophesying to you in my name; I did not send them, says the Lord."

In this letter as in 32:15 the prophet promises only that God's work of blessing will continue among and on behalf of the exiles. It is enough for them that God remembers them for their welfare (*shalom*) and not to their hurt.

In v. 10 the redactor inserted a bit of data which at that point Jeremiah had no authority to announce, and which the Deuteronomist spoke after the fact (v. 12f. follows on v. 10): "When seventy years are completed for Babylon, I will visit you," and you will be freed and can return home. It is actually—contrary to our too narrow understanding of "historical" and "unhistorical"—completely understandable that the Deuteronomist here inserts an oracle of salvation which Jeremiah could then not have spoken, but which corresponds to the oracles of the exilic and postexilic times.

12f.   "Then you will call upon me . . . hear . . . seek . . . find
         . . . .

14   I will restore your fortunes and gather you from all the nations and all the places . . . and I will bring you back to the place from which I sent you into exile."

Jeremiah did not say this in the letter which he wrote to the exiles. At that time the proclamation of speedy deliverance through the destruction of Babylon was false prophecy (vs. 8, 9). What he could announce to the exiles then is said in vs. 5–7, 11. Verses 5–6 say, "Build houses . . . plant gardens . . . take wives . . . multiply." And verse 7 continues: "Seek the welfare of the city where I have sent you into exile." And verse 11: "For I know the plans I have for you, says the Lord, plans for welfare." Seldom is it as clear as in this deuteronomistic form of Jeremiah's letter to the exiles that a promise or a message of salvation can never be understood simply in terms of its content, but that only together with the situation out of which and into which it is spoken does it take its meaning. The deuteronomistic form of the promise in vs. 12–14 shows, however, that the collection of oracles, as they are cited here, could have taken shape only after the collapse in exilic and postexilic times.

Jeremiah 24:1–10: The Two Baskets of Figs

1–2   Yahweh shows Jeremiah a vision of baskets of figs

3–4   He asks Jeremiah what he sees. Introduction to God's answer

5–7   Yahweh's answer:

(5–6a)   The good figs: Yahweh will restore the people and lead them home.

(6b)   Restoration and planting; (7a) inner transformation, so that they will know that they are my people and that I am their God; (7b) they shall return to me with their whole heart.

8–10   The bad figs: Judgment on Zedekiah and the others.

The passage 24:1–10 is an account of a vision, similar to that in chapter 1. The question in v. 3 should have been followed by Jeremiah's answer and then Yahweh's brief interpretation of the vision. Instead we have the deuteronomistic reworking of the passage. Originally God's answer was a word of judgment on Zedekiah and the others. In spite of the reworking, the judgment is preserved in vs. 8–10. The explanation of the basket with the good figs was not really necessary; it was perhaps a quite short allusion to the exiles and their fate. In place of that the Deuteronomist inserted in vs. 5–7 a complete oracle which corresponds sentence for sentence with the exilic and postexilic announcement of deliverance. It is in the form of an oracle in two parts: God returns to his people (5–6a) and God restores them (6b–7), with the motifs of rebuilding and replanting (6b), inner transformation (7a), and the formula "my people—their God" (7a). The text shows that the form of this oracle was so firmly fixed that the Deuteronomist could simply incorporate it as it stood. Compare also 27:11.

Oracles to Individuals in Narratives

Jeremiah 39:15–18, to Ebed-melech; 45:1–5, to Baruch

Jeremiah announced both to this companion Baruch and to Ebed-melech, who had rescued him from the cistern, that they would escape with their lives. In both cases we have an announcement of deliverance that is formulated in terms of the situation in which the announcement is delivered, as is also the case in Isaiah 38:5.

Jeremiah 35:19, to Jonadab ben Rechab

After the comparison of the disloyal people with the faithful Rechabites, Jeremiah announces to the latter, "Jonadab son of Rechab shall never lack a man to stand before me."

Jeremiah 28:1–4, the Oracle Spoken by Hananiah

This is included here because it too is an oracle of salvation in the context of a narrative.

1 Introduction with date.
2 "Thus says the Lord of hosts, the God of Israel: I have broken the yoke of the king of Babylon.
3 Within two years I will bring back to this place all the vessels of the Lord's house. . . .
4 I will also bring back to this place Jeconiah . . . and all the exiles . . . for I will break the yoke of the king of Babylon."

Hananiah proclaimed to those who were left behind in

Jerusalem after 597 B.C., as if it were a word from Yahweh, that before two years would pass Nebuchadnezzar would be slain and the temple furnishings, the king, and the prisoners of war would return to Jerusalem. Jeremiah confronts him and denies that this message came from Yahweh. After two years it was seen that Hananiah was a false prophet. It should be noted that the structure of Hananiah's message is that of the later announcements in two contrasting parts: destruction of the enemies, deliverance for Israel. Note also that among the captives in Babylon there were prophets with the same message, chapter 29. These were also proven to be false prophets.

Summary of the Motifs

Motifs of God's Return to the People and Their Liberation

These motifs are chiefly found in 30:1–31:22.

Prehistory: God's earlier saving deeds; Israel's apostasy; judgment on Israel; lament.

Proclamation of deliverance: God is again favorable to the people; deliverance, gathering together, leading home. In addition we find in several passages a statement about restoration, but this is not a necessary part of this series of events.

God's Earlier Saving Deeds
(only in deuteronomistic passages)

3:19: "I thought how I would set you among my sons and give you a pleasant land." References to the promise of the land are found in 3:19; 7:7; 30:3.

Israel's Apostasy

(Deuteronomistic): "Because your guilt is great" (30:15). " . . . like an untrained calf" (31:18b).

God's Judgment on Israel

"For I have dealt you the blow of an enemy" (30:14b). "Thou hast chastened me" (31:18b; see also 30:5–7a; 30:11; 31:10).

Lament

"Why do you cry out over your hurt?" (30:12–15; implied in 39:5–7). "With weeping they shall come" (31:9). "I will turn their mourning into joy" (31:13b). "A voice is heard in Ramah, lamentation and bitter weeping" (31:15–16). "Keep your voice from weeping, and your eyes from tears" (16a).

Returning of God (forgiveness)

"I will . . . have compassion on his dwellings" (30:18). "The people who survived the sword found grace in the wilderness" (31:2). "Therefore my heart yearns for him; I will surely have mercy on him" (31:20; see also 31:16a, 17a).

Liberation, Ingathering, Leading Home

"The Lord has saved his people, the remnant of Israel. Behold I will bring them from the north country, and gather them from the farthest parts of the earth. . . . With weeping they shall come (author, "went out"), and with consolations I will lead them back" (31:7–9). "He who scattered Israel will gather him, and will keep him as a shepherd keeps his flock. For the Lord has ransomed Jacob" (10b–11; see also 30:3; 30:7–8; 30:17, 30:18; 31:2; 31:10–12; 31:16b, 17b, 21; 32:37; 33:6).

Assurance of Salvation and Song of Praise

"Then fear not, O Jacob my servant. . . . For I am with you to save you" (30:10–11; see also 31:7–9). Similarities to Second Isaiah are found in many places.

Restoration of Their Fortunes

See 30:1–3, 9–10, 18–21 (22); 31:12–14; 32:44; 33:7.

Motifs of God's Return to His People and Restoration

This second group of oracles is characterized by the proclamation or description of restoration—God's deeds on behalf of his people after the return. The sequence of liberation–ingathering–return is not found except in a few exceptional situations. In place of this unique intervention to save the people we find the motif that God is again favorable to his people. The depiction of restoration brings together individual motifs of salvation.

Reconstruction, Cultivation of the Land, Settling In

These are the first steps after the return that make normal life possible. The counterpart of the collapse is the reconstruction; of the destruction, cultivation of the land. Building houses, reconstructing the city and the temple, cultivating the fields and vineyards are all necessary for a normal life. This reflects the activity of God, who tears down and builds.

The city will be rebuilt on its mound (30:18). "Again I will build you, and you shall be built, O virgin Israel!" (31:4). "Again you shall plant vineyards upon the mountains of Samaria; the planters shall plant, and shall enjoy the fruit" (31:5). The city shall be rebuilt as it was before (33:7, 10–11, 12–13). The people will possess again what they had before (30:3).

Restoration of Honor

"I shall raise them to honour, no longer to be despised"(30:19b, REB; cf. NRSV).

Blessing and Increase

A normal life includes the growth of the community and of the means of life, food, clothing. Thus the proclamation of well-being includes the promise of blessing, as is seen also in the prophecies of Second Isaiah. And the realm of nature, growth, maturity, the bearing of fruit also belongs to a full and normal life.

31:23   "Once more they shall use these words . . .
       'The Lord bless you, O habitation of righteousness,
       O holy hill!' "

31:27   "I will sow the house of Israel and the house of Judah
        with the seed of man and the seed of beast."
31:12a "They shall come and sing aloud on the height of
              Zion,
          and they shall be radiant over the goodness of the
              Lord,
        over the grain, the wine, and the oil,
          and over the young of the flock and the herd."
          (See also 3:16; 23:3; 29:4–7; 30:19; 32:15; 32:42;
          33:12–13)

Feasting, Rejoicing, Singing

Joy, the joy in life itself, is also a part of well-being—
singing, dancing, festivals, and processions. Offerings of
thanks (30:19) and songs of praise shall be heard, and the
people will rejoice.

31:4–5   "Again you shall adorn yourself with timbrels,
              and shall go forth in the dance of the merrymak-
              ers. . . .
            The planters shall plant,
              and shall enjoy the fruit."
33:10b–11 "There shall be heard again the voice of mirth and
            the voice of gladness, the voice of the bridegroom
            and the voice of the bride, the voices of those who
            sing, as they bring thank offerings to the house of
            the Lord: "Give thanks to the Lord of hosts, for
            the Lord is good, for his steadfast love endures for
            ever!" (See also 31:12)

Restoration of a Saving Relationship with God

It goes without saying that such a relationship is essential
to salvation, and that it includes forgiveness. In this group
of motifs the emphasis is not on God's acts of deliverance or
on the rejoicing of those liberated. Instead the "covenant
formula" is often cited: "I will be their God and they will be
my people" (31:1 and elsewhere). Salvation cannot be described in static terms, because it is a reciprocal relationship. In it there is movement from God to this people and
from them to God, 24:7; 31:31–34.

32:40a	"I will make with them an everlasting covenant, that I will not turn away from doing good to them.
50:5; 7:23	"Come, let us join ourselves to the Lord in an everlasting covenant which will never be forgotten."
30:20	"Their children shall be as they were of old."
	(Also 32:38, 41; 33:8f.; 31:34; 30:9; 31:29f.)

God's Presence in Jerusalem

3:16–17	"They shall no more say, 'The ark of the covenant of the Lord.' . . . At that time Jerusalem shall be called the throne of the Lord.
7:3, 7	"I will dwell with you [RSV, let you dwell] in this place." (Deuteronomistic)

Inner Transformation

A part of the new relationship with God is the proclamation of an inner transformation that makes a steadfast relationship with God possible.

32:39	"I will give them one heart and one way, that they may fear me for ever, for their own good and the good of their children after them."
24:7a	"I will give them a heart to know that I am the Lord; and they shall be my people."
	(See also 32:40; 31:31–34)

Well-founded Security

It is significant how often and in what strong language the assurance or the expectation of a bright future, of security, of enduring prosperity is stated. In this we can hear the experience of centuries and a clearly expressed anxiety about the future.

30:20b	"Their congregation shall be established before me."
32:37	"I will make them dwell in safety."
33:6; 31:2	They will enjoy security and peace in all fullness.
23:4; 31:35–37	"And they shall fear no more, nor be dismayed."

Similar strong expressions are found in 32:40f.; 17:24f.; 31:38–40; 33:14–26.

The King of the Time of Well-Being

It is significant for our understanding of what is meant by "well-being" that no political announcements or expectations are mentioned. We would expect to hear an announcement of a king as an expression of political expectations. But that is not the case. The king that is meant is not one who will rule over a great and powerful nation, who will be "mighty in battle," who will defeat his enemies and conquer their peoples, nor is it yet a king ruling in majesty and splendor. There is nothing of all that in these passages. It is instead a king who rules "in right and justice," and, because he is a king, he is steadfast, guarantees safety and prosperity in the land, and brings blessing to his people. "And I will give you shepherds after my own heart, who will feed you with knowledge and understanding" (3:15; 23:4 is similar).

> Behold, the days are coming, says the Lord, when I will raise up for David a righteous Branch, and he shall reign as king and deal wisely, and shall execute justice and righteousness in the land. In his days Judah will be saved, and Israel will dwell securely. And this is the name by which he will be called: "The Lord is our righteousness." (23:5–6; see also 30:9, 21; 17:25; 33:14–26)

People of Other Nations Come to Israel

This striking transformation of the concept of kingship as it was in earlier times is also seen in that other peoples are no longer to be conquered and oppressed, but will come of their own free will to join with Israel.

> 3:17b "And all nations shall gather to it, to the presence of the Lord in Jerusalem."
>
> 16:19b "To thee shall the nations come
> from the ends of the earth.
>
> 4:2b "Then nations shall bless themselves in him,
> and in him shall they glory." (Deuteronomistic)

Reunification

"In those days the house of Judah shall join the house of Israel, and together they shall come from the land of the north to the land that I gave your fathers for a heritage" (3:18). The announcement of the reunification of Judah and northern Israel does not involve a political aspect but a religious expectation. As it was in the past, so now again the history of God's activity involves *one* united people.

6

Ezekiel

In keeping with the redaction procedures in prophetic books, in the book of Ezekiel the oracles of judgment against Israel, chapters 1–24, are followed by judgments on the nations, chs. 25–32, and oracles of salvation, chs. 33–37 (39), to which, with some reservations, chs. 40–48 may be assigned. In chapters 33–37 we are concerned with the following passages: The shepherd and the sheep (34:1–31); the mountains of Israel (36:1–15); purification (36:17–37); the vision of dry bones (37:1–14); reunification (37:15–28). Chapter 33, concerning the watchman, belongs to this group only in so far as it forms the basis for a conditional proclamation of deliverance. Chapters 38–39 contain oracles of deliverance only in the final section, 39:21–29. And chapters 40–48 belong here only in that the motif of the rebuilding of the city and the temple is basic to this whole section as one of the motifs in the proclamation of deliverance.

In chapters 1–24 we encounter several scattered oracles of salvation: 11:14–21; 14:21–23; 16:52–63; 17:22–24; 18:1–32, a conditional promise; and 20:34–44. In the oracles to the nations in chapters 25–32, there are the supplements in 28:24–26; 29:21.

Even at first glance the oracles of Ezekiel in the collection in chapters 33–37 (39) differ from those in the other prophetic books by being longer. This is in keeping with the diffuse style that is typical of Ezekiel.

The Collection in Chapters 34–37

In chapter 34 a proclamation of judgment (1–10) is combined with one of deliverance (11–31). The connection is established by the metaphor of sheep and shepherd (see my book *The Parables of Jesus in the Light of the Old Testament,* 1990). An accusation, vs. 1–6, and a pronouncement of judgment against the evil shepherds, vs. 7–10, is followed by a message of salvation to the good shepherds, vs. 11–31. It has been expanded into a lengthy message with many repetitions. One part follows another without any clear connection between them. Chapter 34:1–10 belongs to the fixed motif of accusation against the leaders which we find in the prophecies of judgment, frequently together with the metaphor of shepherd and flock, the message of salvation. But 34:11–31 departs from the traditional metaphor in that deliverance is promised, not to those on whom judgment was threatened, but to Israel itself; and, for the future, Yahweh himself as the good shepherd is contrasted to the evil shepherds. It is only in vs. 23–24 that a savior king is announced as the shepherd; thus sometimes the good shepherd is Yahweh, and sometimes the savior king.

Only vs. 11b–16 are closely connected with vs. 1–10. They form a self-contained announcement of deliverance, with the sequence of liberation–ingathering–return home, and with a look back to God's judgment on the nation. Verses 17–22 constitute a digression from v. 16. Verses 23–30 are part of the section on restoration, in which the motifs of covenant, security, and blessing are held together only loosely, and with much repetition. The announcement of liberation is repeated in v. 22, but motivation for it is lacking in 21b. Because the metaphor of shepherd and sheep is not maintained in vs. 23–30, those verses are artificially connected to this passage by v. 31.

Verses 11b–16 are clearly based almost sentence by sentence on a tradition that antedated Ezekiel, that of the oracles of salvation in the sequence of liberation–ingathering–return home. Verse 11b is the transition from part one, vs. 1–10, and maintains the metaphor. The motif of God's return to his people cancels the judgment against them: " . . . where they have been scattered on a day of clouds and thick darkness" (12b). This is followed by the series of verbs which we have so often encountered: I will liberate them—gather them together—take them home (12–13). In keeping with the metaphor, the stated goal is that the good shepherd will lead his sheep to good pasture (13–15). It is also a part of the tradition that the weak and sick will also be brought back home (16). It is typical of the style of Ezekiel to add that the strong must be treated in a different manner from the weak (16b). An addition in 17–22 makes this explicit: "I myself will judge between the fat sheep and the lean sheep" (20b). The following verses, 23–30, are not part of the liberation but of the restoration. In vs. 23–24 we have the sudden announcement of a savior king. God, who thus far was the shepherd, will place over the people a single shepherd who shall tend them. In v. 23 he is called "my servant David," and in 24, "prince."

In vs. 25–30 it is announced that God will make a covenant of peace with his people. The metaphor of shepherd and sheep is completely dropped here. Motifs independent of the metaphor are added to each other without any unifying context. God will establish a covenant of peace (v. 25) with his people, that is, he will assume the duty of establishing peace and well-being for them. This will be done through his blessing, which brings rain and fertility (26–27a), "prosperous plantations" (29a), so that they will no longer suffer from hunger. In addition, he will protect them from wild animals (25b, 28a), and from their enemies (27b, 28a), so that they may enjoy security and no one will terrify them (25b, 28b). These motifs are given in no particular order and with numerous repetitions, and in the midst of them there is a straightforward reminder of the coming liberation (end of v. 27). Three times in 25–30 they are reminded that God is their Lord. The conclusion is v. 31 serves to tie vs. 25–30 to the shepherd metaphor, as does the formula "you are my sheep, I am your God."

Ezekiel 36:1–15: Oracle About the Mountains of Israel

This oracle is the counterpart to the condemnation of those mountains in chapter 6. The oracle proper begins in v. 8. It is preceded by a complicated message of judgment on the surrounding nations (1–7), an expansion of the introduction to the oracle. The oracle itself consists of well-known motifs, assembled here in no particular order. The message is that God will return again to his people (v. 9) and bring them home again (8b). God will bless the land with fertility (v. 8): "But you, O mountains of Israel, shall shoot forth your branches, and yield your fruit to my people Israel." Both people and livestock will increase in numbers (10a, 11a), and God will do good to his people (11b). The land will be tilled and sown, the cities inhabited, the ruins rebuilt (9–11). And people will again live in the land and take possession of it (12–13). Their shame in the eyes of the nations will be taken away. These motifs have been brought together mechanically, with repetitions, and with no logical connection. Typical of this situation is that the return of the people in v. 8 precedes God's turning to them in v. 9. This is another indication that we have here a late composition which presupposes all the individual motifs without exception. The great contrast to Second Isaiah is unmistakable.

This passage, 36:1–15, is an oracle of salvation in two parts. The first part is comprised of God's return to his people (9a) and the announcement of their return home (8b), and the second part consists of the restoration and the accompanying motifs: Rebuilding of the cities and ruins (10b), which are inhabited as of old (11b); tilling and sowing the land again (9b); the land is again inhabited and taken into possession (11b, 12a); blessing and increase for the people and livestock (8a, 10a, 11a); no one is any longer childless (12b, 13, 14); restoration of honor (15).

Ezekiel 36:17–37: Cleansing

17–20	The profaning of Israel and God's judgment
21–23	God returns to his people
24	Liberation, ingathering, return home
25–27, 29, 33	Cleansing, and a new heart, restoration
28	The land God gave is inhabited again
33b–35	Rebuilding the cities and houses
37, 29f., 30	Blessing and increase in numbers
37f.	Increase of the population
29f.	Increase of grain and fruit
36 (23)	The nations are to acknowledge God's deeds for his people

This oracle is shaped by the thought of a priestly and cultic tradition. Thus it is set apart from the traditional oracles of salvation. Its features include the following: God returns to his people (21–23); liberation, ingathering, return home (24), and restoration (28, 33–35, 37, 29f., 36, 23). The priestly and cultic influence is dominated by the motif of cleansing. Even vs. 21–23 have been modified by the priestly theology. In the earlier oracles the motive for God's return to his people is simply his compassion for their suffering. Here that has been consciously altered. God is concerned, not for the sorrow of his people, but for the honor of his name, which the Israelites had profaned among the nations. "It is not for your sake, O house of Israel, that I am about to act, but for the sake of my holy name" (v. 22). Here a later theology has modified the simple proclamation of salvation. The author did not feel that he had weakened the understanding of compassion as the motif for God's return to his people by making the statement "not for your sake . . . but . . . " Moreover the emphasis is no longer on liberation and the return home as such, but solely on the cleansing. In vs. 25–27 the cleansing and inner transformation occupy the central place; they serve to assure that the people follow the law of God. In vs. 28, 33, we find once more the theme of cleansing, and in vs. 31–32 the necessity for the people to repent is strongly emphasized: "You will loathe yourselves for your iniquities and your abominable deeds. . . . Be ashamed and confounded for your ways, O house of Israel." This strong emphasis on cleansing is found also in the Priestly Code, e.g., Leviticus 18:24–30, and the sharp command to repent points up the transformation of the time of lamentation into the worship service of repentance in the time of Ezra and Nehemiah. This section, 36:16–37, belongs in any case to a later stratum of the books of Ezekiel (so also W. Zimmerli, BKAT, vol. XIII/2).

This passage, 36:16–37, belongs to the oracles of salvation in two parts. The first part presents God's return to the people (vs. 21–23), liberation, ingathering, and leading home (v. 24), plus the corruption of Israel in their preceding history and God's judgment, with expansions. The second part consists of the restoration, in which the whole emphasis is placed on cleansing. Then follow the traditional motifs of reconstruction, renewed cultivation of the land, blessing, and increase in numbers.

Ezekiel 37:1–15: The Valley of Dry Bones

This oracle, distinctive of the prophet Ezekiel, has an extraordinary well-thought-out structure, and can be understood only in the total context of the prophetic oracles of salvation. The beauty of its structure is due to the way in which several quite different structures are combined in a single text.

The basis of this oracle is the structure known to us from many other oracles of salvation: lament of the people— God's answer to the lament. The lament, fragmentary in form, is quoted in v. 11:

> Behold, they say, "Our bones are dried up,
> And our hope is lost; we are clean cut off."

This is a quotation of a lament that was really spoken and which the prophet can assume his hearers were familiar with. It is the part designated as the "we-lament." It is followed by God's response in v. 12:

> Thus says the Lord God: "Behold, I will open your graves,
> And raise you from your graves, O my people."

This answer, which could fit many situations, is applied to a specific situation in the following sentences—liberation from exile:

12 "I will bring you home into the land of Israel."
14 "I will place you in your own land."

The metaphor in the lament of the people, that the people in exile are like dry bones, is expanded into a vision, which God grants to the prophet. The vision has the following structure:

1–2 The vision (the prophet is carried off)
3 God's question, "What do you see?" [modified here]
11–14 Explanation of the vision

In a very complicated way the structure of the call of a prophet is followed here: (4) "Again he said to me, 'Prophesy to these bones.'" (5) "Thus says the Lord," followed by the announcement of salvation. (7) "So I prophesied." This account of the prophet's response is combined with the fulfillment of the announcement. (9) An assignment, "Prophesy to the breath." (10) "So I prophesied." An account of the prophet's response, combined with the fulfillment of the prophesy.

Thus three different events are intertwined. The prophet is shown a vision, which is interpreted to him (vs. 1–3 and 11–14). As the vision unfolds, that which was foretold takes place—the people receive new life. This is similar to a symbolic action. Finally the prophet receives the commission to announce to the people the coming liberation from exile, in such a way that he himself will have part in the fulfillment (vs. 9–10; this also resembles a symbolic action).

If the focus of this complicated literary structure is the lament of the people and God's answer to it, then the whole is an artistic exposition of a simple oracle of salvation, such as is found in many other passages: A lament of the people in their exile, and an oracle that announces their liberation from exile. It should be noted that here Ezekiel used only the liberation part of the oracle, not that of restoration, which here is only implicit (cf. 34:11–16).

Ezekiel 37:15–28: The Two Sticks

This oracle resembles chapter 34 in that it begins with a symbolic action (in contrast to the metaphor in ch. 34), and then proceeds independently of it in the following verses. The symbolic action (vs. 15–22) is based on a motif from an oracle of salvation, that of the proclamation of the reunification of North and South, as, for example, in Jeremiah 3:18. It is not really an action, but is rather an illustration of this proclamation. It actually concludes with the first answer to the question of the significance of the action, that is, vs. 19–20. There then follows a second answer which brings the symbolic action and the traditional oracle (vs. 21, 23–28) together in v. 22: God will make them into one nation with one king. The promise of the king is repeated in 24a and 25b. This repetition is awkward and serves no real purpose. Here the promise is of a "king," and not as elsewhere in Ezekiel, of a "prince" (Heb. *nasi*). The LXX has *archōn*, "prince," indicating that the promise was taken literally.

This is also shown by the structure: announcement of liberation (21), and restoration (22–28). So too in the individual motifs, all of which are found elsewhere. A striking feature is the strong emphasis or intensification of the announcement through the recurring "for ever," "everlasting covenant," etc. This indicates a late date.

This passage is a proclamation of salvation in two parts: first, the announcement of liberation and return (21) and second, restoration (22), 23–28. This structure is, however, modified, in that a motif of restoration, that of reunification, is expanded to an artificial symbolic action and placed at the very first, vs. 15–20 (22). This motif, which occurs once more in v. 22, thus takes on special importance.

The other motifs of restoration can be summarized as follows: (1) Restoration of a wholesome relationship with God (23), through the removal of idolatry. (2) The covenant formula, "You are my people, I am your God" (27b); "They shall follow my ordinances" (24b); an eternal covenant with the people (26a); God's sanctuary will be forever in their midst (26b, 27a, 27b). (3) The promise of a king: God will make them one people with one king (22); "My servant David shall be king over them" (24); "David my servant shall be their prince for ever" (25b). (4) Permanent residence in the land: "They shall dwell in the land where your fathers dwelt that I gave to my servant Jacob . . . for ever" (25). (5) Conclusion: "Then the nations will know . . . " (28).

Chapters 38–39: Gog and Magog, Fury Against Yahweh's People

This apocalyptic text is discussed here because the conclusion, 39:21–29, is an oracle of salvation for Israel. There is already an allusion to such an oracle in 38:6–9, the attack of the world power against Israel, who is "gathered from many nations," "brought out from the nations," "restored from war," and whose people "dwell securely."

Judgment on the world power on the mountains of Israel, 38:17–23 and 39:1–8, is followed by the oracle of salvation for Israel, 39:21–29.

21 "And I will set my glory among the nations; and all the nations shall see my judgment which I have executed . . .

23   And the nations shall know that the house of Israel went
     into captivity for their iniquity. . . . I hid my face from
     them. . . .
24   I dealt with them according to their uncleanness . . . and
     hid my face from them."

These three verses (22 is a later addition) explain that the
fall of Israel was not due to the impotence of their God, but
to Israel's guilt, for which God punished them. By his judgment over the nations Yahweh showed that he is the Lord of
history. Thus 39:25–29 is an oracle of salvation that concludes chapters 38–39 for Israel.

25   "Now I will restore the fortunes of Jacob, and have mercy
     upon the whole house of Israel; and I will be jealous for
     my holy name.
26   They shall forget their shame, and all the treachery they
     have practiced against me, when they dwell securely in
     their land . . . ,
27   when I have brought them back from the peoples and . . .
     through them have vindicated my holiness in the sight of
     many nations.
28   Then they shall know that I am the Lord their God because
     I sent them into exile among the nations. . . .
29   And I will not hide my face any more from them, when I
     pour out my Spirit upon the house of Israel."

This oracle, 39:(21) 25–26, differs from the previous
ones in that it especially develops the first part of the traditional oracle, liberation; restoration is only alluded to. An
overview shows that the text announces that God will return to his people and give them freedom, and it says what
this means for Israel and the nations: (1) Looking back to
the time of judgment (21, 23–24). (2) God returns to his
people, restores their fortunes, and shows them mercy. (3)
God liberates them ("vindicate my holiness"), gathers them
together, and leads them home (27), and they "shall know
that I am the Lord their God" (28). (4) This happens "in the
sight of many nations" (v. 27; this is developed in vs. 21–
24). (5) They shall forget their shame (26a), and dwell securely in their land with none to make them afraid (16b).
(6) "I will not hide my face any more from them" (29).
Typical of Ezekiel is the formula of recognition: The ex-

perience of liberation will make Israel know, and the sharing of this experience will make the nations know. What they will know is, for both Israel and the nations, that God is working for his people.

Chapters 40–48: The Vision of the New Temple

Only by virtue of its basic motifs does this great body of text belong to the oracles of salvation. Fundamental to it is the proclamation of the reconstruction of the city and the temple. That the two belong together in Ezekiel 40–48 can be seen in that the text begins in 40:1–3 with the rebuilding of the city, even though this is only alluded to: " . . . and set me down upon a very high mountain, on which was a structure like a city" (40:2); and at the very end, 48:30–35, the gates of the city are listed as being part of the reconstruction of the city.

Two additional motifs of the oracles are found in Ezekiel 40–48. The first is that in the time of salvation God will dwell with his people. This is portrayed in 43:2–9, where God's glory returns from the distant East (v. 2), it moves into the temple (3f.), and the temple is filled with the glory of God (5). "This is the place of my throne . . . where I will dwell in the midst of the people of Israel for ever" (v. 7). Thus vs. 7–9 are united with the motif that apostasy will be eliminated. This text is the counterpart to 10:18–22, where the glory of Yahweh leaves the temple. The two texts bring together priestly and prophetic speech.

The stream of water in 47:12 has only a loose connection to a motif in the oracles of salvation. It belongs to the pre-Israelite Zion tradition, but has in common with these later oracles the theme that both produce fertility.

Scattered Oracles of Salvation

Ezekiel 11:14–20 (21)

This oracle is a later addition to this context. It is in the form of a dispute and relates to chapter 9. The question in 11:13 is identical with that in 9:8. At issue here is the relationship between those remaining in Jerusalem and the exiles, and it resembles the situation in Jeremiah 24. Those

remaining behind pass judgment on the exiles (v. 15). The
answer to this is found in the composite oracle in two parts
(vs. 16–20). Verse 16 confirms that Yahweh has scattered
them in distant lands and has not manifested himself to
them as "holy," that is, as their powerful helper (see also
36:23). And yet it is to them that Yahweh's promise in 17–
20 is given. It is assembled from well-known motifs. The
one speaking here does not intend to announce new oracles, but is disputing with those left in Jerusalem and wants
to make it clear to them that the promise, which it is assumed is well-known, applies to those in exile. It is these
exiles whom Yahweh will assemble, bring back to the land
of Israel, and give the land to (v. 17). The first thing that
will be done then is to wipe out idolatry (19), and this is
pointedly addressed to those who have remained behind, as
is the case in chapters 8–11. In the same way, those whom
Yahweh brings back will be transformed (36:25–27 is explicitly quoted here). Verse 21, which states that those who
still cling to their abominations will be punished by Yahweh
("I will requite their deeds upon their own heads") is the
same as 9:10.

The distinguishing feature of this oracle, the content of the
dispute (the judgment on those left behind in Jerusalem, v.
15), is that it proclaims liberation to one group in the nation,
those exiled to Babylon (v. 17), and describes the restoration
of a whole relationship with God (vs. 18–20).

Ezekiel 14:21–23

21   "Thus says the Lord God: How much more when I send
upon Jerusalem . . . sword, famine, evil beasts, and pesti-
lence, to cut off from it man and beast!

22   Yet, if there should be left in it any survivors to lead out
sons and daughters, when they come forth to you, and you
see their ways and their doings . . . ,

23   They will console you . . . and you shall know that I have
not done without cause all that I have done in it."

This is a later addition to 14:12–20, and deals with God's
punishment of the nations and of Israel. It is a partial oracle
that limits the judgment, as is often the case elsewhere,
e.g., Amos 9:8b–10. It resembles 11:14–20 in that there

God's judgment falls on those who have remained in Jerusalem. In addition, 14:21–23 says that some of them will survive the catastrophe and encounter those who have long been exiled in Babylon. Thus those who escape will also be recipients of this oracle to the exiles. This passage is not a real oracle but only a deliberation over a remnant who will survive the catastrophe that is yet to befall them.

Ezekiel 16:53–63

This text is a supplement to the major historical allegory of the two sisters, Israel and Judah, and can be recognized as such by the distinctive expression, "I will restore their fortunes." It is in two parts: vs. 53–55 (expanded in 56–58) and vs. 59–63.

The clause "I will restore your fortunes," seems to apply only to Sodom (the type of the licentious city) and Samaria. It plays the same role as the additions to the oracles to the nations which proclaim wholeness after the judgment. Verses 59–63 are addressed to Judah, or to the whole of Israel, and as a variant of the many promises of a new covenant, remind us of Jeremiah 31:31–34. The special emphasis on the feeling of shame indicates a late date (cf. 36:32f.).

This is not an independent oracle but a supplement which contains only the motif of restoration, in dependence on Jeremiah 31:31–34. The restoration of the relationship to God is preceded by God's return to his people (v. 60).

Ezekiel 17:22–24

This is a supplement to the allegory of eagle and cedar, an accusation of Zedekiah (17:1–21). Thus a promise of the king of the time of salvation is added to the oracle of judgment on a king of Judah (cf. 34:23–34; 37:24–25). This addition maintains the comparison with the cedar tree (cf. vs. 3–4).

22 "Thus says the Lord God: 'I myself will take a sprig from the lofty top of the cedar . . . ; I will break off from the topmost of its young twigs a tender one and . . . plant it upon a high and lofty mountain;

23 On the mountain height of Israel will I plant it, that it may

bring forth boughs and bear fruit, and . . . in the shade of
its branches birds of every sort will nest.

24 And all the trees of the field shall know that I the Lord
bring low the high tree, and make high the low tree, dry
up the green tree, and make the dry tree flourish. I the
Lord have spoken, and I will do it.' "

This oracle surely had its origin in the circle of exiles in
Babylon. It is clearly related to the preceding oracle of
judgment. In vs. 22–23 the breaking off of the "twig" (cf.
Isa. 11:1) and its being planted in another place shows that
the proclamation of a future royal savior belongs to the context of the exile and of the return from exile. The phrase
"mountain height of Israel" is also found in 20:40. The
opening words, "I myself," emphasize Yahweh's activity in
contrast to that of the "eagle," in terms of exalting and
bringing low in v. 24. "Yahweh will bring to honor a member of the then-humbled dynasty of David in Jerusalem, will
grant him growth and sovereignty over wide areas, and under him people will find peace and security" (W. Zimmerli's commentary on this passage). The conclusion is an
expanded acknowledgment of God in the form of a doxology that is unique in the book of Ezekiel. "All the trees of
the field" refers to the surrounding peoples. They will acknowledge that Yahweh is the Lord of history, the one who
lifts up and brings down.

Ezekiel 20:34–44

Chapter 20, like chapter 16, is an accusation against Israel that encompasses the sweep of history, and like chapter 16 it has a supplement in the form of an oracle of
salvation.

The oracle bears a clear relationship to the accusation of
idolatry that precedes it in this chapter. In keeping with the
traditional motif it proclaims God's activity in bringing
them out of captivity, gathering them together (vs. 34, 41),
and leading them back to their land (42b). We also find
God's gracious acceptance of his people (40b), with the difference that here it is on the basis of worship that is purged
of idolatry (40–41a). Verse 43, with its shamefaced looking
back on the people's evil deeds, is also related to this

theme. Apart from this the oracle contains only fixed, frequently recurring expressions, which, together with the many repetitions, show the composite nature of this late oracle.

The oracle is almost entirely limited to the announcement of liberation (with the return to the promised land), motifs that permeate the entire oracle. Restoration is limited to the new, purified worship (vs. 40–41). The only additional features are the acknowledgment formula, typical of Ezekiel, here applied to Israel and to the nations, and the confession in v. 43.

Ezekiel 28:24–26

These verses are a supplement to an oracle on the nations.

24 "And for the house of Israel there shall be no more a brier to prick or a thorn to hurt them among all their neighbors who have treated them with contempt. . . .
25 Thus says the Lord God: When I gather the house of Israel from the peoples among whom they are scattered, and manifest my holiness in them in the sight of the nations, then they shall dwell in their own land which I gave to my servant Jacob.
26 And they shall dwell securely in it, and they shall build houses and plant vineyards . . . when I execute judgments upon all their neighbors who have treated them with contempt. Then they will know that I am the Lord their God."

This is a composite oracle, based on the allegory addressed to Sidon. The proclamation of salvation has the usual themes of gathering those who are scattered, bringing them back to their land, letting them live in security, building houses and planting vineyards (25–26a). This is preceded by a reference in v. 24 to the allegory on Sidon, and in 26b there follows an explication of the oracle threatening Sidon for all they have done to Israel.

Ezekiel 29:21

A positive oracle as supplement to a message of judgment on Egypt.

On that day I will cause a horn to spring forth to the house of
Israel, and I will open your lips among them. Then they will
know that I am the Lord.

Exactly what the author of this supplementary addition
means here it is impossible to say (W. Zimmerli agrees). At
the time of Nebuchadnezzar's victory over Egypt, Israel
will receive new power (something that is improbable, and
seen from the historical point of view, unintelligible), and
the prophet will again be able to speak freely. But it is not
clear whether the message proclaims judgment or salvation.
The meaning of this oracle remains inaccessible to us.

Chapter 16:53–55 can be included among the messages
of salvation that are supplements to oracles on the nations:
Sodom and Samaria will once again attain their former
state.

Chapters 33 and 18: Warning and Exhortation

These two chapters have a structure different from that of
oracles of judgment and oracles of salvation. They do not fit
into the forms of prophetic speech. How is this to be
explained?

As a result of the unusually pregnant and impressive nature of the comparison of prophet and watchman in chapter
33, all the exegetes (I know of no exception) have regarded
it as obvious that this understanding of the prophet Ezekiel
as a watchman applies to his total mission. The two statements have been regarded as saying the same thing: Yahweh called Ezekiel as a prophet, and Yahweh appointed
Ezekiel as a watchman. This identification is improbable,
first of all because the office of watchman is a continuing
responsibility, while that of a prophet is intermittent, as the
designation as "messenger" indicates. It is also improbable
because this designation as watchman is not found in the
context of the call, but only at the beginning of the oracles.
Nor does Ezekiel, or any other prophet, ever speak of himself as a watchman.

This identification by the commentators of prophet =
watchman does not take it into account that chapter 33 has
a different literary structure from the rest of Ezekiel's proclamations, and that therefore the term "watchman" must

belong to the same context as this distinctive literary structure in ch. 33 (this is also true of ch. 18, of which more later). The chapter is marked from the very beginning by conditional sentences:

2   "If I bring a sword upon a land and . . . "(completion in vs. 4, 5).
6   But if he does not warn, I will require his blood.
8   "If I say to the wicked . . . " (completion in 8b).
9   "But if you warn the wicked . . . you will have saved your life."

And so on to the end of the chapter.

The warnings given by the watchman in the form of "when—then" are parallel to a similar form of speech, the exhortation.

10   Some of the people come with the question, "How then can we live?"
11   An exhortation follows as the answer:
       "Say to them, As I live, says the Lord God, I have no pleasure in the death of the wicked . . . ; turn back, turn back from your evil ways; for why will you die, O house of Israel?"

This exhortation too has a conditional structure: If you repent, then you can remain alive. (Cf. Amos 5:5–6, 14–15, 23–24.) This totally different form of speech is not one of the prophetic forms. It is paraenesis, and its conditional sentences, exhortations, and warnings are found in the Old Testament mostly in the deuteronomic-deuteronomistic literature.

In the postexilic period, with the end of prophecy of judgment and the end of the Judaic state, the conditional forms, exhortation and warning, in most contexts take the place of unconditional proclamation. This paraenesis (termed by many "Levitical preaching") had its origin in the deuteronomic-deuteronomistic school and is regarded as the continuation of prophecy. This is seen with greatest clarity in the deuteronomistic reworking of the book of Jeremiah, especially in the conditional sentences, but also in that paraenetic oracles are ascribed to the prophets. In the book of Ezekiel it is evident in the transformation of the prophetic office into that of a watchman.

Two distinctions result from this transformation. The first is especially emphasized in Ezekiel 33. If the watchman has given warning of a danger, but his warning is not heeded, then he is not responsible for the catastrophe that results; he will have saved his life (v. 9). The fate of the watchman is separate from that of the people over whom he has been placed as watchman. Only after the political collapse of the nation is it possible to postulate such a distinction. For Jeremiah, for example, it would have been impossible.

The other distinction is stressed in Ezekiel 18:1–32. Here too there are conditional sentences, and in v. 32 the exhortation:

> 21 "But if a wicked man turns away from all his sins . . . and keeps all my statutes . . . he shall surely live; he shall not die."
>
> 32 "So turn, and live."

The sons are no longer responsible for the sins of their fathers, but each will be judged only according to his own conduct. Here the distinction between the righteous and the wicked begins. The destiny of each person depends on that person's conduct. The individual is no longer a prisoner of the destiny of the nation, but is treated by God as an individual on the basis of his conduct

This transformation parallels that between a conditional and an unconditional proclamation. Warning and exhortation take the place of unconditional oracles of judgment and salvation.

Ezekiel 33 and 18 provide a clear starting point for texts in this form of speech (conditional statements, exhortation, warning) in all the other prophetic books. Thus they all belong to the postexilic period, the time after the ministry of Ezekiel. Another indication that these two chapters are late is clearly seen in that they make reference to "our fathers" and their guilt.

Summary: Forms and Motifs
of the Salvation Oracles in Ezekiel

The independent oracles in the collection, chapters 34–37 (39): Proclamation of liberation (34:11b–16; 37:1–14;

38:6–9, alluded to in 39:25–29). In addition it is found as a motif in many oracles in two parts.

Oracles in two parts: Liberation/God's gracious return—restoration (34:23–30; 36:1–15; 36:16–37; 37:(15) 21–28).

A motif that has been expanded into an oracle: Reunification, 37:15–22; Rebuilding of city and temple, chapters 40–48. Such an expansion is typical of Ezekiel, e.g., the parable of shepherd and sheep, cleansing, new life for the dead bones.

Scattered oracles: They are distinguished from independent oracles of salvation in that they are a supplement or a brief addition to the preceding text: Announcement of liberation, 14:21–23; 20:34–44; (28:24–26); Oracle in two parts: 11:14–20, a controversy. Motif that has been expanded into an oracle, 16:60–63; 17:22–24. Addition of a word of salvation to a popular saying, 16:53–55; 28:24–26; 29:21.

Motifs of the Proclamation of Liberation (34:11b–16)

The individual steps in liberation:

Looking back on the judgment, 34:12b; 36:18f.; 38:6–9, 23f.; 11:16, 17; 14:21; 16:59.

Lament of the people prior to God's return, 37:11.

God's return to his people, 16:60; 20:40; 34:11b, 12, 16; 36:9, 21–23; 39:25.

Restoring the fortunes of the people, 16:53, 55; 39:25.

Liberation, gathering, leading home, 20:23, 41; 28:25; 34:12–16, 27; 36:8, 24; (37:1–14); 37:12–13, 21; (38:6–9); 39:27; (14:21–23 survivors).

Living in safety, 28:24; 34:13, 14, 15, 27; 39:26.

Motifs of Restoration and Blessing

Reconstruction and replanting: 11:17; 28:25–26; 36:9, 10, 11, 12, 28, 33, 35; 37:25.

Building the city and the temple: chapters 40–48; the city, 40:1–3; 48:30–35.

Safety from wild beasts and enemies: 34:25, 28; 28:34.

Restoration of Israel's honor among the nations: 34:29; 36:15.

Blessing, fertility, and increase of people and animals: 27:29; 34:26; 36:8, 10, 11, 29b, 30, 35, 37; 37:26.

Restoration of a whole relationship with God: An end to idolatry, 11:18 (21); 37:23; 43:7–9; purified worship of God, 20:40 (chs. 40–48).

The new covenant: 16:60–62; 34:25; 37:26.

The covenant formula: 11:20; 30:31; 34:23; 36:28; 37:23b.

The formula of acknowledgment, for Israel and the nations: 16:62; 20:42; 28:24; 36:36, 37; 37:28; 38:16, 23–24; 39:28.

God is in the midst of his people: 37:26f.; 39:29; 43:2–7.

Cleansing, a new heart: 11:19; 29:33; 36:25, 26.

Feelings of repentance, shame, disgust: 16:54, 61, 63; 20:43; 36:21, 22.

Following God's law: 11:20; 36:26f.; 37:24b.

Promise of a savior king: 17:22–24; 34:23, 24; 37:22, 24, 25b.

Reunification: 37:15–20, 22.

7

Trito-Isaiah

Salvation Oracles as the Core of Trito-Isaiah

The salvation oracles in Isaiah 56–66 differ from other,
similar oracles by their greater length, and in this they resemble those in Ezekiel. Here too we find literary expansion, but of a different sort from that in Ezekiel 33–37. First
of all, there is the change from the announcement of liberation to announcement of well-being in a general sense, then
proclamation of wealth, splendor, and magnificence far beyond simple restoration.

Isaiah 60:1–22

The beginning (v. 1) and the conclusion (v. 22b) of this
elaborate oracle are clearly marked. The division into two
parts, liberation (1–9) and restoration (10–22), is clear. The
first part consists of liberation (1–3) and the gathering of
the people and their return (4–9); the second includes the
rebuilding of city and temple (10–14), security (11a) and
peace (17b), dwelling in the land (22a), and blessing and
growth in numbers (21–22).

There are also numerous expansions. Liberation is expanded by an epiphany of Yahweh (1–3), and by the return
of the exiles, bringing the treasures of the nations to Israel
(5b–9, 11, 13). Foreigners rebuild the city and bring to it

the wealth of the nations, and the reconstruction uses magnificent, costly materials.

Isaiah 61:1–11

This too is an oracle in two parts, liberation (1–3) and restoration (4–11), with the speech of the messenger about himself in vs. 1–3. The message of liberation is possible because God is once again gracious to his people, with a message of comfort which turns mourning into joy (2–3). The messenger's functions as mediator are concentrated in 1–2, and his good news is directed to the poor in general. Israel is to enjoy the wealth of the nations and be decked out with their splendor, while foreigners do the hard work. The oracle ends, as in Deutero-Isaiah, in a song of praise in v. 10 (which is to be read after v. 11).

Isaiah 62:1–12

This passage (minus vs. 8–9, which are repeated in 65:21–22) is a dramatic paraphrase of the coming of salvation and is reminiscent of 40:1–11. In place of liberation, which in 10–12 is only alluded to, we find the account of God's being once again favorable to his people, but this leads only to a vague description of the nature of the salvation. The text falls into two parts: 1–5 and 6–12. The high point of these two parallel passages, which both move toward an eager expectation of a "new name," is in v. 11, "Behold, your salvation comes." This is the dramatization of an arrival for which they pleaded in the lament, "How long?" This passage gives the impression of being the high point and climax of the entire message of Trito-Isaiah.

The Three Separate Oracles in Chapters 57, 65, and 66

Isaiah 57:14–19 (21)

This oracle resembles chapter 62. Here too God's gracious return to his people takes the place of liberation. It begins with a call to prepare the way, which is meant as hyperbole and like Deutero-Isaiah is introduced by praise of God. The cry is supported by an oracle in two parts: looking back to the time of judgment (16–17), and God's gracious return to his people, in the language of the Psalms. In vs. 20–21 we have a supplement which belongs to an announcement in two parts.

Isaiah 65:16b–25

An apocalyptic framework was added to this text in vs. 17 and 25. Part one (16b, 18, 19a) resembles the songs of praise in Deutero-Isaiah: call to rejoice, God's saving acts as the basis of joy. The second part (19b–24) corresponds to the restoration in other oracles, but a description of the circumstances has replaced the events. The first part of the oracle closely resembles Deutero-Isaiah, and the second part resembles traditional oracles of salvation.

Isaiah 66:6–16

This text gives the impression of not being a unit. It can be understood if we recognize vs. 6 and 15–16 as an apocalyptic framework, an epiphany at the judgment of the world. The framework makes the oracle into a proclamation in two parts: destruction of the enemies and salvation for Israel.

Without this framework, 66:7–14 has almost the same structure as 65:16b–25: A call to rejoice (10–11), with the metaphor in 7–9, based on the oracle, "I will extend prosperity to her like a river" (12a). The coming of salvation is compared to a miraculous birth (7–9), as is done in Isaiah 49:20–23. But here the metaphor is intensified beyond what it is in Deutero-Isaiah. It is a miraculous birth in which the birth itself corresponds to the beginning of the labor pains. The section in 12–14 resembles a promise of blessing. In the mind of Trito-Isaiah the wealth of the nations will be involved here too, as in chapters 60 and 61. A climax is reached in 12–14, "As one whom his mother comforts, so will I comfort you." For the prophet the real salvation is provided by God's presence, the basis of the joy to which we were summoned at the beginning of the oracle.

Summary: Structure and Motifs

The six texts from Trito-Isaiah include four in two parts (60:1–22; 61:1–11; 65:16b–25; and 66:6–16) and two with one part (57:14–19; 62:1–12). The freedom with which they were rearranged can still be recognized, but the changing situations have appreciably modified that freedom.

The motifs of the first part, Yahweh's earlier saving deeds, are referred to in only a few situations. But Israel's falling away from God and God's law is mentioned in 57:16–17. Repeatedly we hear the lament of those suffering under God's punishment (e.g., 62:1–12). Liberation is mentioned in 61:1–3 and 62:12, "the redeemed of the Lord." Usually, however, it is mentioned in paraphrases or in metaphors, "until her vindication goes forth as brightness" (62:1b). It is compared to birthing in 66:7–9. Trito-Isaiah speaks in fuller detail of God's gracious return to the people (60:10; 62:12). For the gathering together and the return home, see 60:4; 62:10–11. In the context of the return there are numerous imperatives which urge the people to set out on the journey (e.g., 62:10–11) and to rejoice, a theme that permeates Trito-Isaiah's entire message.

Motifs of restoration, that is, of rebuilding and replanting, are often found at the beginning of an oracle (60:10–14; 65:21–22). Here Trito-Isaiah follows the style of traditional oracles, although his situation and that of his hearers has changed, a sure sign that his oracles presuppose the traditional oracles. The promise of security and quiet is significant here, "They shall not labor in vain, or bear children for calamity" (65:23; see also 60:11, 18; 65:19b).

The whole emphasis rests on the state of salvation, as is seen in the prominence of the nouns *shalom* and *ṣedaqah*. Many metaphors are drawn on to describe the situation: "Behold, I will extend prosperity to her like a river" (66:12); "he has clothed me with the garments of salvation . . . as a bride adorns herself with her jewels" (61:10). In these metaphors a new concept of salvation as a state is formed. This state is also represented by the descriptions in chapters 60, 61, 65, 66, intensified by the mention of splendor, brilliance, and abundance: "You shall be a crown of beauty in the hand of the Lord, and a royal diadem in the hand of your God" (62:3). Especially in 60:15–18 we read of the transition from the simple and unadorned to precious and costly. Here we see the way in which for Trito-Isaiah the announcement merges into expectation and longing. This is connected with the effect of "peoples and kings" on the great transformation, as described in the expanded section, 60:5b–16. The motif combines the section on liberation and the section on restoration. The other nations, the former persecutors of Israel, have an effect on both.

> The abundance of the sea shall be turned to you,
>   the wealth of the nations shall come to you.
> A multitude of camels shall cover you. . . .
> They shall bring gold and frankincense. (60:5b–6a)
>   (See also 60:9–16; 61:5–6b; 66:12)

Also a part of this vision of the future filled with longing and expectation is the thought that "nations and kings" will have to acknowledge what Yahweh has done (60:3, 14). This vision goes beyond the traditional motifs of restoration. It was never fulfilled, but the proclamation that Israel's shame will be taken away, and that Israel will again be honored among the nations (61:7, 9), was also a part of the traditional proclamation of salvation.

It is striking that the oracles in Isaiah 56–66 have little to say about the healing of the relationship to God (61:8; 65:24), and especially striking that the announcement of forgiveness is lacking in what is said about restoration. But this should probably be understood as a result of the passage of time. For Trito-Isaiah the restoration of a whole relationship with God is included in God's gracious return to his people.

PART THREE

Prophetic Oracles
of Salvation, Group 2

8

Group 2:
The Twofold
Proclamation

Introduction

In two respects these texts differ from those on Group 1.
First, they all have the same basic structure: Proclamation
of judgment on the enemy—Proclamation of deliverance
for Judah-Israel. Second, these texts contain only proclamation. No objective depictions of deliverance or of restoration of a state of salvation are ever encountered in them.
The reason for this is that the full weight is placed on one
event, the destruction of the enemy. Within this one section, "destruction of the enemy," however, there is a division into three subgroups. The other section, "salvation for
Israel," consists chiefly of motifs that are taken from the
oracles of Group 1.

Among the three subgroups of the section "destruction of
the enemy," the major subgroup presents two contrasting
motifs. It is further subdivided into (1) oracles in which the
twofold proclamation contains supplements; (2) oracles in
which the destruction of the enemy is portrayed as retribution for their behavior toward Israel; (3) oracles in which
Judah is God's instrument for the destruction of the enemy.
A further parallel group announces that Judah will take possession of the territory of the neighboring nations.

In the second of these subgroups the approach of the
enemy is described prior to their destruction.

In the third subgroup the simple structure of destruction

of the enemy—salvation for Israel is expanded into a drama between Israel and the enemy. These oracles cross the boundary into apocalyptic discourse.

The way to salvation in Group 2 is distinctly different from that in Group 1. We have here a group of political oracles, and salvation as a relationship between God and God's people is absent. Destruction of the enemy is here the only turning point that can be conceived of as leading to salvation.

The Simple Form: Destruction of the Enemy, Salvation for Israel

Isaiah 14:24–27

> 24 "The Lord of hosts has sworn . . . : so shall it be . . .
> 25a I will break the Assyrian in my land . . . , trample him under foot . . .
> 25b and his yoke shall depart from them . . .
> 26–27 This is the purpose . . . concerning the whole earth. . . . For the Lord of hosts has purposed, and who will annul it?"

These verses are characteristic of the passages dealing with the oracles to the nations. Verse 24a begins with God's oath, such as is often used to reinforce the simple promise of the land and is found only in late passages (see my *The Promises to the Fathers*, 1980). Verses 26–27 also serve to reinforce the promise. The inclusio, vs. 24, 26–27, underlines the twofold proclamation of the destruction of Assyria in the land of Judah and the liberation of Israel from the Assyrian yoke.

H. Wildberger (together with B. Duhm, K. Marti, G. Fohrer, and others) holds that v. 25b is a later addition. Against deleting it is the fact that God's oath is elsewhere always found in connection with a promise, but never together with a proclamation of a disaster on a foreign land. Wildberger also wants to delete 25b because it presupposed a lengthy foreign occupation, and according to him this could not have been written by Isaiah. He disagrees with Marti, who regards it as a later text, as follows: "Marti's interpretation is wrong. What is really spoken of here is a sharp defeat on the mountains of Judah" (p. 567). But the two verbs in 25a ("I will break," *shbr;* and "I will trample," *bus*) mean elsewhere to destroy. The text announces the destruction of Assyria in Yahweh's land, not a severe defeat.

If we recognize that the sentence has a large number of parallels in the group of twofold proclamations, this issue can be regarded as settled. Moreover the enemy here is not a historical nation: "This is the purpose that is purposed concerning the whole earth; and this is the hand that is stretched out over all the nations" (v. 26). Here as often elsewhere, Assyria is a designation for the hostile world powers as such.

Isaiah 10:24–27

24a	"Therefore thus says the Lord . . . "
24b–26	The destruction of Assyria
24b	"Be not afraid of the Assyrians. . . .
25	For in a very little while . . . my anger will be directed to their destruction . . . .
26	As when he smote Midian at the rock of Oreb . . . .
27	His burden will depart . . . his yoke will be destroyed."

The announcement of the coming destruction, introduced by the words of reassurance combined with a glance at the past, is followed by the announcement of Israel's liberation from the foreign yoke. The oracle is clearly based on the message of judgment against Assyria in Isaiah 10:5–19. Note in v. 5 the use of "rod" and "staff" (see also 30:31f.) and "anger" and "fury." As in many of the late oracles (among which H. Wildberger includes this passage and many others) it is proclaimed that God's anger against Israel will soon be ended and will then be turned against Israel's enemies. But this text says nothing about God's return to his people with mercy. The only important thing here is that God's enemies will feel his wrath. The same message is seen in the look at past history (a rare feature in the twofold proclamation): Israel's history is shaped by the mighty deeds through which God destroyed Israel's ene-

mies (Ex. 14:16; and Judg. 7:25). This shows an understanding of history in distinctly one-sided political terms.

Isaiah 14:3–4a, 22–23

> 3   "When the Lord has given you rest from . . . the hard
>   service which you were made to serve,
> 4   you will take up this taunt against the king of Baby-
>   lon . . . ."
> 22–23 " 'I will rise up against them,' says the Lord of hosts,
>   'and will cut off from Babylon name . . . and poster-
>   ity . . . .' "

14:1–2 is a supplement to chapter 13, and 14:3–4a is a
redactional transition from the oracle in vs. 1–2 and at the
same time an introduction to the oracle about the king of
Babylon in vs. 4b–21. The conclusion in 14:22–23 belongs
together with 3–4a and thus marks the inclusio 4b–21. The
two parts are held together by the structure of the twofold
proclamation.

Isaiah 14:28–29, 31

Verses 30 and 32 are a later supplement to 14:28–29, 31,
an oracle from Isaiah about the nation of Philistia, which is
structured as follows:

> 28   Introduction and date
> 29   Warning to Philistia (plus 31a)
> 31b Announcement of the foe from the north

This oracle about Philistia has a clear structure, reflecting
its function as an announcement of woe. It would however
be disrupted if we followed Wildberger in regarding 30a as
an addition, and 30b as following directly on 29b. That
would be awkward. This difficulty is avoided if we take 30
and 32 together as a later supplement which assures the
poor in Zion of safety. In 30b destruction is proclaimed to
the Philistines, and, by contrast, safety to Zion. Thus, and
this points to a late date, the Israelites are called the poor
and needy, while the Philistines suffer the fate of the ungodly. The political contrast has been replaced by that between the godly and the ungodly. The text was probably

disturbed by the late insertion of vs. 30 and 32. I attempt to reconstruct them as follows:

32a What will one answer the messengers of the nation?
30b I will kill your "posterity" with famine
    and your remnant will "I" slay.
30a The poor will feed in my pasture
    and the needy lie down in safety.
32b For the Lord has founded Zion,
    and in her the afflicted of his people find refuge.

Isaiah 8:9–10

This oracle proclaims both the destruction of Israel's foes and God's help for Israel, and its two parts reveal the structure of the twofold proclamation. Thus it clearly is connected with Isaiah 7:4–9 and the Immanuel name in 7:14. It differs, however, from the oracles in chapter 7 in that it is addressed, not to the foes now threatening Jerusalem, but to all the peoples. "Be broken, you peoples, and be dismayed; give ear, all you far countries" (v. 9). It refers to the attack of all the peoples of the earth against Israel in the end time. The support which Budde gave to this interpretation (cited by Wildberger at this passage) is still valid today: "Nowhere else has Isaiah promised so unconditionally that Yahweh will protect his people against the whole world." As is often the case with late oracles of salvation, the final sentence is formulated as a confession of trust.

Joel 2:18–20

18 "Then the Lord became jealous for his land . . .
19 'Behold I am sending to you
    grain, wine, and oil . . .
  and I will no more make you
    a reproach among the nations.' "
20 Destruction of the enemies

This oracle is God's first answer to the lament of the people during the plague of locusts, which then is interpreted as the onslaught of the enemy nations. The answer in v. 19 promises blessing, fertility in the face of the plague, and, surprisingly, that God will not make them again a reproach

among the nations, in response to v. 17. In v. 20 there follows the proclamation that the foes will be scattered and
destroyed, described in coarse, emotional language, "the
stench and foul smell of him will rise." The added comment
at the end of v. 20, "for he has acted arrogantly" (my
trans.). The whole oracle is loosely structured, and only the
form of the twofold proclamation holds it together.

Joel 2:28–32

28–29 Salvation for Israel (supplement?)
       "I will pour out my spirit on all flesh; your sons and
       your daughters shall prophesy . . . ."
30–31 Judgment of the world; apocalypse; signs in heaven
   32 Salvation for Israel: " . . . all who call upon the name
       of the Lord shall be delivered; for in Mount Zion and
       in Jerusalem . . . ."

The destruction of the enemy is not made explicit, but is
implied in the announcement of the "great and terrible day
of the Lord," the day of judgment on all the nations. On the
other hand we have the security of God's people on Zion,
v. 32, expanded in v. 28 by an apocalyptic portrayal of the
pouring out of the Spirit, now no longer limited to specific
charismatics, but bestowed on all the people. Since vs. 28–
29 are separate from vs. 30–32 and the latter is a complete
oracle, it is possible that 28–29 are an apocalyptic supplement.

Joel 3:15–17

15–16a Judgment of the world, apocalyptic
16b–17 Salvation for Israel
   16b   "But the Lord is a refuge to his people . . . "
   17a   "So you shall know that I am the Lord your God,
            who dwell in Zion, my holy mountain.
   17b   And Jerusalem shall be holy and strangers shall
            never again pass through it."

A random collection of various motifs, held together only
by the structure of the twofold proclamation. The text consists of expressions that are also found elsewhere. (Compare
the following: v. 15 and 2:10, 31; v. 16a and Amos 1:2; v.

17a and Joel 2:27; Ezek. 28:23.) That this is not really an announcement is shown by v. 16b, where we have instead a confession of trust. The appearance of God for judgment is based on an epiphany, and through v. 15 it is transformed into apocalyptic. After v. 15b the formula of acknowledgment does not fit well. The feeling for the style of the particular formulas of speech has been lost.

Joel 3:18–21

18 "And in that day . . . "
Blessing for Israel: "The mountains shall drip sweet wine."

19 Destruction of the foes: "Egypt shall become a desolation, and Edom . . . ."

20–21 "But Judah . . . for ever. . . . The Lord dwells in Zion."

21a "I will avenge their blood, and I will not clear the guilty."

In this passage also the first part is a promise of blessing. The core of the oracle is in 19a and 20, and since this core has a distinctly rhythmic form (two stichs of three beats each) the prose supplement in 19b, 21a is especially conspicuous, with its secondary reason for the judgment on Egypt and Edom. As elsewhere, supplements are often found in the wrong place in the text. Here 21a is separated from the other part of the supplement in 19b. Behind the twofold proclamation there is a double wish, and this explains the supplement. The reason is part of the prophetic proclamation but not of a double wish. As in most twofold proclamations, Judah-Jerusalem is not promised deliverance but survival. This is in keeping with the two motifs of the old Zion tradition that are preserved here: That Yahweh dwells in Zion (21b), and the spring of water at the temple (cf. Ezek. 47:12; Zech. 14:8).

Comments on the Joel Texts

Of all the prophetic books only Joel contains so great a number of texts that have the structure of the twofold proclamation. The first part of the book (1:2–2:17) is marked by the call to fasting and lament in the face of the plague of locusts, or the Day of Yahweh which the plague represents. It ends with the plea for deliverance in 2:15–17. The second part (2:19–3:21) gives God's answer to the lament (2:19), "The Lord answered and said to his people . . ." The answer is given in 2:18–20 as a twofold proclamation, and in 2:21–27 it is expanded in a broad portrayal of the promised blessing. In what follows in 2:28 to the end of the book we find only twofold proclamations.

The book of Joel is widely regarded as late (H. W. Wolff dates it to the first half of the first century B.C.), and evidence is found in the fact that at this late date the twofold proclamation replaced the traditional proclamation of salvation in those circles from which the book of Joel came. Also significant are the emphasis on the promise of blessing and the resemblance to apocalyptic.

Zechariah 9:1–8

1–3	"For to the Lord belong" the cities and lands
4	The Lord will take possession and punish
5–7	Ashkelon, Gaza, the people of Philistia
8	Salvation (security) for Israel
8a	"I will encamp . . . as a guard"
8b	"For now I see with my own eyes"

In vs. 1–7 of this oracle there is merely a long enumeration of peoples who will come under God's judgment. It is through v. 8 that it becomes a part of the structure of the twofold proclamation. The list of peoples sounds like a greatly abbreviated collection of sayings about the nations, which is held together by the threat of destruction. In a remarkably abrupt manner the passage ends with the motif of God's coming to his people as found in the oracles of salvation. This text shows the development from the older oracles on the nations to the later twofold proclamations.

Obadiah 15–17

15–16	Judgment as retribution on the nations
15a	"For the day of the Lord is near"
15b	"As you have done, it shall be done to you, . . .

16a   For as you have drunk . . . , the nations . . . shall drink . . . ."

16b   "And shall be as though they had not been."

17   Salvation (security) for Israel

17a   "But in Mount Zion there shall be those that escape . . . "

17b   "The house of Jacob shall possess" those who possessed them.

The day of Yahweh's judgment on the nations is announced. It comes because of the grief that the nations have brought on Israel. The comparison in v. 16 refers to the cup of Yahweh's wrath and is perhaps a reminder of the conquest of Jerusalem. In 17a the judgment on the nations parallels Israel's preservation from the judgment. Verse 17b is a gloss.

The Twofold Proclamation as Formed by a Gloss

Isaiah 10:12

The message of judgment on Assyria in 10:5–19 contains a gloss in v. 12 (so H. Wildberger and most other exegetes) that transfers the proclamation about Assyria into the post-exilic period and applies it to the enemies of that time. It draws on the language of Isaiah. Wildberger applies the phrase "all his work on Mount Zion and on Jerusalem" to the temple buildings. This is unlikely, for in all the other oracles of this group the destruction of the enemy is contrasted to the liberation and restoration of Israel, and that is what is probably intended here. As a gloss to the judgment on Assyria in 10:5–19, verse 12 turns the event of Assyria's destruction into a twofold happening, for at the same time Yahweh will complete his work of salvation for Israel. This demonstrates the power of the structure of twofold proclamation.

Isaiah 30:29, 32b

This message of judgment on Assyria in 30:27–33 is one of the oracles on the nations. And vs. 29, 32b are a gloss to the effect that destruction for Assyria means deliverance for

Israel. They do not directly announce deliverance, but its effects and the reaction to them, as so often is the case in Deutero-Isaiah, as we are reminded by this gloss:

> And you shall have a song as in the night when a holy feast is kept; and gladness of heart, as when one sets out to the sound of the flute to go to the mountain of the Lord, to the Rock of Israel . . . , to the sound of timbrels and lyres.

This depicts a cultic act, a procession by night to the Temple Mount, accompanied with singing and the playing of instruments. This shows how the old tradition of songs of victory lived on. Earlier it was the praise of God after victory over a foe; now it is the praise of God that celebrates the destruction of the foe at some future time.

Isaiah 60:12

The gloss, "For the nation and kingdom that will not serve you shall perish; those nations shall be utterly laid waste," does not at all fit the context of the oracle of salvation in chapter 60. It functions to turn this oracle into part of a twofold proclamation: Destruction of the nations—salvation for Israel.

Jeremiah 30:11b, 16, 17, 20b

In the collection of oracles in Jeremiah 30:4–22 verses 11b, 16, 17, 20b are glosses inserted here to announce the destruction of the enemy so as to change the proclamations into twofold proclamations. This attempt failed utterly. The glosses differ so markedly from the carefully crafted, unified oracles that they are all too clearly recognizable as glosses.

Note the other passages treated above that contain glosses: Isaiah 14:1–2; 14:30, 32; 29:5b–8 (gloss to 29:1–4); 66:6, 15–16; glosses to Micah 5; 4:13; Zechariah 2:12f.

Destruction of the Enemy as Retribution

In some texts the destruction of the enemy is regarded as retribution for what they have done to Judah-Israel, or as punishment for arrogance.

For the violence done to the people of Judah . . .
I will avenge their blood . . . . (Joel 3:19-21)

As you have done, it shall be done to you. (Obad. 15-17)

Therefore all who devour you shall be devoured . . . ;
those who despoil you shall become a spoil.
(Jer. 30:16-17)

(Similar passages are Jer. 30:11, 20b; Joel 2:18-20; 3:2b-3; Zech. 2:8; Isa. 10:12; 34:8; 35:4b; Ezek. 38:10-13.) In many passages the reason for this is given (e.g., Joel 2:19b; 3:19b, 21a). A typical motif is the word-for-word equivalence: "As you have done, it shall be done to you," and "All who devour you shall be devoured."

This motif was not originally a part of the twofold proclamation. Behind the proclamation there stands the double wish, for which no basis was stated, and so the inclusion of the motif brings the oracle into agreement with a prophetic proclamation of justice, which does require such a basis. Only in this group does an oracle from God announce retribution for Israel's foes, and never in the oracles of Group 1.

Judah as God's Implement for Destruction of the Enemy

Obadiah 18-21

Verse 18 goes beyond the twofold proclamation in 15-17. The judgment on Edom will be executed by Judah (comparison with fire and stubble). In vs. 19-20 the proclamation is expanded by the list of the districts which Judah will take possession of. In v. 21 the rescue of Judah is only alluded to.

Malachi 4:1-6

The comparison with fire and straw for destruction is somewhat modified here: "The day comes, burning like an oven." But v. 3 says that those addressed will carry out the destruction: "You shall tread down the wicked, for they will be ashes under the soles of your feet." Here the motif has been combined with another—the destiny of the pious and of the godless: "Once more you shall distinguish between the righteous and the wicked" (3:18). The fate of those who

fear God, however, is given in 4:2, "But for you who fear
my name the sun of righteousness shall rise, with healing in
its wings," an echo of Trito-Isaiah. The beautiful metaphor
in v. 2 depicts the joy of those who have been liberated:
"You shall go forth leaping like calves from the stall." In
stark contrast to this is the next sentence, "And you shall
tread down the wicked" (v. 3a).

Isaiah 14:1–2

Verse 2 is a gloss to the oracle in 14:1. Here it is not the
destruction but the enslavement of Israel's former enemies
that is proclaimed. This implies that the Judeans themselves
have subjugated them.

Isaiah 19:16–17

This is a material gloss to 19:1–15, an oracle about the
nation of Egypt. It lifts out of vs. 1–15 the sentence in 1b,
"and the heart of the Egyptians will melt within them."
Judah will be so strong that mighty Egypt will be afraid of
them. This gloss shows that the oracle is not really a proclamation, but a wish.

Zechariah 9:13–16

The proclamation of the destruction of the enemy in vs.
13–15 is dominated by the motif that Judah itself will carry
out the destruction. Yahweh uses Judah as a weapon of destruction—a bizarre metaphor. The epiphany of Yahweh in
v. 14 is an expansion that reminds us of the ancient wars of
Yahweh. The intensification in v. 15b makes the emotional,
bloodthirsty tone unmistakable. Here the bitterness of
those who had been subjugated is heard.

Zechariah 10:3–6a, 11b

The extent of this passage is uncertain and many details
are not clear. But it is evident that it resembles a twofold
proclamation, such as 9:13–16. Yahweh intervenes for his
people (3b, 5, 6a), but it is Judah itself that wins the victory
over the enemy, empowered by Yahweh.

Zechariah 12:1–9

Verses 7–9 are the heart of this oracle: All the nations will be destroyed, but Jerusalem will remain—Yahweh will protect its inhabitants. This central emphasis is expanded by vs. 2–6, which state that the destruction will be carried out by Judah. Judah will be a "cup of reeling to all the peoples" (v. 2), "a heavy stone" (v.3), "a blazing pot in the midst of wood," "a flaming torch among sheaves" (v. 6). The heaping up of metaphors increases the intensity of the passage.

Micah 4:13

This is a gloss to the oracle in 4:9–12 (Group 1), which H. W. Wolff dates to around 587 B.C. Verse 13 cannot have been an original part of the oracle. It is impossible to think that around 587 Judah would have been able to "beat in pieces many peoples." The comparison with beasts of prey ("horns and hoofs") calls to mind the oracles to the patriarchs (Genesis 49). Micah 4:13 is a typical example of a twofold proclamation which arose from a gloss. According to the parallels, the gloss came into being in late postexilic times.

Micah 5:5–6

This is a gloss to a proclamation of the coming of a savior king. H. W. Wolff sees this also as a late addition. Like 4:13 it results in a twofold proclamation. Verse 5 says "seven shepherds and eight princes of men," a greatly inflated figure for the proclamation of the coming of a peaceful king. Judah will become so strong that it can oppose Assyria with seven or eight military leaders who will destroy that nation's might.

Micah 5:8–9

This gloss has been deliberately brought into harmony with v. 7, "The remnant of Jacob shall be . . . ," but its content is in sharp contrast to v. 7 and cannot have arisen at the same time. Verse 7 announces salvation for Israel, and

8–9 announce the destruction of the peoples, with the participation of Judah: "Like a young lion among the flocks of sheep, which . . . treads down and tears in pieces." Like Micah 4:13, this comparison resembles the oracles of the patriarchs. If 5:9, which departs from the rhythm of v. 8, originally followed 4:13 (as H. Guthe assumes in HSAT), it may have been moved here by the author in order to make the twofold proclamation clearer.

These three glosses are important in that they not only supplement the text but also are in conscious contrast to the oracles which they supplement. Not a peaceful king, but eight powerful military leaders. Not a blessing among the peoples, but like a lion that "treads down and tears in pieces." At least in these three supplements to Micah the authors declare that they await a future which is different from that proclaimed in the oracles. They expect salvation for Judah only through the destruction of their foes.

Judah Takes Possession
of the Neighboring Territory

. . . that they may possess the remnant of Edom (Amos 9:12a)

The seacoast shall become the possession of the remnant of the house of Judah. (Zeph. 2:7, 9b)

The house of Jacob will possess those who possessed them. (Obad. 17b, my trans.; see also Obad. 19–20; Zech. 9:7b)

This motif is found only in short glosses. The statements do not belong directly to the group of twofold proclamations, but that group forms their background. Each of these statements presupposes that the destruction of the enemies must be to the advantage of Israel, for Israel benefits from the destruction by taking possession of their land. There must have been a particular group of people in postexilic Israel who had a special interest in getting more land. In these glosses it is no longer assumed that they are prophetic proclamations. Here voice is given to expectations for the future.

The Foes are Destroyed Before They Can Attack

There are seven passages in which the twofold proclamation is expanded by the addition of the approach of the enemy against Jerusalem or the land of Judah. First, this underlines the threat which the enemy constitutes for Yahweh's mountain and Yahweh's land, and, second, land and mountain become the scene of the destruction of the enemy. These passages mark the first step in the expansion of the twofold proclamation to a drama, and finally to the major compositions.

Isaiah 17:12–14

12–13   The thunder of many peoples, like the waves of the sea. God threatens them, and they flee, like straw before the wind.

14   Terror at evening, gone in the morning, that is the lot of those who would plunder us.

In this brief, poetically expressive oracle, the destruction of the foes who are attacking Judah (Zion) is proclaimed. There are no indications of the time or place, and no names are mentioned ("many peoples") in this description of the attack. Quite the opposite is the case in Isaiah 7–8 and 36–38, when the enemies are approaching Jerusalem. Deliverance is only implied in v. 14b.

Isaiah 29:5b–8

This is an addition to 29:1–4, judgment on Jerusalem (the Ariel oracle). The chapter is much discussed and the text is poorly preserved. It is certain, however, that vs. 1–4 are a pronouncement of judgment on Ariel (i.e., Jerusalem), and 5b–8 are an appended oracle of salvation.

5   "The multitude of your foes shall be like small dust."

6   Epiphany

7–8a   Two similes: "Like a dream," "as . . . a hungry man."

8b   " . . . so . . . all the nations . . . that fight against Mount Zion"

Here too is announced the destruction of the "peoples" that attack Mount Zion. God's epiphany is implied in apoca-

lyptic language, and the enemies are ground to dust as the
attack fails. Behind this passage, and perhaps also behind
17:12–14 as well, there is an old tradition of the destruction of those foes who unleash an attack against the holy
mountain.

Isaiah 33:1–16

This passage does not entirely fit here. The text and the
sequence of verses are questionable, and the motifs in their
present order make little sense (this was also the first impression of H. Gunkel). The motifs can be arranged only
according to their present context.

1	The destroyer will be destroyed.
2, 7–9	Lament and petition for God's help
10	God's answer in the epiphany
3–4, 12–13	Destruction of the enemy
11, 14a	The enemies identified as the ungodly
14–16	Salvation for the righteous

God's intervention against Israel's foes, which follows
from the epiphany, corresponds to the first part of the twofold proclamation. As such it was written by a later hand,
who in the glosses in 11, 14a, and 14b–16 identifies these
foes as the ungodly and contrasts the fate of the ungodly
with that of the righteous by means of an entrance liturgy.
Salvation for Israel is seen only in the gloss in v. 6: "and he
will be the stability of your times." The enemy attack is
presupposed in the word of woe at the beginning and
hinted at in the lament of the people.

Joel 3:1–3, 9–14 (15–17)

The limits of this passage cannot be identified with certainty (cf. the commentary of H. W. Wolff). Verses 4–8, a
folk oracle on Tyre, Sidon, and Philistia, are an independent
unit. Verses 1–3 and 9–14 are a twofold proclamation, held
together by the place name "valley of Jehoshaphat" in 2
and 12. Verses 15–17 may either belong here or constitute
an independent unit.

> 1 "At that time, when I restore the fortunes of Judah and Jerusalem,"
> 2a "I will gather all the nations . . . to the valley of Jehoshaphat"
> 2b–3 Because of what they have done to Israel.
> 9–12a, 14 Ironic summons to holy war in the valley of Jehoshaphat
> 12b There Yahweh will judge them.
> 13 Summons to destroy
> 15, 16a Yahweh makes his voice heard on Zion.
> 16b, 17 Yahweh is a refuge for his people.

A day is proclaimed on which Yahweh will restore the fortunes of Judah and at the same time give judgment on the peoples. In verses 2b, 3, the basis for this is given as the crimes committed against Judah. "All people" are accused, even those whom the accusation cannot affect. The beginning in vs. 1–2a is a modified oracle of salvation, the original of which probably read, "At that time when I restore the fortunes of Judah, I will gather (my sons) and lead them (home again)." The author was familiar with the oracles which began this way and were based on the twofold proclamation. In vs. 9–14 the approach of the enemy is described in detail, but in such a way that Yahweh himself is bringing them to the Valley of Jehoshaphat. Thus the motif "summons to battle" becomes ironic. This includes the transformation in v. 10, "Beat your plowshares into swords," which assumes familiarity with Micah 4:3. If vs. 15–17 are the continuation of 4–14, then the epiphany contains apocalyptic elements.

Zechariah 14:1–9 (11)

In this oracle the apocalyptic coloring is more obvious and the apocalyptic drama takes on clearer form.

> 1–2a "A day of the Lord is coming. . . . I will gather all the nations against Jerusalem to battle."
> 2b The city will fall and half the people go into exile.
> 3 Yahweh will go forth to fight as of old.
> 4 His feet will stand on the Mount of Olives, and the mountain will split in two
> 5a The valley of Hinnom will be filled

    5b   Then Yahweh will come and his saints with him.
6–11   Transformation of the world, apocalypse
    8   Living waters flow out from Jerusalem
    9   Yahweh will be king over all the earth
10f.   Jerusalem will be lofty and live in security

In this passage as well the peoples will be brought near by Yahweh. The "peoples" first of all execute Yahweh's judgment on his people, but then he destroys them in his land in an apocalyptic catastrophe. Victory is followed by the entrance of the king into his city, "and all the holy ones with him" (5b). Because Yahweh has conquered all the peoples he is now king over all the earth. The conclusion in vs. 9–11 constitutes the other part of the twofold proclamation: Jerusalem on its lofty height will abide as a safe refuge. Supplements to Zechariah 14:1–9 (11) are found in vs. 12–15 and 16–19.

Isaiah 66:6, 15–16

    6   "An uproar from the city! . . . the Lord, rendering recompense to his enemies!"
 7–14   Oracle of salvation for Israel
15–16   Yahweh comes with fire to judge the whole earth.

The oracle in 7–14 is framed by a later hand through a pronouncement of judgment on the peoples who, according to 6a, threaten Jerusalem. By means of this framework the author changes a simple oracle into a twofold proclamation. The assault of Jerusalem is not developed here, but only presupposed.

Isaiah 66:18, 20, 22–24

The text is not clear and perhaps it does not belong in this collection of oracles. The text and the sequence of verses in 22–23 is uncertain, but it promises continuous, undisturbed worship on Zion. The gloss in v. 24 makes the passage into a twofold proclamation.

    24   "And they shall go forth and look on the dead bodies of the men that have rebelled against me; for their worm

shall not die, their fire shall not be quenched, and they shall be an abhorrence to all flesh."

The permanence of the temple worship is the goal of this passage, but destruction as the judgment of God, eternal punishment, is also explicit. The passage can be included in this group of oracles on the grounds that those slain by God's judgment lie on or near Mount Zion, and thus the battle must have taken place there.

Major Compositions

Isaiah 34–35: Edom Is Destroyed, Zion Redeemed (*H. Guthe*)

34:1–5   Yahweh is enraged with the nations and gives them up to slaughter so that "the stench of their corpses shall rise; the mountains shall flow with their blood."

6–8   Comparison with sacrificial slaughter

9–15   Description of the desolation

The much-discussed problem of these two chapters, presented in full by H. Wildberger, is seen from a new perspective when we explore it in the context of the oracles of salvation, which explains the relationship between chapters 34 and 35. Each has a different origin (so H. Wildberger and others). They form a whole by means of the structure of destruction for the foes—salvation for Israel. That they were brought together purposely is shown by the insertion of 35:4b, "Your God will come with vengeance, with the recompense of God," to correspond to 34:8 in order to join the chapters together. Chapter 35 is purely an oracle of salvation of Group 1 (Wildberger terms passages in this text group parallels) and closely resembles Deutero-Isaiah.

35:1–4   Call to rejoice, fear not!

5–9   Proclamation of salvation

10   Promise that they will remain in the land

If we compare this with the structure of chapter 34, the latter gives the impression of being an expansion of the simple proclamation of the destruction of the enemy, in correspondence with the other twofold proclamations. The heart of 34:1–15 is:

2   Yahweh is enraged at the nations and gives them over to slaughter.

6   "For the Lord has a sacrifice in Bozrah"

8   "For the Lord has a day of vengeance."

Everything else is expansion, ornamentation, tightening up. The language of these expansions is emotional and bloodthirsty and resembles that of apocalyptic. O. Kaiser calls 34–35 "a little apocalypse." The compiler of 34–35 had before him the oracle in chapter 35, as well as the simple form of the proclamation of the destruction of the enemy. These two chapters testify to a late stage of the twofold proclamation, and the apocalyptic elements indicate the transition to apocalyptic.

Ezekiel 35–36

Chapter 35 proclaims the destruction of Edom, but as an oracle about Edom it does not fit well into the collection of oracles in chs. 33–37. It is easy to understand it in its place in the book when we observe that according to the schema of the twofold proclamation it precedes an oracle of salvation to Judah. That they were deliberately placed together is seen in the beginning of each chapter: Chapter 35 is an oracle against the mountains of Seir, and ch. 36 an oracle to the mountains of Israel. There are several points at which this combination resembles that of Isaiah 34–35.

35:1–4	Judgment proclaimed against Edom (Seir)
5–9	Because you cherished enmity against Israel
10–15	"Because you . . . , therefore . . . "
36:1–4	To the mountains of Israel: "because the enemy . . . , therefore . . . "
5–7	The nations must bear their reproach
8–13	Proclamation of salvation to Israel
8	"But you, O mountains of Israel, shall shoot forth your branches . . . "
9	"For, behold, I am for you . . . "
10–13	I will increase the number of people and animals.

Ezekiel 35:1–4 is a proclamation of judgment against Edom in rhythmic form, and probably originated with the prophet Ezekiel. There follow two long prose expansions,

with many repetitions, 5–8 and 10–15, both with the same structure: "because you . . . therefore . . . ," and with little difference in content. As in Isaiah 34 the language is pointed and bloodthirsty. Here too we should distinguish between the brief announcement of judgment (4) and the increasingly expansive 5–9 and 10–15.

In chapter 36, verses 2b–7 take up the proclamation of judgment on Edom and base it on God's message to Israel, which then in vs. 8–13 moves into a proclamation of salvation for Israel, in agreement in each sentence with the salvation oracles in Group 1, as in the case for Isaiah 35.

The combination of Ezekiel 35 and 36 is closely related to that in Isaiah 34–35, and it too has a brief proclamation of judgment and a message of salvation to Israel.

Ezekiel 38–39: Gog and Magog

Apart from chapters 35–36 and the hints in 28:24–26, the twofold proclamation is found in Ezekiel only in chs. 38–39, which W. Zimmerli and others regard as not a genuine part of the book of Ezekiel. These two chapters clearly have the structure of judgment on the enemy—salvation of Israel. The proclamation of the destruction of the peoples on the mountains of Israel is followed by an oracle of salvation for Israel. The distinctive feature of this long passage is the detailed description of the events preceding and following God's judgment. This act of judgment on Israel's foes is portrayed in a drama in three acts. This in itself is the clearest example in the Old Testament of the transition from late prophecy to apocalyptic.

38:1–17	Gog's advance on Israel.
38:18–23; 39:1–8	God's judgment on Gog
39:9–24	The subsequent events
39:25–29	Proclamation of salvation to Israel
25	"Now I will restore the fortunes of Jacob . . ."
26	They shall dwell securely in their land
27	I will gather them, bring them home
28–29	They will know that I am their God

The two parts differ widely from each other in both form and content, and the greatest emphasis is on the first part.

The heart of the large first part is the brief proclamation of God's judgment on Gog:

> 38:18, 22   "On that day, when Gog shall come against the land of Israel . . . , my wrath will be roused. . . . I will enter into judgment with him."

The proclamation of judgment is expanded in vs. 19–22 by the description of an apocalyptic catastrophe, which is continued in the account of the subsequent events, 39:9–24. The account of the events preceding the invasion (38:1–17) negates God's judgment on his people in the commission he gives to Gog to attack the land of Israel. This is a sign that here true history has been integrated into the apocalyptic drama. This drama comes to an end with 39:17–20. The concluding verses, 21–24, which mark the transition to the oracle of salvation, are a return to true history.

The oracle of salvation in 39:25–29 has nothing at all to do with the apocalyptic drama of Gog, and a radical change in style is apparent. It is an oracle of salvation of Group 1 and contains in concentrated form all the motifs of liberation and return; that is, it is a text which has a different origin from that of the Gog drama and which the author of the drama found ready at hand for his use. In this, all three major compositions (Isa. 34–35; Ezek. 35–36; and Ezek. 38–39) agree. Thus it becomes clear that these texts can be explained only as expansions of the twofold proclamation and not in terms of their context in the prophetic books. For example, only in this way is it clear how the approach of the enemy in short passages such as Zechariah 14:1–11 was expanded in these texts to become the action of an apocalyptic drama.

This subgroup of twofold proclamation makes it possible to define more closely the transition from the prophecy to apocalyptic.

Group 2: Conclusions

Characteristic of Group 2, in all three of its subgroups, is the twofold contrasting proclamation. This form displays a particular strength in that in many passages it is constructed by the use of glosses. This in itself leads to the conclusion that a fixed form was already in existence. Secondary combinations are also seen in that in the majority of these texts a condition of permanence and security is contrasted with the act of destroying the enemy.

The major emphasis is placed on the destruction that is foretold. Only in this part do we find the intensification of language by emotional expressions of power, exaggerated metaphors, and a large vocabulary of terms that denote destruction. The destruction of the "peoples" that is announced here is frequently grotesque. Words such as "devour," "tread down" (Zech. 9:15), "the mountains shall flow with their blood" (Isa. 34:3), "The Lord has a sword; it is sated with blood, it is gorged with fat" (Isa. 34:6, 7; 63:1–6). We find this type of language especially in groups of metaphors which serve to sharpen the language: "I will make the clans of Judah like a blazing pot in the midst of wood, like a flaming torch among sheaves" (Zech. 12:6). Another characteristic feature is that the early traditions of the wars of Yahweh are drawn on, such as the call to battle (Micah 4:13), the devoting of the booty to God (Micah 4:13), and the epiphany of Yahweh (Zech. 9:14). The comparison of the "remnant" with a lion (Micah 4:13; 5:8) awakens memories of the oracles to the tribes in Genesis 49.

As for the "peoples" whose destruction is announced, there is a striking absence of anything concrete. This applies to the names of the peoples and the time and place of their destruction. Even where names are mentioned, such as Edom or Egypt, these are only formal designations for the "peoples," the enemies of Yahweh and his people. The only time mentioned is the future; the only place, the mountain of God. The conception that in one act all the peoples of the world of that time would be destroyed already carries us into the world of apocalyptic. In this the foundation of the biblical language of creator and creation is abandoned. In the primal history the peoples come into being through God's blessing, as in the genealogies of Genesis 10. This is explicitly preserved in the proclamation of Deutero-Isaiah, "He did not create it a chaos, he formed it to be inhabited" (Isa. 45:18). If we were to take the expression "all peoples" literally, then after the destruction only Judah-Israel would remain in what would then be truly a desolated world.

The passages in which liberation from the enemy is proclaimed are almost all found in the book of Isaiah, based on oracles of Isaiah, as the frequent use of the distinctive Isaianic language shows. The two passages that call to rejoicing over the liberation remind the reader of Deutero-Isaiah, and Malachi 3:20 is reminiscent of Trito-Isaiah. In the majority of the passages the salvation is not liberation but safety and security, that is, a state of well-being, as for example in Joel 3:20: "But Judah shall be inhabited for ever, and Jerusalem to all generations." See also Isaiah 33:16: ". . . his bread will be given him, his water will be sure." In all that is said about salvation in the twofold proclamations there is nothing said about a new, transformed relationship with God. Not once does it say that God is again gracious to his people, that God is again pleased with his people, or anything similar. The oracles are purely political, and God's work is limited to the destruction of Israel's enemies and the guarantee of security for Israel. It is, moreover, astonishing that in the section on "salvation for Israel" no place is given to the restored and blessed life of the people. There is nothing to the effect that the people can again have a happy life, or can sit in peace under their fig tree. We do not find such words as "quiet" and "peace." This lack is evident in the three major compositions, Isaiah 34–35, Ezekiel 35–36 and 38–39, in which the section "salvation for Israel" is simply taken over from oracles from Group 1.

Excursus: Destruction of the Enemies
in Deutero-Isaiah

It might be asked, Isn't the destruction of the enemies also a component to Deutro-Isaiah's message, so that here we can see a contrast to the twofold proclamation? But here we must point to the difference. In the twofold proclamation the destruction of "the peoples," or "all peoples" is proclaimed, but a specific historical situation is never clearly discernable. In Deutero-Isaiah the proclamation refers to the historical world power Babylon in a clearly definable historical situation.

The distinction is also seen in the three settings in which we encounter the motif in Deutero-Isaiah. First is the context of the praise of God as the Lord of history, especially in Isaiah 40:18–24, where God's actions in history include the fall of the mighty: "who . . . makes the rulers of the earth as nothing" (v. 23b). As the Lord of history Yahweh intervenes on behalf of his people (40:9–10). This never involves the destruction of one or of all the peoples. Second, Yahweh assigns to the emperor of Persia the task of defeating Babylon (44:24–45:7). He rescues his people in a manner different from that which he employed in the time before the collapse of the nation. Third, we also encounter oracles that resemble those found in the twofold proclamation, for example, 41:11–13: "Behold, all who are incensed against you shall be put to shame and confounded." (See also Isa. 41:14–16; 49:24–26; 51:13b; 51:23; Nahum 1:12–13; 2:1–3; Zeph. 3:14–20.) These are parts of traditional oracles with which the prophets comforted their people. The prophets were giving courage to the people in exile through the language of traditional oracles of salvation in answer to the people's laments. The concern of even these oracles is never the destruction of the hostile nations themselves.

The Transition to Apocalyptic in the Twofold Proclamation

With a few exceptions, apocalyptic motifs are not found in the twofold proclamation in its simple form. They are first encountered when the form is expanded by the motif of the approach of the enemy, and they then are seen in the exaggerated portrayal of the approach and sudden destruction of the enemy and in the expansion of the enemy into "the peoples," or "all peoples."

This apocalyptic nature is reinforced in the major compositions, in which the judgment on the peoples takes on cosmic proportions. "And I will give portents in the heavens and on earth, blood and fire and columns of smoke. The sun shall be turned to darkness and the moon to blood" (Joel 2:30). The stars lose their brightness, the Lord's voice makes the heavens and the earth shake (Joel 4:15f. [3:15f. Eng.]). "The Mount of Olives shall be split in two," the rhythm of days and seasons will be broken (Zech. 14:4–7), streams will be turned to pitch (Isa. 34:9). The destruction is unimaginable, beyond all measure. The proclamation of eternal damnation (Isa. 66:24) can also be seen as an apocalyptic motif.

In the form of the twofold proclamation, especially in the glosses, the transition from the late successors of the prophets to apocalyptic is clearly seen. We can also observe here that in the late examples of the oracles of salvation in Group 1, motifs which depict the deliverance are exaggerated to the point of unreality, but in the glosses to the twofold proclamation it is only the motif of the destruction of the enemy that takes on apocalyptic dimensions.

On the Origins of the Twofold Proclamation

A rationale is given for some of the proclamations of destruction for Judah's enemies: It is retribution for what they have done to Judah. This is stated in detail in Joel 3:2–3 " . . . on account of my people and my heritage Israel"; "As you have done, it shall be done to you" (Obad. 15). In some passages the rationale is clearly stated, as in Joel 3:19–22, especially verses 19b and 21a. Such an addition of the reason for God's action shows that it was not an original part of the twofold proclamation, but probably arose in imitation of the prophetic announcement of judgment. This process can be understood if the twofold proclamation has its roots in the so-called "double-wish," which originally led an independent life, as can be seen in 1 Samuel 25:29:

> The life of my lord shall be bound in the bundle of the living in the care of the Lord your God, and the lives of your enemies he shall sling out as from the hollow of a sling.

The double wish contains no rationale in itself because it is a special form of the motif blessing–curse. There was a close relationship between double wish and twofold proclamation, as can be seen in Micah, where the two are found together in 7:8–10 and 14–17.

> 7:9 "He will bring me forth to the light; I shall behold his deliverance.
> 10 Then my enemy will see, and shame will cover her . . . ;
> now she will be trodden down like the mire of the streets."

In the psalms of lament this wish that moves in two directions is a frequent form at the conclusion of the psalm, generally just before the vow of praise. The set formula of a two-sided wish is found almost exclusively in laments of the people, such as Psalm 80:16–17:

16 "They have burned it with fire, they have cut it down;
    may they perish at the rebuke of thy countenance!
17 But let thy hand be upon the man of thy right hand,
    the son of man whom thou hast made strong for thyself!"

See also Psalms 79:10b–12; 71:12–13; 74:18–21. The double wish has its distinctive place in the lament of the people, and this corresponds to its being taken up in the twofold proclamation, which is also concerned with Israel's enemies.

The double wish is found in many places in the lament of the individual, where it is usually transformed into a petition at the end of the psalm, e.g., Psalm 31:17f.:

17 "Let me not be put to shame, O Lord,
    for I call on thee;
    let the wicked be put to shame,
    let them go dumbfounded to Sheol."

In addition to Psalms 32:10 and 54:4–5 there are some 26 other passages. The example above shows that in the laments of the individual, in the place of the contrast between Israel and its political enemies, we usually have the contrast between the ungodly and the pious.

The twofold proclamation agrees with this two-sided wish in its structure. The oracle has two parts, in which it looks in two directions. It agrees in content, in that the contrast is essentially the same: The enemies—I (we). From this we may conclude that the two-sided proclamation, whether directly or indirectly, can be traced back to the double wish, the roots of which lie in the realm of blessing and curse. (See H. Gunkel and J. Begrich, *Einleitung in die Psalmen*, 1933; 2nd ed, 1966, 228f., on "Wishes against the enemy and wishes for oneself," with citations of other passages.)

This origin makes it even clearer that the twofold proclamation is a foreign body in the prophetic oracles of salvation, and that it was added to them at a late stage of their development. It is also a foreign body in that the double wish is a prayer spoken by a member of the worshiping community. Even though in form it was changed into a proclamation, it remains in content a wish. This confirms that the prophetic proclamation was transformed in its late stages into an expectation or a wish.

The Theological Significance
of the Twofold Proclamation

The twofold proclamation represents a late stage in the history of the prophetic oracles and clearly belongs to late postexilic times. In this period there were, in the strict sense, no prophets in Israel. Then when the twofold proclamation took on the form of prophetic oracles (messenger formula and God's message in the first person), this was an imitation designed to give authority to the message. In this proclamation it is no longer the word of a messenger that is transmitted. It is what the speakers of these messages thought God intended for the future. It was their expectations for the future which they transmitted in the honorable conviction that it was God's message.

But what these texts say stands in irreconcilable contrast to the oracles of salvation of Group 1. The only thing they know of a history of God's dealings with his people is that God must take revenge for what the enemy has done to his people. When they draw on traditions, they are the traditions of the early wars in which God helped his people to victory or of the oracles to the tribes. In these texts nothing is said of Israel's guilt in being unfaithful to their God, and naturally nothing is said of forgiveness. Here there is indeed a great historical breach. The authors of these words are close to those preexilic prophets of salvation whom the prophets of judgment called false prophets. They stand in the same contrast to the message of Deutero-Isaiah as that of Hananiah to the proclamations of Jeremiah (cf. Jer. 29).

Thus we cannot avoid the conclusion that during and after the exile the expectation of salvation in Israel moved in two diverging directions. The message of the successors of Deutero-Isaiah is heard in the oracles of Group 1, and those in the contrasting group in the words of the twofold proclamation. These were nationalistic and militaristic circles, which foresaw a future for Judah-Israel only in victory over and destruction of Israel's foes. We must ask whether from these texts of Group 2 there are lines that lead to a continuation of the nationalistic and military renewal, according to which Judah itself was to be the implement by which Yahweh destroyed the enemies, as is proclaimed in a group of these texts.

The contrast between Jesus of Nazareth and that which "had been said to the fathers" can be found not only in individual scattered words in the Old Testament, but in a large, clearly defined complex of "oracles of salvation" in the exilic and postexilic periods which understood salvation for Israel as possible only through the destruction of Israel's foes. The expectation of salvation held by this group is radically negated by the proclamation, the life, and the suffering of Jesus.

PART FOUR

Nonprophetic Oracles
of Salvation

9

Group 3:
Conditional Oracles
of Salvation

Introduction: Deuteronomy
and the Deuteronomic History

In his book *Preaching to the Exiles: A Study of the Prose Tradition in the Book of Jeremiah* (1970), E. W. Nicholson demonstrated that the book of Jeremiah developed in two stages: oracles of Jeremiah, and the modification and expansion of those oracles by the Deuteronomists during the exile. In this process Jeremiah's words were transposed in such a way that they could serve as sermons and instructions for the exiles. This is the case for both the discourse texts (Mowinckel's Source C) and the narrative texts (Mowinckel's Source B).

According to Nicholson, this deuteronomistic modification and expansion includes the majority of oracles of salvation in the book of Jeremiah, as the language of these oracles shows.

While we can agree with Nicholson's thesis in its essentials, what he says about the oracles in Jeremiah needs to be supplemented. He is concerned only with the question of whether the oracles in the book of Jeremiah come from Jeremiah or whether they are deuteronomistic. But he does not ask whether the oracles that were not spoken by Jeremiah (and according to Nicholson, these were the majority) were shaped by the Deuteronomists themselves or whether they were adopted and adapted from a tradition of already existing oracles. In addition he hardly at all considers the form and content of these oracles. The thesis that all these oracles were deuteronomistic, however, is inadequate, because there are too many differences among them.

At one point we can agree with Nicholson without reservation, a point that was seen earlier by many other scholars. Language shaped by the Deuteronomists is characteristic of some prophetic oracles of judgment as well as of many oracles of salvation. A deuteronomistic reworking of these prophetic oracles is unmistakable. (The basic work here was done by W. Thiel, *Die deuteronomistische Redaktion von Jeremia 1–25*, WMANT 41, 1973. He deals with chapters 26–45 in WMANT 52, 1981.)

But the matter is not settled when we have once answered this question. In fact the questions are only beginning. I will confine my comments to the question of what the adoption and reworking of these oracles in the deuteronomic and deuteronomistic writings means in itself.

Deuteronomy 4 as the Classic Form
of Deuteronomistic Paraenesis

A majority of scholars agree that Deuteronomy 4 is deuteronomistic. It includes all the essential elements of deuteronomistic paraenesis in a clear, carefully thought-out arrangement.

1–2	Exhortation: "Give heed to the statutes and the ordinances . . . , that you may live . . . , go in . . . , take possession . . . ."
3–4	Reminder of history: "Your eyes have seen . . . "
5–8	Continuation of the exhortation
9–14	Warning and exhortation based on history
15–24	Warning against idolatry
25–28	Conditional proclamation of judgment
29–31	Conditional proclamation of blessing
32–38	Reminder of history: v. 35, "That you might know . . . "
39–40	Concluding exhortation

The whole passage is marked by an inclusio in which the framework is exhortation (vs. 1–2, the opening exhortation; vs. 39–40, the conclusion). Exhortation holds special significance for deuteronomistic paraenesis. In each instance it is exhortation to heed God's commands. As an element of moral instruction it was ready at hand for the writers.

Within this framework the remembrance of history is inserted in vs. 3–8 and 32–38. It provides the basis of the exhortation with the words, "Your eyes have seen . . ." The hearers are called on to remember their history and that of their ancestors. The command to heed God's word is based on Israel's experiences with their God.

The remembrance of history brackets the two sections, warning and exhortation, especially the warning against idolatry (vs. 9–14, 15–24) and the conditional section (vs. 25–31), conditional proclamation of judgment and salvation. The carefully thought-out structure of this paraenetic discourse, with its looking both back and forward at history, discloses the following outline:

1–2	Introductory exhortation
3–8	Remembrance of history
9–24	Exhortation and warning
25–31	Conditional judgment and salvation
32–38	Remembrance of history
39–40	Concluding exhortation

This outline reveals the meaning and intention of the deuteronomistic paraenesis. At its midpoint we find the proclamation of judgment, to which is added the conditional proclamation of salvation. Thus here paraenesis takes up the prophetic proclamation of judgment, v. 27: "And the Lord will scatter you among the peoples." In its form as a conditional warning it can maintain its validity beyond the exile. Thus the preexilic proclamation of judgment is based on accusation, and the conditional proclamation on warning. The change is due to the new situation following the execution of punishment (so also Nicholson).

The second change is that in this altered situation the proclamation of judgment can be combined with a conditional promise of salvation. Both of them are no longer restricted to a specific, limited situation, but now their validity is timeless.

In Deuteronomy 4 we have the deuteronomistic work in a nutshell, a model of this whole work. Its object is to unite history, law, and prophets as a whole and thus to make the history of God's dealings with Israel, and his word to Israel in law and prophets, present to them, to make it real in the situation after the execution of judgment and to awaken a new awareness of it. The structure of Deuteronomy 4 confirms the end of preexilic prophecy: In the time following the judgment, exhortation takes the place of prophecy.

The conclusion to be drawn for the history of the oracles of salvation is that the break between unconditional and conditional oracles is found here. The conditional oracle derives its function for the time after the fall of the kingdom as the result of the rise of the deuteronomistic paraenesis during the exile. The conditional oracle of salvation takes its place beside the conditional oracle of judgment as expressing the new possibility of the "life" to which the exhortation summons it. This possibility depends on obedience to God's commands (Deut. 30:15–20). This exhortation contains several bound expressions. The statement in 4:35, " . . . that you might know that . . . " is not mere form. Israel is to recognize the great events in its history and from this knowledge learn to heed the warnings and exhortations.

Prophecy in the Deuteronomic History

In the deuteronomic history, prophecy is an essential element in the story of God's dealings with his people. The function which it has there is set forth in detail in Deuteronomy 18:15–22.

15–18   God promises Israel that when they come into the promised land he will raise up from their midst a prophet like Moses. He will proclaim God's word to Israel, and they are to heed what he says.

    19   God will demand a reckoning from those who do not heed the prophet.

20–22   A false prophet, who does not speak God's word, must die. Any prophetic word that is not fulfilled did not come from Yahweh.

2 Kings 17:13–18 also refers to preexilic prophets of judgment.

    13   Yahweh has warned his people through his prophets.

14–17   But they refused to listen.

18 So he was angry with them.

This text shows that the prophetic accusations and pronouncements of judgment were understood as exhortations and warnings. Thus the prophets believed that it was justified, when after the fall of the kingdom, paraenesis continued the prophetic message. From this it follows that oracles from the mouth of the prophets contained exhortations and warnings which were derived from the deuteronomic updating of the words of the prophets after the collapse of the nation.

Conditional Proclamations of Salvation in the Deuteronomic History

In Solomon's prayer at the dedication of the temple the Deuteronomist foresees the exile, 1 Kings 8:46–51.

46   Apostasy, God's judgment, exile
47–48 Reflection, repentance, confession of sin, fervent prayer to God
49–50 "Then hear thou in heaven . . . and forgive, and grant them compassion from their oppressors,
51   for they are thy people."

In this oracle, which already presupposes the destruction of the temple that is only now being dedicated, the deuteronomic author declares that it will still be possible to beseech God to be gracious to his people when he judges them, even though that judgment includes the destruction of the temple. Even in a foreign land, in exile, it is possible to pray in the direction of the temple in Jerusalem. God hears them, and it is not impossible that he will forgive them. This passage is particularly important for Deuteronomy, because it deals with the possibility that there will still be a future for Israel after the judgment. Only because of God's return to his people, which presupposes their turning again to him, is the proclamation of salvation once more possible. But this passage also declares that now the proclamation of salvation can only be conditional. An example of this is Deuteronomy 30:1–10.

1a   When the curse which Yahweh sends has come upon you
1b–2 If you then return to Yahweh . . .

3a Then Yahweh will restore your fortunes.

3b–4 He will have mercy on you . . . gather you . . . bring you back,

5b Make you happier and more numerous than your ancestors were.

9 Yahweh will give you abundance . . . will take delight in you

10 If you obey his voice . . . follow his commands . . . turn to him.

The traditional proclamation of salvation in 3b–9 is made conditional by the framework in 1f. and 10 and thus corresponds to the deuteronomic paraenesis. The familiar, traditional proclamation, however, is unconditional. The author had such oracles at hand and changed them into conditional oracles. In that case, Nicholson's distinction between oracles which Jeremiah spoke and deuteronomistic oracles is invalid. It is rather the case that in addition to oracles of Jeremiah the deuteronomic revision also had other oracles at hand which were contained in various other prophetic books with the same motifs and the same sequence of motifs. Even the oracles in the book of Jeremiah which were revised by the Deuteronomists must be investigated in the context of all the exilic and postexilic oracles of salvation.

Deuteronomy 28:1–13

The two concluding chapters, Deuteronomy 28 and 29, speak of blessing to those who keep the law that has been given to them and of curse to those who disobey this law. Even blessing and curse, which essentially are unconditional (for only so can they be effective), become conditional blessing and conditional curse, as indicated in the paraenesis.

1–2 "If you obey the voice of the Lord your God . . . , the Lord your God will set you high above all nations. . . . And all these blessings shall come upon you."

3–8 "Blessed shall you be in the city, and . . . in the field . . . ."

9–13 And God will bless you with abundance, if you obey his commands.

In the middle section, vs. 3–8, we can discern the old form of the ritual of blessing, in which the blessing was imparted at the sanctuary. That could have had only the unconditional form (Num. 6:24–26). If it is changed into a conditional promise of blessing, the original character of blessing as an effectual word is lost. Through the condition God's blessing becomes dependent on human behavior.

Conditional Deuteronomistic Oracles of Salvation in the Book of Jeremiah

A large number of Jeremianic oracles are like these deuteronomistic passages in that they have been changed to conditional proclamations of salvation. In the analysis of these passages a significant feature is seen. All the passages in chapters 30–33, a collection the language of which shows deuteronomistic influence, have indeed been edited, but in spite of that they are still unconditional proclamations of salvation, while all passages outside this collection are conditional oracles. Those who preserved the tradition must then have consciously drawn a distinction between the two types. Thus they acknowledge that there were indeed unconditional proclamations of salvation. The texts in chapters 30–33 will therefore be discussed with the group to which they belong. These passages are 30:1–3 (31:27–28); 32:37–44; 33:1–13.

The conditional oracles, on the other hand, belong to the wider context of deuteronomistic paraenesis, as has been shown in the examples examined above. These passages are: 3:6–13; 3:19–4:4; 7:3–8, 23–24; 26:2–6; 13:19; 12:14–17; 17:19–27; 18:1–12; 24:4–10; 22:1–5; 29:10, 12–14; (42:10–18).

Oracles Calling on Israel to Repent

Jeremiah 3:6–18

Two originally independent units, 6–13 and 14–18, have been combined. The latter belongs to the group of texts that proclaim liberation and restoration.

3:6–13 is a typical deuteronomistic call to repentance, combined with a conditional proclamation of salvation. It

begins with an interpretation of history that is typical of
Deuteronomy, in this case, a comparison between the apostasy of Judah and that of Israel, and the conclusion in 11–
12a that Israel is less guilty than Judah. In 12b we have a
call to repentance coupled with an offer of God's grace, if
Judah will own its guilt.

> 12b   "Return, faithless Israel, says the Lord; . . . for I am mer-
>   ciful . . . ; I will not be angry for ever.
> 13   Only acknowledge your guilt, that you rebelled against
>   the Lord your God . . . .
> 14   Return, O faithless children, says the Lord."

Jeremiah 3:19–4:4

This passage resembles 3:6–13 in that the call to repent in
4:1–4 also follows a retrospective look at history (3:19–25).

3:19	God's earlier deeds of salvation
20	Israel's apostasy, accusation of unfaithfulness
21	Lament of the people, confession of sin
22a	Call to repent, offer of forgiveness
22b–25	Repentance, confession of trust
4:1–4	Offer of conditional acceptance
1–2a	The conditions: If you . . .
2b	The Lord will send blessing
3–4	Exhortation and warning

It is probable that behind 3:19–25 there lies an older
unconditional oracle of salvation, but it is not possible to
reconstruct it. This oracle is an example of how in the time
after the exile a worship service of confession (Ezra 9; Neh.
9) replaced lamentation. The structure of the lament of the
people can be clearly recognized here. The decisive change
is that in place of God's unconditional response we have the
call to repentance and the conditional proclamation of salvation (4:14). The deuteronomistic paraenesis must have
had the same context as the service of confession before
God, as can be seen from Isaiah 48:1–8.

Jeremiah 7:3–8, 23–24; 26:13

It is widely recognized that Jeremiah's temple address
was expanded by the Deuteronomist. The expansion in vs.

3–8 contains an exhortation, "Amend your ways . . . " as a condition for the promise: "If . . . then . . . " In v. 8 there follows the transition to accusation. The same is found in vs. 23–24. To the account of the temple address in chapter 26, a conditional proclamation of blessing is added: "amend your ways and your doings . . . and the Lord will repent of the evil which he has pronounced against you" (v. 13).

In 22:1–5 Jeremiah receives the commission to speak the word of Yahweh to the king (vs. 1–2). It consists of a list of exhortations: "Do justice and righteousness . . . " This is followed by a conditional proclamation of salvation and punishment. The whole passage is typical paraenesis.

Oracles in Which the People Are Divided Into Two Groups

In two passages, 24:4–10; 29:1–14; (plus 42:10–18?) the proclamation of salvation is found in the context of a distinction drawn among the people of God, in which one group is promised conditional salvation and the other conditional punishment. These passages show how both serve the Deuteronomist's interpretation of history. It is also possible to include 3:6–13 here (see above, pp. 233f.), insofar as here the differing destinies of northern Israel and Judah are concerned. In 24:4–10 and 29:1–14 at issue is the differing destinies of those already in exile and those who remained in Jerusalem.

Jeremiah 24:4–7: The Two Baskets of Figs

The account of the vision in vs. 1–3 probably belongs to an older version of the text. There is no interpretation given, which would in any case have been quite brief. It was replaced by the interpretation in vs. 4–10 in clearly deuteronomistic language. It is a prophecy *ex eventu*. In retrospect it explains why at this point in God's actions with his people the salvation and punishment were separated, in agreement with the proclamations of salvation, as they came into being after the catastrophe and were collected in Jeremiah 30–33. The order of motifs is the same: Judgment on the people; God's grace bestowed; the people are led home, restored, and then undergo inner renewal. The final state-

ment (7b) interprets the change in their fortunes in terms of
a conditional proclamation: "for they shall return to me
with their whole heart."

Jeremiah 29:10, 12-14: Jeremiah's Letter

This letter is closely related to the promise in 32:15. In v.
10a the deuteronomistic redactor inserted a date (seventy
years), which Jeremiah had no power to give. This is followed by a conditional promise in vs. 12–14 (cf. 27:11;
39:17–20).

> 10 "For thus says the Lord: When seventy years are com-
>   pleted . . .
> 12 Then you will call upon me . . . , and I will hear you . . . .
> 13 You will seek me and find me; when you seek me with all
>   your heart,
> 14 . . . I will restore your fortunes and gather you . . . and I
>   will bring you back . . . ."

Jeremiah 42:10-18: Survival in the Land

After the conquest of Judah, Jeremiah addresses a group
of survivors, promising that they can continue to live in the
land if they remain there and do not go to Egypt (vs. 10–
12). But if they do go, he declares that God will punish
them (vs. 13–18).

Oracles Concerning God's Dealings with the Peoples

Jeremiah 18:1-12: The Potter

Based on the work of the potter, 18:6b–10 offers an interpretation of God's dealings with the nations in their history. The passage contains conditional sentences in the
form that is typical of Deuteronomy.

> 6b "Like the clay in the potter's hand, so are you in my hand,
>   O house of Israel."
> 8 "And if that nation . . . turns from its evil . . . "
> 10 "And if it does evil in my sight . . . then I will repent of
>   the good which I had intended."

Jeremiah 12:14–17: The Evil Neighbors

The conditional statements in this passage are also directed against the hostile peoples.

Jeremiah 17:19–27: An Oracle Concerning the Sabbath

This late text differs from the foregoing passages in that its conditional proclamation of salvation or punishment is concerned with the keeping or violating of the sabbath (cf. Isa. 56:1–2; 56:3–8; 58:13–14).

24 "But if you listen to me . . . and . . . keep the sabbath . . . ,
25 then there shall enter by the gates of this city kings who sit on the throne of David. . . . "
27 "But if you do not listen to me . . . I will kindle a fire in its gates . . . ."

In all the above instances of conditional proclamations we can observe the drastic transformation of the unconditional messages of the prophets in the direction of the interpretation of history that is found in Deuteronomy and in the deuteronomic history.

Conditional Proclamations of Salvation in the Minor Prophets

There is a group of ten oracles in two parts that combine the proclamation of salvation with an exhortation (Amos 5:4–6; 14–15; Zeph. 2:3; Hos. 10:12a, 12b; 12:6, 9; Joel 2:12–14; Zech. 1:1–6; Mal. 3:6–12; Zech. 6:15b; 8:14–17).

Not only is the twofold structure the same in all these passages, but the first part almost always consists of an exhortation: "Seek me"; "return unto me"; "seek righteousness"; "speak the truth." Once there is a conditional sentence, "If you will diligently obey the voice of the Lord" (Zech. 6:15b). In the second part the conditional promise is expressed in many different ways, usually an expression for turning to God: "Return to me and you shall live"; "until you receive the fruit of your salvation"; "to do good to Jerusalem." All these statements are paraenesis, exhortation and warning, conditional proclamations of salvation or disaster. This is supported by the parallels in Deuteronomy (see C. Westermann, ThB 73, 107–118), where conditional sentences of warning or exhortation, as well as imperatives and conditional proclamations of salvation, are found in large number. The feature that most clearly distinguishes these forms of speech from the words of the prophets is the "perhaps," which makes the proclamation of salvation relative, a mere possibility.

Amos 5:15   "It may be that the Lord . . . will be gracious to the remnant of Joseph."

Zeph. 2:3   "Perhaps you may be hidden on the day of the wrath of the Lord."

Joel 2:14   "Who knows whether he will not turn and repent, and leave a blessing behind him."

Mal. 3:10   "Put me to the test, says the Lord of hosts, if I will not . . . pour down for you an overflowing blessing."

This "perhaps" is incompatible with the way the words of the prophets were introduced, "Thus says Yahweh." The unconditional nature of the prophetic message is a function of prophetic authority. With it the prophet steps out from behind the cover under which the messenger of a conditional word of salvation or condemnation is secure. The unconditional oracle is a feature of "charismatic" presence, which occurs only in specific situations that demand it. The conditional message is a function of a permanent office, as is the "Levitical sermon."

The agreement of the above-mentioned passages in four different prophetic books is so striking that it must follow from this that the context of each of these statements is unanimous testimony to the larger context of deuteronomistic paraenesis.

There are in addition two quite different texts to be considered: Haggai 2:6–9, 15–17 and Zechariah 3:6–7. In both passages the conditional message of salvation is part of a narrative: In Haggai 2 the account of the command to Haggai to rebuild the temple, and in Zechariah 3 the consecration of Joshua as a priest. In Haggai 2, the prophet promises God's richest blessing if the temple is completed: "From this day on I will bless you" (2:19b); "The treasures of all nations shall come in, and I will fill this house with splendor" (2:7). In Zechariah 3, Joshua is promised blessing, but under the condition in vs. 6–7, "If you will walk in my ways and keep my charge" (cf. Zech. 6:15b).

These two passages agree with the deuteronomistic shaping of history, but here in connection with events in the postexilic age.

Hosea 3:2–5

This passage bears a close resemblance to the conditional oracles.

1a   "Go, take to yourself a wife . . . " [my trans.]
1b   Idolatry
3   Symbolic action
4–5 Word to the woman: For yet a little while, then repentance.

God's commission and its being carried out (2–3a) correspond to God's accusation of Israel. The symbolic action that is interpreted in v. 4 corresponds to the proclamation of judgment. The consequences of this procedure are interpreted by the history of Israel from its apostasy to its repentance, in agreement with the deuteronomic history (similarly in Gen. 15:13–15), and even the language is deuteronomistic. Just as elsewhere an oracle of salvation is added in a new situation to a word of judgment on Israel, so here the message in 3:1 is added to Hosea 1 by a deuteronomistic interpretation of history.

Conditional Proclamations of Salvation and Exhortations in Isaiah 1–39

These forms are seldom encountered here and then only in glosses: 1:19–20; (33:14–16); 2:5; 2:22; 31:6.

Isaiah 1:19–20: Conditional Proclamation of Salvation and Judgment

19   "If you are willing and obedient,
       you shall eat the good of the land;
     But if you refuse and rebel,
       You shall be devoured by the sword."

H. Wildberger ascribes these verses as a unit to Isaiah and believes that "the topic of 17f. is derived from the covenant tradition." He bases this conclusion on the vocabulary in these verses, which have their parallels in Leviticus 26, Deuteronomy 28, and elsewhere. This is correct, even for the late form of conditional announcement of salvation and disaster. But there is almost universal agreement that these two verses are postexilic. They are typical examples of paraenesis.

Moreover the isolated exhortations in three glosses are paraenesis similar to that found in many other passages:

2:5   "O house of Jacob, come, let us walk in the light of the Lord."

2:22 "Turn away from man in whose nostrils is breath, for of what account is he?"

31:6 "Turn to him from whom you have deeply revolted, O people of Israel."

In a larger sense the language of the liturgy for entry to the temple in 33:14–16 resembles a conditional promise. It is likely that these forms are closely related.

Conditional Proclamation of Salvation and Exhortation in Isaiah 40–55

In these chapters there are two exhortations with glosses containing conditional assurance of salvation.

Seek the Lord while he may be found,
   call upon him while he is near;
let the wicked forsake his way,
   and the unrighteous man his thoughts;
let him return to the Lord, that he may have mercy on him,
   and to our God, for he will abundantly pardon. (55:6–7)

This exhortation and the conditional oracle are similar to those in the Minor Prophets. Here too we find the call, "Seek the Lord," and the exhortation to repent, in expectation of God's mercy. That this is a late addition to the text may be recognized in that the "for" at the beginning of 55:8–11 refers to vs. 1–5 and not to 6–7.

The other oracle, 48:18–19, is an exhortation in the form of a wish:

18 "O that you had hearkened to my commandments! Then your peace would have been like a river, and your righteousness like the waves of the sea;

19 your offspring would have been like the sand, . . . like its grains; their name would never be cut off . . . from before me."

This is a wish that paraphrases an exhortation to keep the commandments. It has a parallel in Psalm 81:13–14, an exhortation that follows an oracle of salvation (C. Westermann, "Jesaja 48 und die Bezeugung gegen Israel," in ThB 55, 138–148). As an element in worship it is related to exhortation and conditional promise. The parallel confirms that it is an oracle which belongs together with a conditional proclamation of salvation in a text used in worship in exilic or postexilic times.

Conditional Proclamation of Salvation in Isaiah 56–66

These chapters contain four conditional proclamations of salvation: 56:1–2; 56:3–8; 58:1–12; 58:13–14. They are highly significant for this form and its history.

Isaiah 56:1–2: Thus says Yahweh

> "Keep justice, and do righteousness,
> for soon my salvation will come,
>   and my deliverance be revealed.
> Blessed is the man who does this
>   and the son of man who holds it fast,
> who keeps the sabbath, not profaning it,
>   and keeps his hand from doing any evil."

Isaiah 58:13–14

This passage urges the keeping of the sabbath; it is in the form of a conditional sentence.

> If you turn back your foot from the sabbath,
>   from doing your pleasure on my holy day,
> and call the sabbath a delight . . . ;
> if you honor it . . . ,

> then you shall take delight in the Lord . . . ;
> I will feed you with the heritage of Jacob . . . .

Both these passages show that the form presupposes the conditional proclamation of salvation and closely resembles a conditional exhortation. That can have come into being only in the exile, or later, when the sabbath took on great significance for the stability of the Jewish community. The same holds true for the third passage.

Isaiah 56:3–8

Here is another passage emphasizing the sabbath.

> 3   "Let not the foreigner . . . say . . . .
>   and let not the eunuch say,
>   'Behold, I am a dry tree.'
> 4–5 For thus says the Lord:
>   'To the eunuchs who keep my sabbaths . . .
>   I will give . . . a monument and a name . . . .
> 6–7 And the foreigners who join themselves to the
>   Lord . . . ,
>   every one who keeps the sabbath . . . ,
>   these I will bring to my holy mountain . . . ;
>   for my house shall be called a house of prayer
>   for all peoples.
> 8   Thus says the Lord God,
>   who gathers the outcasts of Israel . . . ."

This oracle opens the way for proselytes and eunuchs to join the Jewish worship. This also has the form of a conditional oracle of salvation—keeping the sabbath is the condition for admission to worship.

Isaiah 58:1–12

This passage is completely different, a condemnation of false fasting and exhortation to true fasting.

> 1–5   Condemnation of false fasting
> 6–7   True fasting: To loose the bonds of wickedness
> 8–9a Your light shall break forth like the dawn
> 9b–10 If you deal with oppression and hunger

10b–11   "Then shall your light rise . . .
            and you shall be like a watered garden. . . .
    12   And your ancient ruins shall be rebuilt . . . ."

In two stages in the form of a conditional proclamation of salvation, false fasting is contrasted, in words that remind us of the preexilic prophets of judgment, to the fasting that God desires. Note that there are added to both detailed oracles (56:3–8 and 58:1–12) motifs from the traditional— that is, unconditional—oracles: the gathering of the scattered people (56:8); the rebuilding of the cities (58:12); the promises of blessing (58:10b–11); and the universal extent of the promise (56:7). This shows that the conditional proclamations of salvation build on the earlier unconditional proclamations. All four of these passages have the function of furthering the security of the postexilic Jewish community. Paraenesis has replaced the prophetic oracle.

Conditional proclamations of salvation in the book of Ezekiel (chs. 18 and 33) have been discussed under Group 1 (pp. 182–184).

Summary: From Prophecy to Paraenesis

In Deuteronomy and the deuteronomistic history, the history of Israel is seen from the one point of view of obedience and disobedience as the factors that determine salvation or disaster. Deuteronomy develops this viewpoint in retrospect: God's judgment was called forth by Israel's disobedience; and in prospect: Israel is exhorted to return to God and to seek his mercy after punishment has fallen on them. If they do, God will again be gracious to them.

The possibility of repentance after judgment has come upon them, of pleading with God and confessing their sin, is based on God's saving deeds for Israel before their apostasy, when he rescued them from Egypt and made a covenant with them. The texts show, however, that the conditional proclamations presuppose an unconditional proclamation that has already been made. There is ample textual evidence for this in the oracles of Group 1, just as in Deuteronomy 28 and 29 the conditional blessing and curse presuppose the unconditional. Likewise in the historical books from 1 Samuel through 2 Kings the conditional oracles presuppose the unconditional. In specific situations the unconditional oracles from older texts are transformed into conditional ones, for example, in the deliverance from the Philistines in 1 Samuel 7 and 12, two texts that bear the unmistakable imprint of Deuteronomy. The establishment of Solomon's kingdom (1 Kings 9:1–9) is made conditional, so that God's judgment on Israel is proclaimed as potential, the fault of Israel itself, and then openly proclaimed as the result of Israel's sin in 1 Kings 11:9–13.

For the Deuteronomist it was important to make repeated reference to the promises made earlier to the patriarchs and to Moses, and which had now been fulfilled. They served to strengthen the exhortations to repent. Likewise continuity with preexilic prophecy was also important to the Deuteronomist.

Conditional oracles in the book of Jeremiah are so similar to those in Deuteronomy and the deuteronomic history that there is clearly a connection between the two. They are part of a deuteronomic reworking of the text. In them Israel is personally addressed and called to repentance as is frequently the case in Deuteronomy and the deuteronomic history. It is also evident that in Deuteronomy there is a tendency to trace the lines of history back into the past or forward into the future, and to explain divisions in the people (Jeremiah 24 and 25) in terms of the conditional proclamation of salvation and judgment. This interpretation of history is extended still farther in Jeremiah 12 and 18 to include the fate of nations with whom God deals on the basis of their conduct.

Of the thirteen passages in the Minor Prophets, ten form a clearly defined group of short twofold oracles that consist of an exhortation and the proclamation of salvation conditional on heeding the exhortation. Both the form and the vocabulary are remarkably homogeneous. This indicates that behind the oracles there is a stylized form of exhortation and conditional proclamation of salvation, an example of oral paraenesis such as could have arisen in the liturgy during the exile. The most important parallel is Deuteronomy 30:15–20, even though here a brief paraenesis has been expanded into an address. The text makes it clear that the paraenesis arose out of oral address to a group.

In the book of Ezekiel there are no conditional proclamations of salvation that were added subsequently. But chapters 18 and 33 give expression to the belief that with the end of the state of Israel prophecy itself, with its unconditional proclamation of salvation and judgment, was at an end. The "watchman" (33:2–9) took the place of the prophet. He can only warn. Anyone who does not listen to his warning will die, but the watchman is free of guilt. The two chapters are a sort of etiology for the way in which paraenesis replaced prophecy from the time of the exile on.

The four passages in Trito-Isaiah demonstrate the new function of paraenesis after the exile, that of serving the reconstruction and the security of the postexilic Jewish community. In this, paraenesis consciously built on the prophetic tradition. On the one hand there was an awareness of another way of speaking to the community, and on the other an awareness of continuity with the prophets, even in this quite different situation.

As was pointed out in the foregoing, a step had been taken from an earlier unconditional proclamation of salvation by the prophets to a later conditional, nonprophetic proclamation. That step was confirmed by the same step in the tradition history of the promises as we find it in the history of the patriarchs. The promises to the patriarchs, like those made by the prophets, are by their very nature unconditional. Only at a later stage does conditional proclamation take its place through glosses or expansions of the text, e.g., Genesis 22:15–18. (See C. Westermann, *The Promises to the Fathers*, 1980, 121f.)

10

Group 4:
Fate of the Godly,
Fate of the Ungodly

Introduction

In a group of additions to the text—for the most part it is
such that we are dealing with here—the fate of the ungodly
is contrasted with that of the godly. This is the case in seven
passages in Isaiah 1–39 (1:27–28; 3:10–11; 10:12[?];
11:4b[?]; 14:30; 29:19–21; 33:14–16; chapter 32:6–8 contrasts the actions of the two groups). In the Minor Prophets
there are five passages (Amos 9:8b–10; Hab. 2:4; Zeph.
3:11–13; Zech. 13:1–2a; 14:20–21); in Trito-Isaiah, three
glosses (57:1–2; 65:1–16a; 66:5). Additions of this type are
not found in Jeremiah, Deutero-Isaiah, or Ezekiel.

When in fifteen passages we encounter additions based
on this motif, we may assume that those who handed them
on saw a connection with the prophetic oracles. That is understandable insofar as these oracles deal with the fate of
the godly and the ungodly in reference to their future salvation or doom. Yet the differences between these oracles and
prophetic oracles are obvious. In the sayings about the
godly and the ungodly the speaker is never a prophet, but
rather one of the people, someone like the "friends" in the
book of Job. A second difference is that in the prophetic
oracles salvation is proclaimed to Israel, but here to individuals, the "godly." The passages indicate a differentiation
that had arisen in Israel between godly and ungodly. A
third difference is that the statements about the fate of the

godly and the ungodly are not proclamations in the strict sense. It is rather that a cause-and-effect relation is established. The fate of the godly and the ungodly is the result of their conduct. This pointing out of a sequence of events does not require a specific divine authorization. All these differences are especially clear when a comparison is made with the oracles of the prophets.

Wisdom Sayings in Their Pure Form

Only twice do we encounter a wisdom saying of this type in its pure form: Isaiah 3:10–11 and Proverbs 28:14.

Isaiah 3:10–11

> Tell the righteous that it shall be well with them,
>   for they shall eat the fruit of their deeds.
> Woe to the wicked! It shall be ill with him,
>   for what his hands have done shall be done to him.

The oracle consists of a simple contrast. Its meaning is given in a sentence that describes the success or the misery that results.

Proverbs 28:14

> Blessed is the man who fears the Lord always;
>   but he who hardens his heart will fall into calamity.

This is the same contrast that characterizes Psalm 1, and Isaiah 3:10–11 could appear without any change in the book of Proverbs. Compare Proverbs 12:14b; 16:20; Psalm 128:1–2. The contrast between the fate of the godly and that of the ungodly is one of the main motifs in the speeches of Job's friends.

There is also a wisdom saying in Habakkuk 2:4:

> Behold, he whose soul is not upright in him shall fail,
>   but the righteous shall live by his faith.

Wisdom Sayings in Connection with Oracles

This motif is combined in many different ways with oracles of salvation.

Oracles of Zion

Isaiah 1:27–28

> Zion shall be redeemed by justice. . . .
> But rebels and sinners shall be destroyed together,
>   and those who forsake the Lord shall be consumed.

These verses describe the fate of the ungodly in the language of wisdom literature. Yet they do not speak of the destiny of the godly, but use the language of Isaiah to say that Zion will be redeemed by justice and righteousness. Verse 27 uses the language of a prophetic proclamation of salvation.

Isaiah 33:14–15

> 14 "The sinners in Zion are afraid;
>   trembling has seized the godless:
>   'Who among us can dwell with the devouring fire? . . . '
> 15 He who walks righteously and speaks uprightly."

In 33:1–16 the motif is again combined with an oracle in a distinctive manner. The epiphany in which Yahweh intervenes against Israel's enemies is followed by 14a, "The sinners in Zion are afraid." The contrast to the godly is then given in the language of the entry liturgy, "He who walks righteously . . . "

Yahweh Determines the Destiny of the Godly and the Ungodly

In the oracles that contrast the destiny of the godly with that of the ungodly, it is not stated that the destiny is controlled by Yahweh; rather, their destiny is the result of their actions. But in order to bring these oracles into harmony with prophetic oracles the activity of Yahweh is mentioned in several passages (Isa. 10:12; 14:30; 29:19; Zeph. 3:11–13; Zech. 13:1–2; Isa. 57:1–2, 13; 65:13–16).

The Godly Remnant Is Separated from the Ungodly

A group of texts proclaim a separation between the godly remnant of Israel and the ungodly, who will be destroyed.

Zephaniah 3:11–13

11b " . . . for then I will remove from your midst
your proudly exultant ones . . . .
12a For I will leave in the midst of you
a people humble and lowly. . . . "

Here we can note a change from an earlier use of the term "remnant." Formerly it designated the remnant of the people of God who had survived the judgment. In later usage God draws a distinction among his people, eliminating the ungodly and leaving a humble and godly remnant.

Amos 9:8b–10

8b " . . . 'except that I will not utterly
destroy the house of Jacob,'
says the Lord.
9a ' . . . I will command,
and shake the house of Israel
among all the nations . . . .
10a All the sinners of my people shall die by the
sword . . . .' "

God's judgment on Israel is understood here as a cleansing by which the sinners are destroyed.

Zechariah 13:8–9

8 " . . . two thirds shall be cut off and perish,
and one third shall be left alive.
9 And I will . . . refine them. . . .
They [the remnant] will call on my name. . . .
I will say, 'They are my people';
and they will say, 'The Lord is my God.' "

This text is typical of the purifying judgment. The godly now understand themselves as those whom God has separated from the ungodly, the elimination of whom makes it possible for the remnant to have a healed relation with God.

Isaiah 65:1–16a

This text is so extensive because it contains not only accusations against the ungodly and the proclamation of judg-

ment on them but also the removal of the godly from among
them.

    1–7   Accusation and judgment on the ungodly
    8–10   I will not destroy them all
  11–12 Repetition of 1–7
  13–16 The process of separation is carried out

The distinguishing feature of this text is that the preexilic
form of accusation and proclamation of judgment is no
longer applied to Israel but only to the ungodly among
them. Then in 13–16 we have the detailed, bitter process
of separating the godly and the ungodly, in which the deep
chasm between them is revealed in all its terror. "My servants shall eat, but you shall be hungry; . . . my servants
shall drink, but you shall be thirsty" (13a).

Isaiah 66:5

> Hear the word of the Lord,
>   you who tremble at his word:
> "Your brethren who hate you
>   and cast you out for my name's sake
> have said, 'Let the Lord be glorified,
>   that we may see your joy';
>   but it is they who shall be put to shame."

In this oracle we see the beginning of a separation in the
words, "Your brethren who hate you." They are still regarded as brothers among whom the godly are living. But
they ridicule the godly, who hold on to the promises, and
because they are powerful they push the godly aside. In
this situation the godly can hold to the hope that "it is they
who will be put to shame."

Isaiah 32:6–8

> 6 "For the fool speaks folly,
>   and his mind plots iniquity:
> to practice ungodliness,
>   to utter error concerning the Lord,
> to leave the craving of the hungry unsatisfied,
>   and to deprive the thirsty of drink.

7 The knaveries of the knave are evil;
     he devises wicked devices
   to ruin the poor with lying words . . . .
8 But he who is noble devises noble things,
     and by noble things he stands."

This passage too is in the wisdom tradition. The contrast
between the destiny of the godly and the ungodly involves
their conduct. This is a gloss to the promise of a king in vs.
1–5 and picks up the statement in 5b, "The fool will no
more be called noble."

Conclusion

The additions to the text that deal with the fate of the
godly and the ungodly differ from the additions to the twofold proclamations in that the latter draw a political contrast, while in the former the contrast is between groups in
Israel. The destruction of Israel's enemies is drawn in
highly realistic language, while the difference between the
fate of the godly and the ungodly is theoretical and abstract.
Nowhere is it made clear, or even hinted at, how the anticipated division between the godly and the ungodly will take
place. It is hard even to imagine, since it involves two
groups in the same community. It sounds more like a theoretical procedure, the general validity of which is disputed,
as for example in the book of Job.

To arrive at a comprehensive evaluation it would be necessary to place the few passages in the prophetic books,
which in this case are merely additions, in the larger context of sayings about the godly and the ungodly in the late
wisdom writings about piety. This group of oracles cannot
be included in the prohetic oracles of salvation.

Excurses

Introductory Formulas to the Oracles of Salvation

The Messenger Formula koh 'amar yhwh

At first glance the distribution of the introductory messenger formulas seems arbitrary, and it appears impossible to determine why a formula may be present in one oracle and not in the next. But a survey of all the roughly 150 oracles of salvation reveals several distinctions that deserve attention.

The starting point for the following investigation is the significance of the difference between the function which the formula plays in the prophetic oracles of judgment and that which it has in the oracles of salvation. It is common to both that the formula introduces the words of a messenger. The one who speaks these words is authorized by God to utter them. There is a difference in that in an oracle of judgment the place of the formula was between two parts of the oracle. It marks the transition from the accusation to the announcement of judgment, usually with the word *laken*, "Therefore thus says Yahweh . . ." (*Basic Forms of Prophetic Speech*, 1967, 149). In an oracle of salvation, however, it has the function of the introduction, a function which at a later stage it also acquired in the oracles of judgment. As a consequence, it does not perform the same vital function in an oracle of salvation that it does in an oracle of judgment. It is clear from the message itself that an oracle of salvation is commissioned by God. Thus it is that the messenger formula was not used consistently as an introduction to these oracles. The differences in usage are as follows.

Deutero-Isaiah. The formula is found in the vast majority of oracles, in 26 out of 37, usually in its full form, but occasionally with variations. It is found only where it performs a function integral to the oracle, and is never repeated. It is not found where it would be awkward, such as with songs of praise or in disputes (e.g., 40:12–31). In any case the formula is an organic part of the text. On this point Deutero-Isaiah is fully in the tradition of the preexilic prophets of judgment.

Oracles in Narrative. In ten passages in Isaiah and Jeremiah there are ten such instances, almost always with "Thus says the Lord." This too agrees with the earlier tradition. In these passages the formula is to be explained in terms of the situation, for example, when a prophet speaks an oracle of salvation in a city under siege (Isaiah 7). The announcement that the city will be rescued is the unexpected element in this situation, and it must carry authority.

Ezekiel. The frequent use of the formula in Ezekiel is especially striking. It occurs in fifteen passages, always in the form *koh 'amar 'adonai yhwh*. It is lacking only in two glosses to oracles against the nations, 29:21 and 16:53–55. In all the other passages it is almost always repeated, sometimes more than once, for a total of 43 occurrences. Here as in Haggai and Zechariah it has become a set formula. The phrase as we find it in this frequency can be explained as the result of an early postexilic redaction, and is in contrast to the way it is used as an organic part of the message in Deutero-Isaiah.

Isaiah 1–39 and the Minor Prophets. Here its use is in contrast to that in Ezekiel and in Deutero-Isaiah. The majority of the oracles do not have the introductory formula *koh 'amar yhwh*, "Thus says the Lord." In Isaiah 1–39 it is found only in oracles in narrative material (see above, pp. 67ff.), with the announcement of deliverance (8 times, with only one exception), in brief glosses (10 times), and in the expansion of a motif (5 times). It is found in 25 passages

in the Minor Prophets: In the two major groups of oracles
(announcement of liberation, 11 passages, and God's turning again to the people and restoring them, 8 passages), the
formula is found only twice. It occurs only once in an expansion of a motif (6 passages), and not at all in the Judah
glosses (5 passages). The situation in the Minor Prophets
thus agrees essentially with that in Isaiah 1–39.

These peculiarities require an explanation, even if only a
tentative one. There must have been a form of the oracle of
salvation that differed from and was independent of that in
Deutero-Isaiah and did not contain the messenger formula.
This other form began with an indication of the time, "in
that day," or something similar, followed by an announcement or a description of a situation. The time element indicates that a long time will pass, and this is strengthened by
the expression "in that day," *bayyom hahu'*. Wherever the
expression introduces a brief gloss in Isaiah 1–39, it seems
to assume that the proclamation of salvation was given in
the past, "in that day." Therefore the formula "Thus says
the Lord" can be omitted as inappropriate at this point. This
is indicated by passages in which the two expressions are
combined; for instance, Jeremiah 31:31–34: "Behold, the
days are coming, says the Lord." So also Jeremiah 33:14–
18. The formal nature of the expression is seen in that the
words "In that day," or "A day is coming when . . . " are
not spoken by God but by human beings, especially where
the annunciation passes into a time of waiting. When God
announces a time when what he has promised will be fulfilled (as in Jeremiah 33:14–18, "Behold, the days are
coming, says the Lord, when I will fulfil the promise I
made . . . "), that is an artificial, abstract construction. A
real promise says what is promised. All this leads one to
think that this was a later combination of two originally independent introductions.

Jeremiah. Here the situation is different. In the passages
in 30:1–31:22, where liberation is proclaimed (seven texts),
the formula is found with only one or two exceptions. In the
six texts outside these passages, three have the formula and
three do not. In the group of seven texts of twofold oracles,
the formula is found in all, even the glosses to oracles on the
nations (four texts), and in narratives (six texts). That Jeremiah differs from Isaiah 1–39 and the Minor Prophets in

having a large number of passages introduced with "thus
says Yahweh" is probably the result of redactional activity,
probably deuteronomistic.

Trito-Isaiah. The phrase *koh 'amar yhwh* is found in five
of the six texts, but, as in Ezekiel, there is never a heaping
up of the phrase. We may assume that in this Trito-Isaiah is
following Deutero-Isaiah.

This study shows that the use of the formula *koh 'amar
yhwh* as an introduction to salvation oracles corresponds to
its use in the oracles of judgment in preexilic times. This is
clearest and least ambiguous in Deutero-Isaiah. Likewise
the use of the formula in preexilic oracles of salvation in
narratives precedes its use in exilic and postexilic oracles.

We have also seen that there was a form of oracle that
was not introduced by the messenger formula but by "in
that day," or "the days are coming . . . ," or a similar
phrase. This form probably presupposes an oracle that had
been given earlier and to which it refers. This is the predominant form in Isaiah 1–39 and in the Minor Prophets.

In the oracles in Jeremiah the predominant introduction
is "thus says Yahweh," which probably can be traced back
to a redaction (the deuteronomistic?). In the book of
Ezekiel another redaction has introduced multiple occurrences of the formula. Trito-Isaiah, where this is the predominant formula, but is never heaped one on another,
follows Deutero-Isaiah.

The Expression bayyom hahu'

This expression is found 105 times in the prophetic
books. It introduces oracles of judgment in 35 instances and
oracles of salvation in 57, and in the other occurrences it is
simply an indication of time.

It is found in Isaiah 44 times, in Jeremiah 7, Ezekiel 12,
Hosea 5, Joel 1, Amos 6, Obadiah 1, Micah 3, Zephaniah 5,
Haggai 1, Zechariah 19, and Malachi 1. It is striking that
although it occurs 44 times in Isaiah 1–39, it does not occur
at all in Isaiah 40–66, but is relatively frequent in Zechariah
(19 times), where it always introduces a salvation oracle.

It is obvious that the expression is very much at home in
the prophetic books, but it is not limited to them. It is found
as a simple indication of time in narratives and reports.

Some examples are Genesis 15:18: "On that day the Lord made a covenant with Abram . . . "; Genesis 26:32: "That same day Isaac's servants . . . "; and Esther 5:9: "And Haman went out that day . . . " It is also found in the prophetic books, for example, Zechariah 6:10: "go the same day to the house of Josiah"; Ezekiel 23:39: "on the same day they came into my sanctuary"; also Ezekiel 38:18; 45:22; and frequently. Thus an ordinary designation of time was taken up into prophecy.

Like the expression "days are coming," the expression "on that day" was first used in prophecies of judgment and later was taken up by prophets of salvation. It can be demonstrated that it served its proper function in the prophecies of judgment. The proclamation of judgment had the structure: God intervenes—the results of the intervention. The expression "on that day" belongs in the second part, results of the intervention, and thus presupposes the intervention. It introduces a continuation of the proclamation of judgment which precedes it. Thus in Micah 2:1–4 we read the following:

> 3 "Therefore thus says the Lord:
> Behold . . . I am devising evil . . . .
> 4 In that day they shall take up a taunt song . . . ."

Isaiah 2:19f. and 7:17f. are similar. The case is the same for the use of the expression in reports—it always presupposes what has been said earlier, which "day" is meant. In oracles of salvation it also refers back to something that has already happened, the act of liberation, even though this is not said. The expression occurs in Isaiah 1–39 twenty-five times as an introduction, but never in Deutero-Isaiah, and the reason for this is clear. All oracles of salvation in Deutero-Isaiah announce deliverance; later oracles only refer back to it.

Such passages as Isaiah 10:24–27 show that the expression denotes the consequences of the intervention even in the oracles of salvation:

> 25 "For in a very little while my indignation will come to an end . . . .
> 27 And in that day his burden will depart from your shoulder . . . ."

In general, however, this original function of the expression has weakened, and it has become merely a formal introduction. But even in this usage it remains an indication that the prophetic oracles of the exilic and postexilic times were in fact related to a "day," to the event of deliverance.

The meaning of the expression "in that day" is that those who use it are announcing a relationship to a future day which they take it for granted is known to their hearers. The expression presupposes a tradition that speaks of that day. Written in full it might read, "In that day, the coming of which the prophets have announced." Three stages can be identified in the use of the expression. Well before the time of Amos people spoke of the "day of Yahweh," on which Yahweh would intervene on behalf of his people, as we can see from Amos 5:18. The prophets of judgment turn this expectation of salvation into a proclamation of judgment, as is also seen from Amos 5:18. After the occurrence of the judgment the expression once again serves to introduce oracles of salvation. From these three stages we may conclude that when an oracle of salvation is introduced by the phrase "In that day," it is *a priori* likely that this oracle was spoken after the prophecy of judgment had been given.

In late usage the term defines a distance from the present: "Not today or tomorrow, but . . . " This marks the distinction between a prophecy of judgment and one of salvation, which signifies the end to the dire threat in an acute present situation.

The Expression yamim ba'im

This expression occurs in twenty passages (Isa. 39:6 = 2 Kings 20:17; 1 Sam. 2:31; Jer. 7:32 = 19:6; 9:24; 16:14 = 23:7; 23:5; 30:3; 31:27; 31:38; 33:14; 48:12; 49:2; 51:47, 52; Amos 4:3; 8:11; 9:13). It can be translated, "Behold, days are coming . . . " or "Behold, a time is coming . . . " In contrast to "in that day," the expression introduces in each of its occurences a prophetic proclamation, and is thus a part of the proclamation itself. Fifteen occurrences are found in Jeremiah, three in Amos, and one in Isaiah. In addition 1 Samuel 2:31 and 2 Kings 20:17 are also prophetic proclamations. It can be accepted as certain that the expression served first as a proclamation in an oracle of di-

saster or punishment and was then taken up by later proclamations of salvation.

A small· group of prophetic proclamations of judgment
show the original use of the expression, and Amos 4:2 is
especially clear: "Behold, the days are coming upon you,
when they shall take you away with hooks." See also Samuel's oracle against the house of Eli (1 Sam. 2:31); Isaiah's
oracle against Hezekiah (2 Kings 20:17 = Isa. 39:6); and
the oracle in Jer. 7:32 (= 19:6; 9:24). The significance of
this introduction is that it stresses the contrast between the
coming disaster and the present in which the message is
given and all is still at peace. A secondary formation is
found in the gloss of Amos 8:11 (see H. W. Wolff's
commentary).

The expression is used in only a few oracles against the
nations in Jeremiah 46–51 (48:12; 49:2; 51:47, 52).

There are in addition eight passages in which the expression introduces an oracle of salvation (Jer. 16:14 = 23:7;
23:5; 30:3; 31:27, 31, 38; 33:14; and Amos 9:13). Aside
from the Amos passage, this usage is found only in the book
of Jeremiah and generally begins in a formal manner:
"Therefore, behold, the days are coming, says the Lord,
when I will . . . " (as also in the four oracles against the
nations).

An indication of its late origin is that this formal introduction combines two originally separate introductions, that is,
"Behold, the days are coming" and "Thus says the Lord."
Even clearer evidence is that the content of what is announced in these passages may be found without the formal
introduction, as in 30:3: "I will restore the fortunes of my
people"; 23:5: "I will raise up for David a righteous
Branch"; and 31:38: "The city shall be rebuilt." This confirms the late origin of these proclamations of salvation. In
Deutero-Isaiah neither this introduction nor the introduction "in that day" is found.

The Expression shub shebut = Restore the Fortunes

This expression occurs in 24 passages, a total of 27 occurrences. The prophetic books contain 18 of these passages
(Jeremiah, 10; Ezekiel, 3; Hosea, Joel, Amos, one each;

Zephaniah, 2), the Psalms, 4 passages; and one each in Lamentations and Job.

The most striking features in the use of the expression are that Yahweh is always the subject (even in Lam. 2:14 Yahweh is the semantic subject) and that the function of the sentences in which it is found is in almost every instance to make a proclamation—that God brings about a restoration of the fortunes of his people from disaster to salvation, a reversal of the prior judgment of God. Thus the turn in their fortunes brings what we term a proclamation of salvation. In almost every instance it is a restoration of Israel's fortunes, but in a few passages that of another people. Only once, Job 42:10, is it a restoration of the fortunes of an individual, a clearly secondary meaning.

In a recent article, *"šūb šebūt*: A Reappraisal" (ZAW 97/ 2, 1985, 233–244), John A. Bracke has defended this meaning of the restoration against the attempts of E. Preuschen (ZAW 15, 1895, 1–74) and E. L. Baumann (ZAW 47, 1929, 17–44) to explain the meaning by etymology. It agrees in the essentials with E. L. Dietrich (BZAW 40, 1925). Bracke examined the contexts in which the expression occurs and concluded that it represents "a model of restoration, whose primary character is God's reversal of his judgment" (p. 233); "a technical term indicating a restoration to an earlier time of well-being—*restitutio ad integrum*" (p. 244).

I agree completely with this conclusion. The meaning, however, can be defined even more precisely in terms of its time frame and the areas in which it was used (e.g. Jer. 29:14; 30:3).

> I will restore your fortunes and gather you from all the nations and all the places where I have driven you, says the Lord, and I will bring you back to the place from which I sent you into exile. (Jer. 29:14)

> For behold, days are coming, says the Lord, when I will restore the fortunes of my people, Israel and Judah, says the Lord, and I will bring them back to the land which I gave to their fathers, and they shall take possession of it. (Jer. 30:3)

The first passage, 29:12–14, is a part of the deuteronomic version of Jeremiah's letter to the exiles, and 30:3 is part of the redactional introduction, 30:1–3, to the collection of oracles of salvation, chapters 30–33. The expression is a later, retrospective designation of all the exilic and postexilic oracles which deal with the liberation, gathering together, and return from the exile and the subsequent restoration. It is based on the experience of Israel's deliverance from exile and reflects that experience. Since it is connected with the experience of liberation, return, and restoration it bears testimony to the survival of that which was expressed by the concept in postexilic times. The absence of the expression in Deutero-Isaiah indicates that it arose after Deutero-Isaiah, but was interpreted in the tradition of his proclamation.

Through the numerous passages brought together in the collection of oracles in Jeremiah 30–33 (which Bracke rightly chose as his starting point), the expression depicts the way in which God restored the fortunes of his people. There are in addition several later developments.

1. In Jeremiah 29:12–14 and Deuteronomy 30:2–3 the unconditional proclamation of salvation is turned into a conditional proclamation.

> Then you will call upon me . . . and I will hear you . . . and I will restore your fortunes . . . . (Jer. 29:12–14)

> [And when you] return to the Lord your God . . . and obey his voice . . . , then the Lord your God will restore your fortunes, and have compassion on you. (Deut. 30:2–3)

This is not prophetic speech and does not pretend to be, but is paraenesis in deuteronomistic and deuteronomic language. Since here a message ascribed to Jeremiah and a message spoken by "Moses" in the farewell address in Deuteronomy agree, this is a sure proof that the word of the prophets was taken up in the exhortations of the deuteronomistic preaching.

2. Through the reworking of the text and proclamation of the restoration of fortune, which originally and in its true sense was meant only for Israel, came to be applied to other peoples.

> Jer. 48:47 "Yet I will restore the fortunes of Moab in the latter days, says the Lord."

49:6   "But afterward I will restore the fortunes of the
      Ammonites, says the Lord."
49:39 "But in the latter days I will restore the fortunes
      of Elam, says the Lord."
Ezek. 16:53 "I will restore . . . the fortunes of Sodom and
      . . . Samaria."
29:14 "I will restore the fortunes of Egypt, and bring
      them back to the land of Pathros."

These late glosses to oracles on the foreign peoples in
Jeremiah and Ezekiel belong to a universalistic redaction
which was no longer able to approve of the proclamation of
the eternal destruction of these peoples.

3. Just as the expression became a part of deuteronomistic preaching, it also entered the language of the later
psalms, without losing its significance.

Ps. 14:7 = 53:7 [6] "When the Lord restores the fortunes
      of his people . . .'"
85:1   "Thou didst restore the fortunes of Jacob."
126:1 "When the Lord restored the fortunes of
      Zion,
      we were like those who dream."
Lam. 2:14 "Your prophets . . . have not exposed your
      iniquity to restore your fortunes."

In their present form these passages must be exilic or
postexilic. In Psalm 82:1 the restoration became a part of
the praise of God and continued to be handed down in that
tradition. In Psalm 126:1 the remembrance of liberation
from the exile is expressed in terms of this concept.

4. Only once is the expression applied to the destiny of an
individual, and in this variation the expression lived on.

Job 42:10 "And the Lord restored the fortunes of Job, when
      he had prayed for his friends."

Observations on Some Recent Studies
of the Prophetic Oracles of Salvation

S. Herrmann, *Die prophetischen Heilserwartungen im Alten
Testament, Ursprung und Gestaltwandel*, BWANT 85/5,
1965.

Herrmann divides his study into two parts: Part A, forms
of expectation of salvation outside Israel; the origin of the
expectation of salvation in the Old Testament; the adoption
of the salvation traditions by classical prophecy; and Part B,
the changing form of the prophetic expectation of salvation.
He is not really concerned about the oracles of salvation
themselves, and he does not explore their form and structure, but deals instead with the hopes and expectations for
salvation held by those who were speaking in these oracles.
This is a classic theme of Old Testament scholarship, but
also one of its most disputed themes. The question is again
and again that of the great personalities, and the distinction
between "authentic" and "inauthentic." His first step is the
exploration of the relationship of the expectation of salvation to the whole of prophecy, of which it is a part. The
prophetic oracles give expression to the expectations,
hopes, thoughts, and concepts of the future that were held
by those who gave voice to them. These are the subject of
Herrmann's study, arranged according to the prophetic
books (but not all of them) in which they are found. The
difficulty here is that there is considerable dispute about
whether the prophetic oracles of salvation come from the
prophet in whose book they are found.

Since Herrmann's study concentrates on the oracles in
the individual prophetic books, and because he always sees
them in relation to the prophet in whose book they are
found, it is understandable that he does not notice the extensive agreement in form and content among oracles in
quite different prophetic books. At no place in his book
does he deal with the style and form of oracles that belong
together though they are found in different books. Conse-
quently he cannot see that there emerges from the group-
ings and arrangements of the oracles of salvation a history
of these oracles that is relatively independent of the history
of the great prophetic figures. In any case this history of the
oracles cannot be identified unless we include the oracles in
the exilic and postexilic books of the Minor Prophets, something that Herrmann does not do. He sees merely a change
in the "gestalt" of the prophetic expectation of salvation
between the prophets of the eighth century and those of
the sixth. For the history of the oracles, however, the decisive dividing line is the collapse of the state and the exile.

As long as the oracles are understood in terms of the great prophetic personalities and are regarded as "constructs of ideas" (*Ideenbildungen*), "which were born in the course of intellectual debates" (p. 154), Herrmann's thorough and stimulating research will be of further significance. But his work will be viewed differently if the oracles are understood, as they are understood in the biblical texts, as the words of messengers.

W. Werner, *Eschatologische Texte in Jesaja 1–39, Messias, Heiliger Rest, Völker*. Forschung zur Bibel 48, 1982.

This study explores the exilic and postexilic oracles of salvation in the book of Isaiah (chs. 1–39). The author starts with the question (p. 12) of whether Isaiah, the prophet of the eighth century B.C., proclaimed salvation as well as judgment, and comes to the conclusion that he did not do so. Isaiah is seen rather as exclusively a prophet of judgment, and the oracles of salvation in Isaiah 1–39 belong almost exclusively to exilic and postexilic times. I agree with the author in this major thesis, except for ch. 7 and chs. 36–38. I also agree with him that the oracles of salvation in chs. 1–39 should not be judged, at least not exclusively, by whether they originated with Isaiah or not (in his introduction Werner himself begins with this question), but by the context of all the oracles of salvation in Isaiah 1–39. I also agree with him that these oracles of the exilic and postexilic periods have their important function as "an attempt to interpret the present with the help of the experiences which the people had in the past" (p. 15). It follows from this that it is necessary to classify the oracles in groups by their form and content. He establishes, however, only three groups: "The messianic prophecies" (his chapter 1), "the sacred remnant" (his chapter 2), "the role of the peoples in the eschatological events" (his chapter 3). In all he discusses a total of fifteen passages. According to my count there are thirty-seven passages (exclusive of chs. 24–27) which can or must be classified as oracles of salvation. In my opinion the author should at least have identified all the passages not discussed and to have arranged them into groups. The necessity of doing so is apparent from the fact that in his excursus "Der Name Jacob in Jes 1–39," Werner

demonstrates effectively that the name "Jacob" can correspond to the term "remnant." From this it follows that the
texts that speak of "Jacob" belong to the same group as that
which speaks of "remnant." Werner did not draw this conclusion. How is it possible to state that the oracles of salvation in Isaiah 1–39 without exception (!) date to the exilic
and postexilic periods, when only fifteen of the thirty-seven
oracles have been investigated?

It comes to this, that if the author has correctly determined the function of these oracles in the exilic and postexilic periods, then the oracles from the same period in the
other prophetic books have the same function. It would
then be necessary, at least potentially, to include those passages in the investigation, but this he has done only for the
promises concerning kingship. Since he has not made an
overview of the entire body of salvation oracles in Isaiah 1–
39, the division followed in the first three chapters is unfortunate, since it is based on a subjective selection. This subjective selection was also criticized by P. R. Ackroyd in *The
Book List*, 1984, 85. Only the first group is appropriately
identified, the messianic prophecies. Werner includes only
five passages in the second group, "The Sacred Remnant."
The title of the third group, "The Role of the Peoples in the
Eschatological Events," is especially inappropriate, since
the peoples in those passages are often mentioned only in
passing (as for example in 12:1–6), and the majority of the
passages belong to the group "Liberation for Israel—destruction for Israel's foes."

In the introduction, pp. 13–16, Werner gives his reasons
for classifying all the oracles of salvation as "eschatological."
He builds on the definition given by G. Wanke, but neither
Wanke nor Werner gives any basis for the position that only
oracles of salvation, but not oracles of judgment, can be "eschatological." It appears that it is on the basis of this designation as "eschatological" that the author does not include
among the oracles of salvation the passages in chapters 7–11
and 36–38 in which Isaiah announces the deliverance of Jerusalem, because there is no way in which they could be
regarded as "eschatological." But if a proclamation of deliverance is not a message of salvation, then what is it?

Werner's monograph, while it has correctly identified the
essential elements, demonstrates that an investigation of

prophetic oracles of salvation must be based on an overview
of all the relevant material.

H. Wildberger, *Jesaja*, Biblischer Kommentar Altes Testament X/1. 2nd ed., 1980, sec. 2, "Das Heil," 1672–1681.

This section of the final part of the commentary contains
a valuable summary and arrangement of the oracles of
salvation in Isaiah 1–39. Central to Wildberger's understanding of "salvation" (*Heil*) is his distinction between deliverance and salvation: "Naturally it is easy to make the
transition from a proclamation of rescue out of a concrete
historical situation of peril to a promise of salvation in the
sense of a condition of permanent peace and uninterrupted
well-being. . . . " This distinction is relevant, but it raises
problems if by oracles of salvation in the strict sense only
those oracles are meant that describe a state of well-being.
"When Isaiah speaks of the destruction of the Assyrian
army outside Jerusalem, that means . . . in the strict sense,
not salvation for the city, but only that it will be rescued
from a perilous situation" (p. 1672). This would mean that
Deutero-Isaiah did not give any oracles of salvation, because his message proclaimed the rescue of Israel from exile. Moreover, such a basic distinction is not possible,
because even in Isaiah 1–39 many oracles of salvation combine the proclamation of deliverance with that of a state of
well-being. There the proclamation of deliverance is primary and that of a state of well-being secondary. The difference in literary form clearly marks the distinction between
the two.

In particular, section *f*, "Zion as the Site of Salvation" (p.
1678), shows that the literary form must be taken into con-
sideration. In that section simply the name "Zion" is taken
as evidence of a "Zion tradition," and the section "The Salvation Recension" (pp. 1565–1569), in which the passages
are only enumerated according to the sequence of the
chapters, lacks even the slightest attempt to arrange the
passages according to their content. There can be no talk of
a "salvation recension" in connection with the passages
enumerated there. What we do find are additions and
glosses of such differing nature that it is impossible that all
of them could have resulted from one recension. The items

enumerated include independent oracles of salvation, additions, and marginal glosses, some of which are not oracles of salvation at all, but motifs from the pious wisdom tradition, exhortations, and paraenesis. A precise arrangement of these items according to form and content would produce a clearly differentiated posthistory of the collection of the messages of the prophet Isaiah. But in order to do this it would be necessary to include the corresponding oracles of salvation in the other prophetic books.

R. Rendtorff, *Das Alte Testament, Eine Einführung*, 1983. E.T., *The Old Testament: An Introduction*, 1986.

The brief presentation of the oracles of salvation in the Old Testament given here (pp. 127–129) deserves positive recognition, first of all because Rendtorff sketches the history of the prophetic oracles of salvation in their entirety, from beginning to end, and in addition because he explores the total corpus of these oracles in terms of their form and does not neglect the situation in which they were given nor the audience to which they were addressed. Rendtorff does not use the term "eschatological"; the oracles speak of "a future for Israel that is characterized by well-being (*heilvoll*)."

H. D. Preuss, ed., *Eschatologie im Alten Testament*, 1978.

This volume renders a great service in bringing together articles on eschatology in the Old Testament written between 1929 and 1974, with the intention of helping produce greater care in the use of this term. The book is consistent throughout with the statement at the beginning, that everyone who uses the concept "eschatology, eschatological" in the exegesis of the Old Testament must begin by saying how he or she understands this term. None of the authors whose writings are found in this book have been able to explain convincingly why this term, which comes to us from and was coined for use in dogmatic theology (Abraham Calovius, *Systema locorum Theologicorum Tomus duodecimus et ultimus ESCHATOLOGIA SACRA* . . . , 1677; I am indebted to my colleague J. Baur, Göttingen, for this citation) is needed to clarify Old Testament texts. That some defend this usage by saying that it is not a dogmatic term does not alter the fact that that is what it is and what it remains. The term eschatology can signify only a logical, conceptual summary. This is not found in what the Old Testament says about the future. The Old Testament does not contain any doctrine of the last things.

When the use of the terms eschatology, eschatological is defended on the ground that in the oracles of salvation we encounter apocalyptic elements, the answer must be that apocalyptic texts and motifs should be characterized as such only because they can be identified by clear criteria. They are apocalyptic, not eschatological, texts and motifs. Moreover it must be said that in the exilic and postexilic oracles of salvation these texts and motifs are for the most part late supplements, or are not really salvation oracles at all.

When, in the oracles of salvation in two parts, one part proclaims restoration, this is to give expression to the fact that God is returning once again to his people, that things will again be as they were before the catastrophe. Frequently this is explicitly stated, as in Amos 9:11–12; Nahum 2:3; also: "Your wounds I will heal, says the Lord" (Jer. 30:17; 33:6); "Their children shall be as they were of old" (Jer. 30:20); "I will . . . rebuild them as they were at first" (Jer. 33:7). Such reconstruction has nothing at all to do with eschatology.

We must not fail to see that the application of the concept eschatology, eschatological to Old Testament texts or issues is not a natural step, but is to be explained on the basis of the history of the exegesis of the Old Testament, in which there was a tendency to borrow concepts from dogmatics and systematics to explain Old Testament terms and contexts. Thus we are justified in asking whether the continued use of these terms which are foreign to the language of the Old Testament is really an appropriate way to approach the texts.

Summary
and Conclusions

An early stratum of prophetic oracles of salvation is found in narratives in the books of Isaiah and Jeremiah. These narratives date from the preexilic period, the same era as that of which they are speaking. The deliverance that is proclaimed in them is always a partial deliverance, within a narrow frame of reference. This deliverance is proclaimed as protection before destruction comes and never as deliverance (of a remnant) after a catastrophe.

From the catastrophe of 587 B.C. on, deliverance of a remnant is announced in terms of rescue from exile. These are new oracles of salvation such as had never before been heard. They begin with Deutero-Isaiah's proclamation, which is explicitly a new message of salvation. Scholarly research shows that the proclamation of salvation after the judgment was more extensive in scope than had previously been assumed. It is heard not only in the individual voices of well-known prophets like Deutero-Isaiah, Trito-Isaiah, Ezekiel, and several of the postexilic minor prophets, but also in the proclamation which extended for decades, or even longer, that God was again attentive to his people. This proclamation is comparable in extent to a major prophetic book. It is a great choir of many voices, proclaiming a message of salvation that to a remarkable degree is consistent and harmonious. Previously the entire scholarly emphasis was on the work of individual prophets of judgment in the preexilic period, but now the emphasis is carried further in the prophecies of salvation after the collapse of the nation, even though these were for the most part transmitted anonymously, and, since they are scattered throughout various prophetic books, their full scope is difficult to recognize. It is significant that what we have here is not the same thing that had occurred hundreds of times in the ancient world following the rise of the great empires, namely, that the worship of a god or a pantheon ended with the destruction of a sanctuary and the exile of the population. These prophecies of salvation constitute a bridge to the life of a "remnant" in the land of their ancestors after return from exile.

At the outset the continuity of the many oracles, some gathered together and others widely scattered, was termed a "layer of tradition," but it can now be described more precisely. All traditions arise out of events. The oracles of the exilic and postexilic times have as their basis the collapse of the Judean state and the end of the worship in the temple. What remained was above all the occasions when those left behind joined in lamenting their plight (e.g., the book of Lamentations), and God's answer to the laments was a part of these occasions. Out of these occasions of mourning (which we may assume were observed by both those who were in exile and those left behind in the land) there arose a new tradition of oracles of salvation. This is shown by the frequent combination of oracles of salvation with motifs of lament, first of all in Deutero-Isaiah, but then also in a whole host of anonymous oracles.

The further developments, beginning with the addition of the proclamation of restoration, show that the oracle gradually became separated from its *Sitz im Leben.* Many brief oracles which contained only a short motif following an introduction give the impression of being a response from the congregation to a preceding proclamation of salvation. Thereby the proclamation completed its transformation into an expression, or an expectation, of hope. To be sure, the form of the proclamation was retained in whole or part, but the claim to speak with prophetic authority was no longer made. Traditional oracles of salvation, especially those from Deutero-Isaiah, were updated and in the process underwent change and further development. The transformation is seen, for example, in the concluding statement, "The zeal of the Lord of hosts will accomplish this" (Isa. 37:32).

In addition to the response made in worship to a lament in an oracle, there was also a literary development. Oracles of salvation were added as supplements to individual oracles that were preexilic prophecies of judgment. This development was influenced by the reading of the prophetic books in the exilic and postexilic services of worship.

The various expansions were also a feature of the literary stage: the expansion to an oracle of salvation in two parts; the addition of a promise of blessing; and the description of the state of well-being, plus many and manifold variants, such as the expansion of a motif to an independent oracle of salvation, etc.

The most significant development in the history of the exilic and postexilic oracles is the separation between the line which came from Deutero-Isaiah and that which developed from the contrasting twofold proclamation.

The feature that was new in Deutero-Isaiah's proclamation was the total absence of any suggestion that political and military power would be regained. This was expressed by directing the proclamation to the "remnant," those who had survived God's judgment on his people and who now acknowledged this judgment and affirmed it. Deutero-Isaiah perceived that the basis of what was "new" was that the liberation was the work of the one who rescued his people, the work of the Creator and the Lord of history, who entrusted this task to the king of a foreign nation. As Creator and Lord of history he does not intend that the peoples of the world shall be destroyed (Isa. 45:18; Genesis 10). He created the world that it might be inhabited, and even those Babylonians who survived the destruction of their nation are invited to partake of salvation.

The ongoing life of the remnant is possible because God is again present to them and forgives them. The remnant can enjoy a wholesome existence only when their relationship to God is once again whole, and this includes the necessity that all other areas of life be whole. The promised wholeness includes God's saving acts and God's blessing.

There is an unreconcilable contrast between this promised wholeness and the twofold proclamation, in which salvation for Israel is possible only through the destruction of their enemies. This contrast has its prehistory in the same contrast between the prophets of judgment and the prophets of salvation before the fall of the nation, as seen with particular clarity in the opposing proclamations of Jeremiah and Hananiah (Jeremiah 28).

The termination of the exilic-postexilic prophecy of salvation is documented in the nonprophetic oracles of salvation—the conditional proclamations of salvation and the oracles about the fate of the pious and the ungodly.

Significance for a Biblical Theology

The significance of the exilic and postexilic prophecies of salvation for the relationship of the Old to the New Testament is not to be found primarily in a list of individual statements in individual oracles, nor in the prediction of a coming savior king or a future kingdom of peace. It can be perceived and evaluated only in the light of all the oracles of salvation in the tradition of Deutero-Isaiah. The whole is defined by God's return in mercy to his people, which includes forgiveness and makes possible a new and whole life, and which, in contrast to the twofold proclamations, does not include the regaining of political power, and victory over and destruction of the people's enemies. Only one line of tradition, that which follows the message of Deutero-Isaiah, moves toward fulfillment in the New Testament; the others do not.

But neither do the texts permit us to establish a direct correspondence between the proclamations of the exilic and postexilic period and the account of its fulfillment in the New Testament. There is a difference between the way that salvation was understood in the two periods. The understanding of salvation that is proclaimed in the texts investigated in this study always involves a community, the people of Israel, as the remnant. In the New Testament, on the contrary, the salvation that is proclaimed in the gospel primarily involves individuals who believe this message. Justification by faith means primarily the faith of each individual. It is impossible to speak of the salvation of a local congregation, or of the justification of the church or of a congregation. In addition, while in the message of the New

Testament salvation can be limited to the wholeness of one's relationship to God, the salvation proclaimed in the oracles of the exilic and postexilic period is in itself the wholesome relationship with God, together with the wholeness and healing of all areas of life. We have not yet become sufficiently aware of the difference which continues to exist here between the Old and the New Testament. The word *shalom*, which so often occurs in the oracles of salvation, means both salvation and peace. Never does it mean simply the cessation of war, and never does it mean only the relationship of an individual to God, that is, what we call "peace with God." The salvation that all those oracles proclaim is made possible by God's being gracious to his people once again, as that grace was made real through deliverance from exile. The salvation that results from deliverance means first of all the restoration of a whole relationship with God. This, moreover, includes of necessity the restoration of all other areas of life as well. The people rescued from the catastrophe receive the promise of renewed community. The individual participates in this salvation only as a member of the community.

Thus it is not true to the meaning and the intention of these oracles to isolate out of what they proclaim one of the many elements that belong to the proclamation. Each element is alive and derives its meaning only from the whole. Thus it is a misunderstanding to take the proclamation of the cessation of wars and apply it to the present or the future as an isolated anticipation of a transformed world, as if here the end of war were prophesied. We cannot have peace without the restoration of a true relationship with God and all that belongs to it.

It is also a misunderstanding if we isolate the restoration of a relationship with God as proclaimed here and think the proclamation is fulfilled in a relationship between God and individuals apart from the rest of life. It is not possible to have the "peace with God" that is announced here without the effect of that peace on the rest of life and on the life of men and women in community. These Old Testament oracles know nothing of a peace of soul in isolation. It would not be salvation or peace if there were no awareness, for example, of what the terror of all war means for the elderly and for little children:

> Thus says the Lord of hosts: "Old men and old women shall again sit in the streets of Jerusalem, each with staff in hand for very age. And the streets of the city shall be full of boys and girls playing in its streets. (Zech. 8:4–5)

But peace among the nations can come only through the work of the God who is again gracious to his people and has delivered them. The proclamation of peace among the nations is not the result of a political concept. The oracles that are universal in content can mean only that the merciful presence of the God who saves is universal in extent. It involves the whole of humanity and the whole of creation, as Deutero-Isaiah's message of salvation makes clear. Forgiveness and God's new presence with his people are granted to a remnant, whose future no longer includes victory over other nations and destruction of their enemies. This remnant now lives among the nations on behalf of that peace, in the comprehensive sense which is disclosed in the oracles of salvation.

Bibliography

Alt, Albrecht. "Jesaja 8, 23–9, 6: Befreiungsnacht und Königstag." *Kleine Schriften* II, pp. 206–244.

Begrich, J. *Studien zu Deuterojesaja.* Theologische Bücherei 20, Munich, 1963.

Bracke, J. M. *"šūb šebūt:* A Reappraisal." *Zeitschrift für die alttestamentliche Wissenschaft* (ZAW) 97 (1985): 233–244.

Budde, Karl. *Jesajas Erleben.* Cited in H. Wildberger, *Jesaja,* Biblischer Kommentar Altes Testament (BKAT), X/1–2. Neukirchen-Vluyn: Neukirchener Verlag, 1972–78.

Conrad, E. W. "Second Isaiah and the Priestly Oracle of Salvation." *ZAW* 93 (1981): 243–246.

———. "The 'Fear Not' Oracles in Second Isaiah." *ZAW* 96 (1984): 129–152.

Duhm, Bernhard. *Das Buch Jesaja.* Handkommentar zum Alten Testament III. Göttingen: Vandenhoeck & Ruprecht, 1892; 4th ed. 1922.

Eichrodt, Walther. *Jesaja.* Die Botschaft des Alten Testaments 17. Stuttgart, 1960; 2nd ed. 1976.

Elliger, Karl. *Deuterojesaja.* BKAT XI/1. Neukirchen-Vluyn: Neukirchener Verlag, 1978.

Fales, F. M., ed. *Assyrian Royal Inscriptions.* Orientis Antiqui Collectio XVII. Rome, 1981.

Fohrer, Georg. *Das Buch Jesaja.* Zürcher Bibelkommentar. Zurich: Theologischer Verlag, 1960; 2nd ed. 1966.

Gunkel, Hermann, and J. Begrich. *Einleitung in die Psalmen.* 1933; 2nd ed. 1966. See also *Psalms: A Form-Critical Introduction.* 1967. Repr. Minneapolis: Fortress Press, 1990.

Guthe, H. *Das Buch Jesaja.* Die Heilige Schrift des Alten Testaments. Bonn, 1922.

Herrmann, Siegfried. *Die prophetischen Heilserwartungen im AT.* Beiträge zur Wissenschaft vom Alten und Neuen Testament, n.s. 5. Stuttgart: W. Kohlhammer, 1965.

Jenni, Ernst, and Claus Westermann, eds. *Theologisches Handwörterbuch zum Alten Testament.* 2 vols. Munich: Chr. Kaiser, 1971–76.

Kaiser, Otto. *Introduction to the Old Testament.* Minneapolis: Augsburg Publishing House, 1977. E.T. of *Einleitung in das Alte Testament.* 1969; 5th ed. 1984.

―――. *Isaiah 1–12.* The Old Testament Library (OTL). London: SCM Press; Philadelphia: Westminster Press, 1972; 2nd ed. 1983. E.T. of *Das Buch des Propheten Jesaja, Kapitel 1–12.* Das Alte Testament Deutsch (ATD) 17. Göttingen: Vandenhoeck & Ruprecht. 2nd ed. 1963; 5th ed. 1981.

―――. *Isaiah 13–39.* OTL. London: SCM Press; Philadelphia: Westminster Press, 1974. E.T. of *Der Prophet Jesaja: Kap. 13–39.* ATD 18. 1973 (2nd ed. 1976).

Kittel, Rudolf. *Gestalten und Gedanken in Israel.* 1925; 2nd ed. 1932.

Köhler, Ludwig. *Deuterojesaja, stilkritisch untersucht.* 1923.

―――. "Der Botenspruch." In *Kleine Lichter,* 1955, pp. 13–17.

Marti, K. *Das Buch Jesaja.* Kurzer Hand-Commentar zum Alten Testament X, Freiburg im Breisgau, 1900.

Mowinckel, Sigmund. *He That Cometh.* Nashville: Abingdon Press, 1954.

Neumann, P. H., ed. *Das Prophetenverständnis in der deutschsprachigen Forschung seit H. Ewald.* Wege der Forschung. Darmstadt, 1979.

Nicholson, Ernest W. *Preaching to the Exiles.* London: Basil Blackwell; New York: Schocken Books, 1971.

Preuss, Horst D. *Eschatologie im Alten Testament.* Wege der Forschung. Darmstadt, 1978.

Rendtorff, Rolf. *The Old Testament: An Introduction.* Philadelphia: Fortress Press, 1986. E.T. of *Das Alte Testament, eine Einführung.* 1983.

―――― and K. Koch, eds. *Studien zur Theologie der alttestamentlichen Überlieferungen: Gerhard von Rad zum 60. Geburtstag.* Neukirchen-Vluyn: Neukirchener Verlag, 1961.

Rost, Leonhard. *Das kleine geschichtliche Credo.* 1965.

Rudolph, Wilhelm. *Jeremia.* Handbuch zum Alten Testament. 3rd ed. Tübingen: J. C. B. Mohr (Paul Siebeck), 1968.

Thiel, Winfried. *Die deuteronomistische Redaktion von Jeremia 1–25.* Wissenschaftliche Monographien zum Alten und Neuen

Testament (WMANT) 41. Neukirchen-Vluyn: Neukirchener Verlag, 1973.

———. *Die deuteronomistische Redaktion von Jeremia 26–45.* WMANT 52. Neukirchen-Vluyn: Neukirchener Verlag, 1981.

Volz, Paul. *Der Prophet Jeremia.* Kommentar zum Alten Testament. Leipzig: Deichert, 1922.

Weippert, Manfred. "Assyrische Prophetien der Zeit Assarhaddons und Assurbanipals." In F. M. Fales, ed., *Assyrian Royal Inscriptions,* pp. 71–115. Rome, 1981.

———. "De herkomst van het Heilsorakel voor Israel bij Deutero-Jesaja." *Nederlands theologisch Tijdschrift* 36 (1982): 1–11.

Werner, W. *Eschatologische Texte in Jesaja 1–39.* Forschung zur Bibel 48, 1982.

Westermann, Claus. *Basic Forms of Prophetic Speech.* London: Lutterworth Press; Philadelphia: Westminster Press, 1967; repr. 1991. E.T. of *Grundformen prophetischer Rede.* Munich: Chr. Kaiser Verlag, 2nd ed., 1964; 5th ed. 1978.

———. *Genesis 1–11, Genesis 12–36, Genesis 37–50.* Minneapolis: Augsburg Publishing House, 1982–86. E.T. of *Genesis.* BKAT I/1, 1974, 3rd ed. 1983; pt. 2, 1981; pt. 3, 1982.

———. *Isaiah 40–66.* OTL. London: SCM Press; Philadelphia: Westminster Press, 1969. E.T. of *Das Buch Jesaja, 40–66.* ATD 19, 1966 (5th ed. 1986).

———. *Blessing in the Bible and the Life of the Church.* Philadelphia: Fortress Press, 1978. E.T. of *Der Segen in der Bibel und im Handeln der Kirche.* 1968.

———. *Forschung am Alten Testament.* Theologische Bücherei. Munich. I, 1964; II (no. 55), 1974; III (no. 73), 1984.

———. *The Promises to the Fathers: Studies on the Patriarchal Narratives.* Philadelphia: Fortress Press, 1980. E.T. of *Die Verheissungen an die Väter.* Göttingen: Vandenhoeck & Ruprecht, 1976.

———. *The Parables of Jesus in the Light of the Old Testament.* Minneapolis: Fortress Press, 1990. E.T. of *Vergleiche und Gleichnisse im Alten und Neuen Testament,* 1984.

———. "Zur Erforschung und zum Verständnis der prophetischen Heilsworte." *ZAW* 98 (1986): 1–13.

Wildberger, Hans. *Jesaja.* BKAT X/1, 1972, 2nd ed. 1980; pt. 2, 1978; pt. 3, 1982.

Wolff, Hans Walter. *Dodekapropheton.* BKAT XIV/1, 1961, 2nd ed. 1965; pt. 2, 1969, 2nd ed. 1975; pt. 3, 1977; pt. 4, 1981; pt. 6, 1986.

Zimmerli, Walther. *Ezekiel I,* 1979; *Ezekiel II,* 1983. Hermeneia. Philadelphia: Fortress Press, 1979–1983. E.T. of *Ezechiel.* BKAT XIII/1–2, 1969.

Index of Scripture References